Wet Behind the Ears
Adventures of a Runaway Sailor

By the same author
As Darker Grows The Night (1975)
White Diamonds North (1990)

WET BEHIND THE EARS
Adventures of a Runaway Sailor

Peter Taylor

HarperCollins*Publishers (New Zealand) Limited*

To
David, Stephen and Joanna,
who always enjoyed a tall tale and
Marita
who was part of it.

National Library of New Zealand Cataloguing-in-Publication Data

Taylor, Peter, 1930-
Wet behind the ears : adventures of a runaway sailor / Peter Taylor.
ISBN: 1-86950-400-3
1.   Taylor, Peter, 1930- 2. Merchant mariners—New Zealand—
Biography. 3. Seafaring life. I. Title.
387.5092—dc 21

First published 2001
HarperCollins*Publishers (New Zealand) Limited*
P.O. Box 1, Auckland

Text and photographs copyright © Peter Taylor 2001

Peter Taylor asserts the moral right to be identified as the author
of this work.

ISBN 1 86950 400 3
Set in Sabon
Designed/typeset by Pages LP
Printed by Griffin Press, Australia on 79 gsm Bulky Book

I'll walk where my own nature would be leading. It vexes me to choose another guide.

Emily Brontë

The sea is the ultimate accomplice of human restlessness.

Joseph Conrad

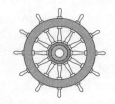

Prologue

Advice to the young is wasted. They have no experience against which to measure its value. And they are tired of being told. So when my schoolteacher tried to bolster my flagging efforts by telling me that the roots of education may be bitter but its fruits would be sweet, he should not have been surprised that my demeanour suggested his declaration was a load of old bollocks. Anyway, I found out shortly afterwards that Aristotle said it first. While some would have doubted it — there are people who would doubt anything — at fifteen I knew everything and doubted nothing. Including Aristotle being a load of old bollocks.

The education process thus satisfactorily concluded, I left school and set off to flash across a black and white world in a blaze of colour. But I was dealt a low blow. The world merely changed my place of incarceration. From a classroom to an office. Worse, a public service office. Boring, so damned boring. It was all the worse for time not progressing as fast as it should, especially between 8 a.m. and 5 p.m. And the tax department was uninterested in my meagre earnings, out of which I also had to pay my parents for the board and lodging previously provided free with the help of the Child Allowance. It was a salutary first demonstration of the reality of the economics of independence.

For a while I was encouraged by the certain knowledge that tomorrow, today would be yesterday. Tomorrow must therefore be better than today. But today was always the same as yesterday and the promise of tomorrow never happened.

Nevertheless, in the belief that there was more to life than merely living, I tried to extract some sort of stimulation from the tedium of it all. But the office was unreceptive to the perpetual motion of teenage enthusiasms. It regularly rebuked them as part of its quiet life-maintenance programme. Occasional smiles while doing so glinted like fixed bayonets.

Eventually, my presence being the one thing keeping us all from total happiness, I left. I also swore never to go near another office.

Huh!

Here I was some years later back in another public service office. This time I had a wife, three young children, one still a baby, and a busted leg supported by a hospital crutch.

But at least someone was asking after my wellbeing. In my first office the main concern had been that unless I tried harder my present and future would be indistinguishable. But as much as I scorned the present, I could raise no interest in the future. Not the one then on offer, anyway. It held nothing new, exciting or interesting.

Now I had to accept anything on offer. I started by taking note of the man in front of me. Except for his tie, obviously a birthday present given the rest of him — corporate black suit, militarily burnished black leather shoes, wonderfully white starched shirt — the chief administration officer seemed to be a man as composed as his office was sober.

A glass-doored mahogany-veneer bookcase along one wall contained the treasury regulations manual, public service manual, ring binders of public service official circulars and similar tomes. A shaft of sunlight through the window illuminated them as if trying to infuse them with life. Beneath the bookshelf a cupboard contained what I later knew to be a clothes brush, a tin of black shoe polish and brush, a plastic raincoat, an umbrella and spare memo pads, paperclips and the like for use in the event the stores clerk died during the night.

His desk being wider than anyone else's acclaimed his superiority. His floor being carpeted in place of the outer office's brown linoleum further endorsed it. So did his blotter. It was unmarked by the doodling whirls and twists that covered all lesser staff's blotters. A man not given to original thought, perhaps. Or a man with clean and tidy official thoughts. On the other hand, he may have believed his job really had something to do with the nation's progress and so had better things to do with his pen.

But the real hallmark of his superiority was his high-backed chair. Its spring base allowed him to lean back with the impassive temperament of a man who knew that while we both may be cogs in a wheel, he was a superior cog.

'Good morning,' he said. 'Settling in OK?'

I thought about it for a moment but concluded *I'm here and that's all there is to it*, in the same way I had looked upon my attendance at boarding school during an earlier part of my education. It was probably where I first learned that fate organises things on the just and rigid basis that no one shall be very happy for very long.

'Well, I'm happy enough, I suppose.'

He seemed to expect more and so I told him that things were certainly different.

'Yes, I suppose they are,' he said. 'Different rules, different people . . .'

Well, different rules yes, but the *people* were not all that different — in my short time in the office a man who smoked cigarettes and ate cakes all day suddenly expired and most of the office went to his funeral; another was caught with his assistant among the files in the records room — the chief administration officer had been cross enough about sex on the premises but probably came near to doodling hangman's nooses when the pair claimed overtime since it was after 6 p.m.

But apart from such understandable human activity the office had been a miscellany of labours so far unexplained. In some cases possibly unexplainable.

'. . . but I'm sure you'll manage, eh?' he went on.

Well, once I understand what I'm supposed to be doing, and can be rid of this bloody crutch, yes, I hope I will. 'I'm sure I will,' I said, although under the circumstances it was impossible to say it with conviction.

He looked at me reflectively as he began a quiet metronomic beat upon his virgin blotter with his upside-down pen. He always did this when about to make an Announcement.

'I must say the staff officer still wonders how you'll fit in,' he said. 'Your background . . . it isn't exactly what would normally suit a job of this kind, is it?'

'Well, I haven't come from *Mars*,' I said, I hoped mildly enough for it not to sound like an Announcement.

The chief administration officer frowned, as if An Important Matter was being trifled with.

'But you think you've arrived there, right?'

His remark surprised me. He was apparently not the sort of man who believed what it said on a bottle of shampoo. My resistive frame of mind began to thaw. Things might work out better than I had imagined. Or not as badly.

'Anyway,' he went on, 'what's the old saying? Worse things happen at sea?'

Like the possibilities of shipwreck and drowning and sometimes having to live with some of the most disagreeable bastards you ever met, yes, mate, maybe they do.

'Yes, perhaps they do,' I said, I hoped light-heartedly.

'But not much worse, eh?' he said, as if trying to be jocular.

'Probably not,' I said flatly.

He pursed his lips and thanked me for my attendance.

Back at my desk and its pile of brown-foldered files, I looked at the faces around me. They seemed enveloped in a stillness of time despite their push of ballpoint pens and the shove of paper. There was a ritualistic air about it all. A socially programmed hypnosis under which everyone did the same thing day after day, week after week, month after month, year after year, until superannuation did us part. And there we were in our pigeonholes, not unlike stuffed pigeons. But I supposed it was just something you had to allow for, like losing your sight or your hearing.

I picked a file from the heap and took up my pen.

'Dear Sir, Thank you for your letter. I have to advise that . . . I remain etc' . . . and so on . . . and so on . . .

God, it was enough to make anyone run away to sea.

Which was what I had done (on a bicycle, actually) after I abandoned my first office.

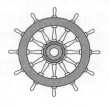

1

Come children, let us shut up the box and the puppets, for our play is played out.

William Makepeace Thackeray, *Vanity Fair*

Adolescent boys believe themselves uniquely different, alone and misunderstood. Adolescent boys are therefore anarchistic, clumsy, complex, errant, egocentric, incomprehensible and ungodly. They are commonly judged as a pain in the collective parental, not to mention public, arse. Fortunately for all concerned, however, they spend much of their time at a place called Out which, if pressed for its whereabouts, is at another place called Nowhere.

When not otherwise engaged in what were generally judged as civil disturbances, although they were really little more than impudent, cheerful havoc, as necessary a part of growing up as chickenpox or the measles, my friends and I spent much of our time at Nowhere.

In that peaceful place we discussed our tribulations and their solutions while coughing over stolen cigarettes. It was commonly agreed that our miserable, tormented lives were because adults were too old-fashioned to understand modern boys and the modern world, and the modern boy's place in it.

Running away was always a popular solution. But it invariably foundered when it came to considering — supposing we eluded the ensuing police manhunt (assuming anyone wished us brought home) — What Then? I sometimes talked of running away to sea. This was always dismissed as *too* venturesome. And in any case much too far from home. But as my parents grew even more old-fashioned, and thus my tribulations grew, the idea gradually resolved into a plan to do so. On my own since no one had the courage to come with me.

Not that it was an entirely new idea. It had in fact been some time in the making.

I don't remember when the sea began to assume sovereignty over me. The original attraction, since water fascinates all children except for washing purposes, may have been the sheer amount of it as much as the element itself.

But while it was to dominate my boyhood, shape the formative years of my adult life and later influence its broader events, our association was no love affair. The sea follows only two rules. The first is that it will drown you at the first opportunity. The second is that it will not break the first. And so I was never carried away by notions of sentimentality towards what Matthew Arnold called the unplumbed, salt, estranging sea. Everything done in relation to it must be a defence against it.

It was what it represented that drew me to it. As a mountain draws some to its summit, despite the undoubted discomfort, not to mention danger, of getting there, to me as an islander at the bottom of the world the sea had come to delineate a boundary beyond which I wished to go. Its flat horizon was my Mount Everest. The sea itself I tolerated as a swimmer tolerates getting wet. I sometimes hated it, sometimes feared it, and sometimes both. I certainly never liked it. I still don't. It is not to be trusted. It is extremely wet and much too deep. A place where nothing is self-evident and nothing can be proved.

It is also one of life's few discomforts you cannot blame on the government. Everybody has always thought so.

Egyptians regarded a sea voyage as sacrilegious. Greeks and Romans weren't greatly impressed, either. It meant leaving their native cities and entering a period of banishment in the pursuit of business or war. It was the results that counted. As for the sea itself, well, it had to be crossed. And the less said about that the better. 'Men do these things, poor fools! For money is life to miserable mortals. Yet it's a dreadful fate to drown,' cried Hesiod, who was rescued by a dolphin.

To Europeans the sea was a symbol of divine anger teeming with monsters — early map makers when they came to the known seas' horizons always warned that 'beyond here lie dragons.' Paintings of it were of shipwreck, storms and similar distresses. In eighteenth-century Britain getting into 'that terrible element' meant taking a bath.

Romantic images of it began when the Industrial Revolution brought the need to work in mines, factories and offices. The only way off such a roundabout was a tangential line to the seaside. English resorts such as Blackpool arose in this fashion. But people did more than escape to the seaside. They built long piers into the sea itself as if to get as far as possible from the clutch of the world when the world pressed in too hard.

Romantic writings of the sea came from such people. It was they who 'loved' it. Those who knew it best, the sailors, had it for a neighbour as much as the air they breathed. If they wrote at all, it was of their ship and those with whom they voyaged.

Towards the sea itself the sailor preserves a certain scepticism. It is best left to poets. If a sailor said to a poet, 'But the sea is not like that,' the poet would reply, 'No, but I am.' Sailors, knowing the sea, unlike poets, therefore confine any 'romance' in their souls to the ships they sail. Once back where the daily papers show no limits to human folly, the sailor tends to gaze upon the world knowing the only thing of real significance he can change is his underwear.

Whatever his level of scepticism, however, he remains attuned to the intangible essence of the sea, although of course he will deny it for fear of being labelled at best a romantic, at worst a romantic fool.

But my own such ripened considerations came only after some years upon it.

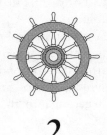

2

There is nothing like a start, and being born, however
pessimistic one may become in later years, is undeniably a start.
William McFee, *Harbours of Memory*

New Zealand was in a doleful mood when I was born. The Great
Depression had taken hold. Over 6000 were unemployed with
numbers rising rapidly (51,000 the following year). Politicians,
one paper said, 'were generally having a bad effect on the country.' The month itself had been cold and stormy, the year one of
the coldest and driest on record and there had already been more
than 700 earthquakes. Children's playgrounds were closed on
Sundays in the interests of Sabbath sanctity and concern that
'swings may lead to worse things.' Of more practical concern, the
minute I arrived I was saddled with $359 as my share of the Na-
tional Debt.

When I was seven I was taken off to the Morrinsville school
with a bellyful of Weetbix, a pencil, rubber, exercise book and
some lettuce and Marmite sandwiches. I was barefoot, my shirt
was new, my trousers patched. I also wore a straw hat because
doctors said children would catch infantile paralysis if the sun
shone on their necks. Without my ears it would have fallen over
my eyes and provided a better excuse for walking in every sloppy
puddle on the way.

Later I was sent to boarding school. My father was the prod-
uct of one of New Zealand's best private schools. It was thought I
would also benefit from an austere regime, tidy uniforms, sports

teams, a tyranny of masters and prefects and early morning cold baths in which we were made to immerse our whole bodies, including our heads.

But it was no use complaining. Ours was a world where anything not compulsory was banned. It was all part of character forming, to which the school was addicted. We were there and that's all there was to it.

We dined in regimental fashion in a large Spartan dining hall with long, scrubbed wooden tables and thick, starch-stiff white tablecloths. Once silence was established we were ordered to give grateful thanks to Him who Delivered Us Our Daily Bread and so was responsible for what we were About to Receive. Our mumbled declarations weren't always true. Some meals were worse than those prepared by our fathers when our mothers were sick.

On Sunday mornings, in our best uniforms and commanded by Hitlerite prefects and taunted by local larrikins who sometimes approached near enough to be left bawling in the gutter with bloody noses, we marched to a nearby church. Robed men then recited the Wonders of the Lord and that we must obey Him or be forever damned.

However, proceedings always concluded with a hymn assuring us that despite earlier statements to the contrary, All Things were in fact Bright and Beautiful. The Lord God, moreover, had Made Them All. Including, presumably, the boarding school which, according to the school hymn, He was also expected to look after: 'Oh Lord, Our Heavenly Father, look down we beseech thee, on this school and visit it with thy blessing.'

But despite my rising scepticism about the whole deal I enjoyed the church in one respect. I sang Eternal Father, Strong to Save with great feeling, particularly its evocative words 'for those in pe—RIL o—n the SEA.'

The hymn may have been the genesis of my fanciful thoughts of going to sea, despite the perils apparently attached thereto.

The sea was influencing my essays, too. Sometimes I was told to read them to the class. My readings earned me the compliments of the teacher who then ordered the class to clap.

Despite such acclaim, however, I finally demanded to be returned to an ordinary school. Perhaps I should have stayed. Some did well enough out of it. One became the country's chief justice and later its governor general. Others became politicians and cabinet ministers. One even became a prime minister. For them Aristotle was spot on — they found themselves in a veritable orchard.

But I nevertheless derived *some* fruits from the experience, although their sweetness may not have tickled Aristotle's palate.

I had learned to live with others while at the same time preserving independence of action and thought. If adversities were imperative enough to need 'counselling' I provided my own. We all did. We didn't dwell on ourselves and so didn't know about problems. We looked life straight in the face. Or perhaps life looked *us* straight in the face. Whatever, we were unquestionably face-to-face, even if the confrontation sometimes ended in tears.

And so at an early age I learned to either tolerate the intolerable or do something about it if I could. If neither was possible, then I learned to be indifferent to it until it became boring.

It was a useful ability when I later had to live among men who were intolerant of other men's problems and ignored their own. Their only counsel, rigorously delivered, was to cut the crap and get on with it.

Just as I was reaching my teens we moved to Russell in the Bay of Islands where I met Old Blom and his friend Mr Worsley. Both had been blue-water men and were the first true sailors I had known.

Whenever I talked of going to sea they tried dissuading me.

'With your brains,' they said, 'you should be capable of greater things.'

I accepted their advice as I would a millionaire's decrying the pursuit of money. As a result they concluded I had no brains at all. Their company was nevertheless a defining point in my life. Their friendly acceptance of my visits and their tales, even if most were cautionary, were constant reminders that I wished to do what they themselves had done — as far as I could tell without the ill effects they forecast should I do the same.

Apart from the First World War, during which as an army captain he won the Military Cross and was gassed in the Somme, Old Blom had spent a lifetime at sea aboard sailing ships and steamers, first as an apprentice and later an officer. He had retired in Russell and lived aboard the blue-hulled ketch he had built and named *Rye* after his hometown on the south-English coast.

His tales in the stuffy cabin accompanied by tinned beef and hot cocoa needed no embellishment. Their simplicity delivered better than any book the taste of the Southern Ocean's salt spray and the screaming chill of Cape Horn's winds.

Mr Worsley lived down the hill from our house. At fifteen he was apprenticed aboard the New Zealand Shipping Company's sailing ship *Waitara*. The ship collided with the same company's *Hurunui* in an English Channel fog off Portland Bill. More than half the crew drowned. But Mr Worsley was found lying unconscious across an oar and revived across *Hurunui*'s saloon table. He later became a rolling stone, wandering and working in Australia and the East Indies and sailing on traders throughout the Pacific.

Mr Worsley's younger brother, Frank, had been a notable New Zealander. He had captained Royal Navy ships and was captain of Sir Ernest Shackleton's 1914 Imperial Trans-Antarctic Expedition ship *Discovery*. After the ship was crushed by ice Frank navigated Shackleton and the second officer on an epic small-boat journey to South Georgia. But Mr Worsley only ever described Frank — Commander Frank Worsley, DSO (and bar), OBE, RD, RNR — as 'my young brother'.

Under such influences it was little wonder the sea dominated my boyhood.

But not completely. According to an early diary there was the occasional other interest: 'Ordinary day at school but think Phyllis wants me to kiss her.' Too damned right she did. Her bold looks across the classroom and coquettish bearing during the lunch hour made it plain enough.

But adolescent girls with ruby lips, swelling bosoms, slimming legs and curving hips are a species apart from adolescent boys with hairless chins and beanstalk bodies, who still don't know whether to wear their socks up or down or their shirts in or out. The flaxen-haired siren's passions in my direction therefore remained unrequited, although she did awaken the realisation that girls and sisters were greatly differing species. But any night-time contemplation of the differences eventually ceded to Old Blom's or Mr Worsley's tale of the day until I was lulled to sleep by the continuous timpani of the sea singing its own siren song on Brampton Reef across the bay.

My share of the National Debt was now $640.

When I left school I joined the local post office. In small-town New Zealand this was a common first step from schoolboy to taxpayer. I polished the floor, counter, vestibule and all the brass in the place. At precisely 9 a.m. the postmaster nodded and I opened the door and hoisted the flag immediately afterwards. I sometimes thought I was expected to do both at once. Then I delivered telegrams by bicycle, wearing a black cap and black uniform with a red stripe down the outside of each trouser leg. Between deliveries I swept the floor and made the tea.

It was hard going, made harder by the accompanying restrictions and the real or imagined limitations, intellectual deprivations and generally crippling mediocrity of small-town life.

'For goodness' sake, Taylor, get on with it,' the postmaster complained yet again while I was polishing the brass in a daydream. This time he sounded weary rather than cross. As if he had given up on his occasional efforts at encouragement, like the long-suffering teacher and Aristotle's alleged fruits.

Then he complained to the telegraphist, 'Whatever's the matter with that boy?' Having one of his own, Charlie said it was a question asked of every boy but that the postmaster, having only a daughter, could not possibly understand the answer even if there was one.

Whatever may have been the matter with me, however, office life had come to represent one of those Gordian knots requiring the implementation of an early boarding-school lesson — if anything intolerable cannot be ignored until it becomes boring, then something must be done about it. And so it was that one morning

I left a note on my bed and another under the post office door for the postmaster. My departure probably made him a happy man for a day or two, a condition to which he was not normally prone. He was one of those factors that made adolescence a difficult if not disagreeable beginning to a man's life.

The stars pinpricked the darkness and the air was as crisp as a cracker biscuit. The small suitcase on the back of my bicycle rebounded against its string strapping when I hit the country gravel road's unseen potholes.

My belongings were few — a couple of shirts, a pair of trousers, toothbrush, jersey, some socks and underwear, wallet, diary and a Box Brownie camera. I also had three books — *Down to the Sea* by Shalimar (F C Hendry), *Sailing Alone Around the World* by Joshua Slocum and a dog-eared copy of the *Rubáiyát of Omar Khayyám* my grandmother had given me some years earlier. It was only on much later reflection I realised that of all my books, these three embodied the essence of the undertaking upon which I had embarked. I must have taken them intuitively. I also had some bread and apples to sustain me until my next meal, which happened to be not for some time.

The populace was stimulated by my departure but soon returned to greater dramas. A small town's peccadillos offer greater appeal than the precipitate actions of a shallow-headed youth. Not that there was anything, in my view, at all dramatic about my leaving.

The only one to see me off had been my cat. He had come with me as I wheeled my bicycle to the front gate. As I prepared to ride off he had rubbed against my leg and I reached down and tickled his chin.

'Hooray, cat,' I had whispered. 'You'll never guess where I'm going.'

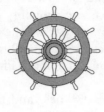

3

He learnt to play when he was young,
And all the tune that he could play,
Was 'Over the hills and far away'.
　　　　Tom, the Piper's Son, Traditional

After six hundred miles by bicycle, foot, bus and train, all the way suspicious of over-friendly men and keeping a wary eye on every policeman, I arrived at my destination, Wellington.

Standing on the railway-station steps looking out on the city, I was acutely aware that for the first time in my life I could rely on no one else for my wellbeing. But I viewed the prospect calmly. I was of an age when we know we can do everything. We doubt it only in later years after some lacerations of the spirit and painful reminders of our limitations imposed by the impudent surprises and twists of fate.

And so after taking a room in a cheap hotel — I was to arrive there again some years later but under very much different circumstances — I set about doing what I had come to do.

Constant newspaper and magazine articles and pictures of *Pamir*, a Finnish sailing ship seized by the New Zealand Government during the war, had fired the imagination of a generation of boys. The few answers to my many letters were always that I had to join the Seaman's Union. To do so there had to be a job. There was none. And anyway, hundreds of boys had the same ambition.

A short, round-bellied, humourless, waddling swine in the Seaman's Union office told me the same.

'Anyway, kid,' he said, 'how old are you?'

'Seventeen,' I lied.

'Well, you don't bloody look it to me. A bloody baby, more like. Still wet behind the bloody ears.'

I did not argue since shaving was hardly yet a matter of necessity. He leaned pugnaciously across his counter and pointed his thick-fingered hand to the door.

'So bugger off, kid,' he said.

Big fat bastard, I thought.

My disconsolation arose as I wandered around the waterfront. But having spread my wings this far I was not about to fall to the ground plucked. And so my determination began to renew itself as my senses of sound, sight and smell became absorbed in the maritime theatre around me.

Ships, scores of them, straining at their mooring ropes and wires, their flags cracking like whips in the southerly breeze as if in countermeasure to the dimly heard sounds of machinery inside their mysterious guts. Ships of every age and size. Beautiful, dowdy, ugly. Rust-streaked, freshly painted. Clean, dirty. Coasters, tramps, freighters, passenger liners. Ships from everywhere. New Zealand, Australia, Britain, Scandinavia, America. Some small enough to be able to peer across their decks, some even into their holds. Others big enough to see little of them except their slab-sided, riveted steel hulls against which their gangways tilted upward like steep stairways to mysterious places.

Lines of waiting lorries and bored drivers. Shunting engines with great puffs of black smoke pushing and pulling railway wagons whose wheel flanges screeched against the steel rails. Rope slings piled with frozen meat and cartons of butter and cheese and bales of wool and all other manner of New Zealand's bounty. Dipping, swinging and grumbling cranes and rattling ships' winches. Watersiders with strong arms and tally clerks with pens and paper.

The imagination was awash with the seagulls' screeching and the tangy bouquets of the sea infusing the air and every action signifying faraway places.

But visits to shipping company offices and agents over the next few days were as discouraging as the man in the union office. I also had to face the fact that, while I was not about to bugger off, independence needed the means to sustain it. I applied for a railway job and was sent to Palmerston North as a junior porter.

After a few weeks, because I was shaping up to be a good railwayman according to the passenger foreman, I was promoted to clipping passengers' tickets on the Main Trunk night expresses and daylight provincial passenger trains. Sometimes I rode in the locomotives, whose drivers occasionally allowed me to blow their whistles. But I had no more hankering for a career in the railways than in the post office.

To earn extra money I peeled potatoes in a fish & chips/steak & eggs/two slices of bread/tea or coffee? café; although to its Greek owner, Mr Papa-something-or-other, it was 'not a café, son, it's a restaurant.'

I continued writing to shipping companies. Few replied. I also called on them whenever the train took me to Wellington. None showed any interest. I was beginning to think I might become a permanent railwayman. Dammit, I may as well have stayed in the post office.

⚓

Acting on impulse can prove more profitable than the best-laid plans. Plans are all very well. But ultimately you must go with what life throws at you. When Mr Papa-something-or-other's wife seemed determined to turn me into a waiter, I made an immediate decision. I left without collecting my pay and replaced a ticket-clipper who had just reported sick. The train took me to Wellington.

At the Railway Wharf to the left of the station, *Pamir*'s masts towered higher than the Waterloo Hotel across the road. As I was studying her mass of yardarms, rigging and running gear, her chief officer came down the gangway. He was a spare man in his mid-twenties in a black uniform with three gold bars on his cuffs and shoulders and a gold anchor on his peaked cap. He walked slowly as he lit his pipe. It was a calm morning and the smoke drifted around him in tendrils until the thing properly combusted.

'Excuse me, mister mate,' I said, 'are there any deck boy's jobs on board?'

He lowered his pipe and pressed a finger into the hot tobacco.

'Afraid not, lad. I've a full crew. And there's a waiting list for our next trip.'

'Where's that to?'

'London. Round the Horn.'

The matter-of-fact mention of London and Cape Horn by a pipe-smoking chief officer standing at the foot of a sailing ship's gangway was a sudden scent of the reality of Old Blom's and Mr Worsley's tales and everything I had read.

Since he was the first not to tell me to bugger off I told him of my fruitless efforts so far.

'Well, you're determined enough, I'll say that for you,' he said. 'You should try to join a Home-boat,' as the British ships were then called.

I felt another sudden impulse.

'And if I got to London, and there was a job?'

He put his pipe to his mouth and puffed a couple of times.

'Well, lad, I meant a Home-boat only as a way of going to sea. But well . . . yes . . . I suppose if there was a deck boy's job . . .' He tapped his bottom teeth with his pipe-stem several times. 'But you'd have to be on the spot. We'll be in London in February. If you're there by then come and see me. You've more chance in a smaller port. Most Poms skin out in places like Napier because they can disappear quickly and the police can't find them.'

'Thank you, sir. Yes, I'll go to Napier. And I'll see you in London.'

'Aye,' the chief officer said, relighting his pipe. 'I shouldn't be surprised if I do.'

During spare time from stacking and unstacking wool bales in a Napier woolstore, I visited every overseas shipping agency impressing upon them my readiness to leave within minutes if called. I also visited ships themselves. But their chief officers said I should keep in touch with the shipping agents.

And so I began a telephone campaign from work. Sometimes the female staff complained that I had become a pain in the neck, the male staff that I had become a pain in the arse. But whatever-ended their opinions of me, I was determined they remembered me.

In the meantime I lived life. It was the heyday of the milkbar, resplendent icecream sundaes, frothy milkshakes, milkbar cowboys, jukeboxes, songs with intelligible if still unintelligent words, white socks, haircream, flared pants, loud ties and sheilas. We stood for God Save the King before the movie and anyone daring to stay seated — few did — was hissed. Penicillin cured everything. Policemen regularly walked the streets. Bicycles were left unchained. Front doors were seldom locked. Prisoners did hard labour. The strongest drugs were aspirins. Elvis Presley was twelve years old. The Beatles were still small boys.

At the Saturday night dance I had no idea at first how to conduct boy–girl smalltalk. Later I began intercepting signals of interest. Once able to decipher them I asked girls to dance. As my experience grew I also asked to take them home. The time of the last bus dictated the duration and intensity of the resulting front door 'pash'. I wore the lipstick residue of my first with some pride and at breakfast the landlady's daughters regarded me with more interest than hitherto although their mother suggested I go and wash my face properly.

My first effort beyond a kiss, however, was roundly repulsed. The girl's warm, pliant lips, her hot breath in my ear and the thrust of her firm breasts against my thin cotton shirt had surely signified only one thing. Apparently not, and it took the bus ride back to the boarding house to overcome my mortification and half the night to regain my equilibrium. I decided female messages were too Machiavellian to be understood. And dangerous into the bargain, if *mis*understood.

Several days later a female message of a different kind produced a tremble of urgency that saturated me like a blush.

'Yes, I can,' I said to the girl on the telephone. 'When?'

'Now,' she said. 'Right away.'

'Yes, OK,' I said. 'I'll be right there.'

I rushed to the foreman and told him I had to leave and would forgo my pay if it meant waiting more than ten minutes.

'Don't worry, lad,' he said. 'Come down to the office and I'll fix up what we owe you. You'll need it where you're going. And some good luck, I shouldn't wonder.'

I sweated a taxation clearance from an official who kept complaining it was impossible, ran to my lodgings, packed my bag and went to sea.

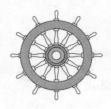

4

You never enjoy the world aright, until
the sea floweth in your veins . . .
                                Thomas Traherne

Algonquin Park's chief officer was pacing up and down outside
the government shipping office. He was impatient enough to not
even look me up and down as my bag and I tumbled out of the
taxi.

'Taylor, is it?' he snapped.

'Yes, sir.'

'Been to sea before?'

I handed him a reference from a local fishing-boat owner
named, the tide of imagination on the ebb when I wrote it only an
hour before, Mr Bill Smith.

He read 'This is to certify that Peter Taylor etc . . .' then said,
'Hmm!' before folding the paper and handing it back.

'Mr Smith, eh?' he said. 'Mr *Bill* Smith?'

He continued looking at me for some moments, as if making
up his mind about something.

'How old are you?'

I told him, adding a few months in case he started asking about
parental permission.

'You don't look it.'

I made no answer and tried to look grown-up instead.

'Can you box the compass?'

'Yes, sir,' I said with a rush of piety at being able to tell the truth for the first time.

'And I suppose Mr Bill-bloody-Smith taught you, eh?' His needling bluntness punctured my piety. But it reflated when he suddenly barked, 'How many degrees in a point?'

'Eleven and a quarter, sir.'

'Tie a bowline?'

'Yes, sir.'

'A clove hitch? A reef knot?'

'Yes, sir.'

'OK. I suppose you'll do. You'll have to, anyway. We're ready to sail so let's get on with it.'

I said a silent thank you to Old Blom and Mr Worsley for their compass and knot lessons. A clerk with the ship's Articles of Agreement open and a pen in his hand made no comment about my reference. He would have known that no one named Bill Smith owned a local fishing boat. But a boy enterprising (i.e. barefaced) enough to present a forged reference, who could box the compass and apparently tie some knots, plainly had a genuine desire to go to sea. And government shipping-office clerks anxious to resume their quiet life took it for granted you were who you said you were. Being a New Zealander meant you were also British. That and proof that you owed the government nothing were all that mattered. Nothing else, no passport or birth certificate or any other documentation.

I signed the Articles and another paper that said that as a first-tripper I would be returned to New Zealand at the conclusion of the voyage. I was then told my pay would be twelve pounds a month. Which was no doubt why the lad I was replacing had deserted his ship — my woolstore job earned that much a week.

Algonquin Park's P flag, the Blue Peter, signalled her imminent departure. It whipped and crackled in the strong salty breeze as if deeply inhaling the sea smell. But it was the ship's port of registry, London, painted on the stern beneath her name, which better spelled out the substance of the coming adventure.

As I followed the chief officer up the gangway, a couple of

off-watch firemen leaned over the bulwarks chewing the tips of the grimy sweat rags around their necks like babies' comforters. The coal-black, broad-nosed, muscular, shirtless Africans personified the rough and tumble life portrayed in most books I had read, particularly where hard-drinking, tough-as-old-boots, coal-burning tramp steamer firemen were concerned. And these two were staring right at me. The sobering glimpse of reality dropped my excitement a notch or two.

The chief officer called the bosun.

'Here you are, bose. Taylor. All yours.'

The chief officer climbed to the bridge after telling several girls milling around the gangway that 'We're sailing so piss off. Christ, the place is like a bloody brothel.' After some lascivious comments to the chief officer's disappearing back and sloppy embraces and slaps on their bottoms from their temporary boyfriends, they put on new lipstick and smoothed down their dresses and headed for a ship on the wharf's other side.

The bosun was the sort of man painters paint and writers write about, a rough-hewn man with leathery face and gnarled hands. He also wore a gold earring in his left ear. All I knew so far about men with earrings was that they usually carried handbags. But he looked the sort who, had he ever held a handbag, had done so only to crush it. I was told later the earring was a customary adornment of the Grimsby Arctic fisherman he had once been. I was also told firemen habitually chewed the ends of their sweat rags. In the heat of the stokehold it maintained saliva in their mouths.

'Right, boyo,' the bosun said. 'Taylor, is it? First name?' I told him. 'Well, it'll be Kiwi from now on.'

Dodging wool bales being swung from the derricks into the holds, I followed him down to the messroom at the stern, beneath what had once been a gun platform and down a companionway to the crew accommodation. He opened a cabin door.

'Well, here we are, boyo. You're with another ordinary seaman and two ABs. The rest of the crowd's in the two cabins across the alleyway.'

He pointed to a spare bunk and I laid my suitcase on its bare mattress.

'Thank you,' I said.

'How old are you?'

'Sixteen.'

'Must say you don't look it. Still, I was fourteen on my first trip.'

It was difficult to believe the bosun had ever been fourteen. At my age he had been at sea two years. I wasn't sure how to reply. Or whether I should. And so I didn't.

'Been to sea before?'

'Only on a fishing boat.'

He didn't answer.

'A small one.'

I was experienced enough by now to know that honesty was not always the best policy. The appearance of honesty was sometimes better.

'But only for a little while.'

'Oh, well, never mind. Get changed and let's have you on deck as quick as you can. We're sailing in about an hour so hop to it.'

The cabin was sparse. Two top and bottom bunks lay fore-and-aft along the inner side with a similar set 'thwartships at the for'ard end. Each had a light, a half-curtain for privacy and leeboards to prevent the occupant falling out. Two drawers were under each lower one. The curving steel outward side of the cabin and the deckhead were insulated with cork. A couple of chairs and a small folding table sat beneath one of two portholes. Below the second was a steam heater. A rough coir mat covered part of the cabin's red-painted deck.

The sparseness, however, was spiced with the smells of rope, Stockholm tar, paint and fish oil, perfumes as agreeable as attar of roses. And all the while the sounds of clattering steam winches and shouting men thrummed through the steel deckhead like distant drumbeats from another world.

⚓

A square, beefy man framed in the doorway ended my daydreaming abruptly.

'Oi, kid! You the new jos?' he demanded.

'Jos?'

'J-O-S. Junior ordinary seaman.'

'Yes.'

'Well, don't sit there like a bloody girl. The bosun wants y'on deck. Now.'

'OK,' I said, discomfited by his imperious tone. 'Be right up.'

'Fuckin' quicker than that, boyo!'

Welcome to the real world, as we say today. Then we said, 'oh shit!'

The bosun was pulling on the end of a guy rope and directing the lowering of the derrick to which it was attached.

'About time, boy,' he said roughly. 'Here, grab this and pull.'

The rope obviously had something to do with lowering the derrick. And so I pulled with a will while a man on the opposite side paid out his rope. The derrick was being lowered by a sailor at a winch at the foot of the mast while we guided it with the guy ropes until it lay in its cradle at the end of the hatch where a fourth man lashed it into place.

The bosun, standing next to me probably as a safety precaution, said quietly, 'Bit bigger than a fishing boat derrick, eh, boyo?'

I began to fear my monumental lie would be exposed before long and I would be bundled ashore at the next port.

But his facial muscles twitched in what was presumably a smile. 'Never mind,' he said, 'everyone has to start somewhere.' He had been through the mill that was about to operate on me, he seemed to be saying. I would have no problems he had not confronted.

After lowering the derricks and covering the hatches with tarpaulins and hammering home their wooden wedges along the coamings, we began clearing the assorted rubbish that accumulates on ships' decks after a stay in port. Dunnage, timber used for stowing and separating various types of cargo, was strewn everywhere. We gathered it up and lashed it against the bulwarks for use at the next port. The radio aerial was then hoisted back into place between the masts. It was always lowered in port otherwise it would interfere with the cargo derricks.

The bosun later took me to the chief steward. I signed for a couple of sheets and blankets, a blue bedcover with an anchor motif, a pillow, pillowcase, knife, fork, spoon and a tin of condensed milk. Like most British tramps, *Algonquin Park* was run to minimum Board of Trade requirements.

I was sitting on my bunk with my new possessions wondering what to do next when a strapping young man entered the cabin. He wore a woollen cap, a polo-necked jersey and a knife and marlin spike in a leather sheath on his belt. Unlike the previous uncompromising bastard who had demanded I get up on deck and be quick about it, this one was friendly. He was also one of those who had slapped the girls' bottoms as they left the ship.

'All right there?'

'Yes, thanks. Are you in this cabin?'

'Aye. I'm the SOS, senior ordinary seaman. Name's Ginger.'

'Who else is in here?'

'Corny's in the bunk above you, Jimmy Southern's in the bunk above me. Corny's all right but a bit quiet. Southern's just a big prick.'

Southern must be the one I had already met.

'Why?'

'Probably because he's got more between his legs than his ears.'

While we were talking I began making up my bunk.

'It's no good doing it like that,' Ginger said. 'This is a cabin, not a bloody bedroom. You need to make a proper sea-bed. Here, I'll show you how.'

He put the sheet, blankets and bedcover together then held them between outstretched arms with the sheet facing outwards then folded them in half backwards. He covered the bunk with the bedding, the sheet on the bottom.

'There,' he said, 'that's a sea-bed. You won't roll out of it when the ship rolls.'

He had created an arrangement whereby the sheet and blankets appeared the same as on any other bed except that instead of being tucked down the sides of the mattress, they were folded in a tube. The occupant burrowed himself into the resulting tunnel so that, lying on either half of the bedclothes, he was prevented from rolling from underneath them when the ship rolled.

The sea-bed, the self-assured young man with his knife, marlin spike and woollen cap, the ship sounds reaching the cabin from the deck, and particularly that big prick Southern were sharp representations of the new life I had entered after the telephone call less than three hours before.

I was still confused at the abruptness of it all. The dream of a goal was one thing. The reality of it was another. Had I been dreaming I might have woken with a sense of relief. I was also feeling an almost perverse sense of anticlimax. Having achieved my ambition there was no one to congratulate me, no one to see me off. I was alone in my triumph.

'OK, lads,' the bosun called down the companionway. 'Gangway. Then stations fore and aft and single up.'

'That means it's time to raise the gangway,' Ginger said. 'We're in the for'ard crowd and stations and single up means we go for'ard and let go all the lines except for one and stand by until we sail. The after crowd does the same aft.'

The engine had already been turned over several revolutions to ensure its readiness when signalled from the brass telegraphs on the bridge. I had felt the tailshaft's grumble and propeller's soft thump earlier in the cabin. There had also been a hissing and clunking from somewhere at the rear of the accommodation. Ginger had explained it was the rudder's steam-driven engine in the steering flat being tested.

More than any other, more even than the P flag, the two actions had manifested *Algonquin Park*'s preparing to sail.

Streaked with rust from more than eighteen months' trekking around the world, the 7130-ton ship had arrived in New Zealand with gypsum from the Red Sea. Now she was loading in Napier, Timaru and Lyttelton, bound for London via Australian and South African coal-bunkering ports, and possibly one in Spain unless she still had sufficient coal to fire her boilers all the way to London.

As I followed Ginger on to the deck I wondered if my parents, who had long since forgiven my precipitate departure from home, had yet received my telegram. I also wondered what the post-office staff and those to whom they would have related it, despite the Official Secrets Act, would have made of it.

'Gone to sea,' it had said. 'Leaving for London 4 p.m. on *Algonquin Park*. Writing soon.'

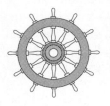

5

*Not fare well
But fare forward, voyagers.*
T S Eliot

The sun was sinking behind the land and the sea turning grey as *Algonquin Park* steamed beam on to the swells with a trail of black smoke behind her. Her gentle rolling caused me to walk a snake-like course. I had yet to develop sea legs.

'Well, Kiwi, you may as well go to the messroom and get yourself a cup of tea,' the bosun had said earlier after we finished lashing the mooring ropes on the fo'c'sle head. 'You're with Ginger and Jimmy Southern in the eight to twelve watch. They'll tell you all about it.'

In the messroom no one took much notice of me. I was not yet part of the normal shipboard routine and so rated little attention apart from the occasional perfunctory hullo and one man who asked, 'D'ya shave yet, mate?' 'Yes,' I said. 'Aye,' he said. 'At least once a week! Christ, you must have just left your mum's apron strings. Still, you're here now. Just do as you're told, learn, and you'll be OK. Otherwise you'll soon fuck it up.'

And so I just listened to the general messroom talk. Most of it was unfathomable. Everything was prefaced and divided with swear words. They were an integral part of seamen's language without which it would be bereft of description or emphasis. But it was not the lack of metaphors, ornaments, literary graces and emphasis that puzzled me. It was the topics. I was in the presence of strangers who obviously possessed much strange knowledge.

Ginger explained the watch-keeping routine. I listened carefully. I would be 'Farmer' — on lookout from nine till eleven o'clock. I would strike the fo'c'sle head brass bell when I saw a light or object. One stroke for port, two for starboard and three ahead. I would answer the bridge bell struck every half-hour by the helmsman. Its strokes signalled the passage of time and the lookout's answer signalled he was still alert. I would spend the first and last of the four hours on standby in the galley amidships. At seven bells, eleven-thirty, I would call the next watch including the second mate. I would call them again at one bell, eleven forty-five. During the first hour I would also peel the next day's potatoes for the cook. In the last I would prepare our blackpan (supper). Southern would be on lookout from eight to nine o'clock, spend the next hour in the galley and relieve the wheel at ten o'clock till midnight. Ginger would be at the wheel from eight to ten o'clock, in the galley for the next hour and relieve the lookout from eleven o'clock to midnight. During subsequent watches the cycle would progress so that we shared each portion equally.

Ginger explained it several times until satisfied he would not be left on lookout beyond his allotted stint; the bell would be properly struck; the third mate would be supplied with kai (a cup of hot cocoa) from the galley when he blew his whistle; the next watch would be called and our blackpan cooked in time.

He stressed again the importance of peeling the potatoes and keeping the galley fires going. This ensured the cook left out blackpan to be cooked by the men coming off their watches during the night. It would also ensure that prick Southern would have nothing to complain about.

During Ginger's patient explanation the other two lay on their bunks. Corny, a Cornishman as his nickname implied, was a small nuggetty man in his thirties. Southern, around the same age, was a cockney, a stocky, melancholy man who when not on watch was in his bunk.

Corny opened his eyes and said hullo. Southern was asleep. His arms were clasped across his barrel chest and his unconscious body swayed gently in time with the ship's light rolling. Otherwise he lay motionless like the horizontal figures in Westminster Abbey.

Sometime before we went on watch we had dinner. I don't remember what it was. There would have been soup, meat and vegetables and a pudding of some sort. However, from Napier to London, Wednesday was oxtail, and since we sailed on Wednesday we must have had oxtail.

There was also a regular night, I forget which, Thursday I think, for a mess of rabbit meat and bones called rabbit stew. The crew called it underground mutton. It floated in what was almost a soup. Sunday's pudding was always plum duff. Throughout the week there were regular ham and pea soups, fatty roast mutton, sometimes fatty beef and a lumpy, glutinous compound that passed for Yorkshire pudding. Occasionally there was curry and rice over which an Indian crew might have mutinied. Breakfast was fatty fried eggs on fatty fried bread with baked beans or spaghetti or black pudding or, occasionally, frizzled fatty bacon and always burgoo (porridge) and toast.

At all times there were tabnabs. These were small, floury, yeasty buns. To disguise their doughiness everyone coated them with Board of Trade jam. Apparently what jam factories could not otherwise use, they sold to Britain's merchant fleet with a Board of Trade label proclaiming it as 'Jam, Merchant Navy, suitable for the use of.' It carried the trade name 'Battle Axe'.

Meals were brought from the galley in kits (tin containers) by the standby man on the watch about to be relieved. In bad weather the journey down the deck could be hazardous. If the man was caught unawares everything ended up in the scuppers. The severity of the waiting diners' reactions depended upon the man's capacity to dispute the issue.

At nine o'clock (two bells) I made my way to the fo'c'sle head for my two hours' lookout with Ginger's 'one bell to port, two to starboard, three ahead' carefully memorised. As Southern disappeared down the deck I was left undisturbed for the first time since the telephone call that afternoon.

I turned to my surroundings. The Cape Kidnappers lighthouse flashed far out to starboard. The red port and green starboard navigation lights glowed each side of the bridge. Occasional sparks drifted with the funnel smoke like cindery fireflies. Behind the wheelhouse windows a soft pool of pale light reflected from the compass and the third mate's cigarette.

I listened to the wind around the mast and rigging; the slough-ing wash of the bow wave; the creaks, squeaks and grindings of the hull and its fittings responding to the strains and stresses placed upon them as the ship rose and dipped over the swells on her way south. The white masthead light swayed against the sky as if stir-ring the stars.

I was at sea!

My confidence, though at times badly dented, had remained unbounded that the time would come. It was only a question of when. Despite earlier misgivings my exultation rose. When was *now*! More than taking hold of life, I had bitten a large chunk out of it.

Stuff the National Debt! Aristotle, too, come to that.

At the end of our watch we sat in the galley next to the hot coal stove eating our blackpan of chips, eggs and sausages. After we finished, Ginger and I washed the dishes and pans. Southern re-turned to our cabin after whacking several cockroaches with a broad-bladed knife — everyone whacked cockroaches but achieved little more than satisfaction at having done so. Despite continual whacking their numbers never lessened. They multiplied anywhere there was warmth, including our messroom.

'Does it every time,' Ginger said as he took over the cockroach whacking. 'Can't wait to get his bloody head down. He's a prick! Aye, he is that. A real right royal *prick*!' he said as he whacked another cockroach as though it was Southern who now lay flat-tened under the knife. He flicked the corpse into the galley fire which devoured it in a flaring instant. 'Go on, y'bastard, die!' he said. Southern was already safely asleep, however, when we reached the cabin.

In my bunk my thoughts were a muddle of excitement and

trepidation pondering the events of the day, culminating in being aboard a ship carrying some of the very wool bales I had been handling only hours ago.

The sea splashing against the hull's thin steel plates and the grumbling tailshaft and regular thump of the propeller were plainly felt and heard. Once used to them, such symptoms of a ship at sea are soporific. Their synchronised rhythms signal that all is well. Sleep comes quickly. But in the palely lit intimacy of my bunk they were all too strange. Last night's boarding-house bed seemed impossibly far away.

Ginger called out from his bunk.

'Oi! Kiwi! Put y'fuckin' light out.'

I did but it was still some time before I went to sleep.

My first full day at sea began at 7.20 a.m. with a rough shake on the shoulder.

'Seven bells, mate,' a voice said.

It was Geordie, a big moustached AB from South Shields and a member of the four to eight watch we were about to relieve. The sun shining through the portholes danced like a twin-pronged solar lance on an opposite bulkhead in time with the ship's slow rolling.

Ginger was already dressing but Southern only swore and turned over at Geordie's call. Southern always swore. Southern's whole method of expression revolved around swearing. Swearing and turning over in his bunk each time he was called was a ritual all the way to London.

So was everyone's response — a dismissive 'well, fuck ya' then!' Southern seldom had the energy to respond to such provocation. All the same, he always turned-to on time. He had been at sea since he was a boy and had learned his job well. That included never being late relieving the watch even if it meant sometimes missing a meal. But at the same time, like all seamen he did no more than necessary for any longer than necessary. As far as Southern was concerned, work was the only dirty word in the language and an occupation he pursued keenly with the utmost lack of vigour. But he seemed afflicted by a desire not so much for laziness as inaction. Sometimes it seemed even a laugh would have been too much exertion. Ginger reckoned that he probably thought manual labour was a Spaniard. Corny once said, in a moment of swearing exasperation, that he should undergo an annual autopsy.

While Ginger and Southern worked on deck with the bosun, it was my turn for the eight to ten stint at the wheel. I had already sought Ginger's advice but 'there's fuck all to it' was all he had to offer. The third mate, who had just relieved the chief officer, nodded as I entered the wheelhouse. The helmsman nodded, too, and said 'G'morning. Course 183,' and was gone in an instant.

The figure 183 pointed to the mark representing the ship's head, at the top of the gyrocompass. It meant she was on her correct course when I took over. But within moments she began swinging to one side. I turned the wheel in the opposite direction. There was no immediate response. I turned it some more. Suddenly the ship began a rapid swing. I quickly turned the wheel the other way. She began a return swing.

The third mate went to the wing of the bridge. He looked at our S-like wake. He returned to enquire, mildly under the circumstances, if I had ever steered a ship.

'Only a fishing boat, sir.'

'How big?'

I began to feel the mythical fishing boat might carry me down 20,000 leagues under the sea.

'Small, sir.'

'Very small, I should think,' he said. 'Well, this isn't a bloody fishing boat. You'll take a round turn out of her if you're not careful.'

The captain stepped through the door from the chartroom. Captains possess a profound sense of the untoward and a change in the general symphony of sound or motion brings them to the bridge within moments. Captain Kilgour had obviously felt his ship being mishandled. He stared at me and went to the bridge wing and stared at our wiggling wake, then returned and stood in front of me with both hands on the binnacle. I kept my eyes on the gyrocompass slightly to the left of it.

'Steered a ship before, son?' he barked.

There was no point in pissing around.

'No, sir.'

'Doesn't look like it, either,' he said, gesturing towards the stern. 'Been to sea before?'

'Only on a fishing boat, sir.'

'How big was this bloody fishing boat?'

'A small one, sir.'

'Yeah,' the captain said. 'Must have been. And owned by Mr Bill-bloody-Smith, so I'm told.'

'Yes, sir.'

'And I suppose his wife's name was *Mary*!'

'Never met her, sir.'

'No, don't suppose you did.'

He shrugged. The third mate also shrugged. For a few moments they watched me struggling to keep the ship on course. I stayed silent under their combined scrutiny.

'D'ya know the compass?' the captain asked.

'Yes, sir!'

'How many degrees in a point?'

'Eleven and a quarter, sir.'

'Well, that's something, I suppose. Keep an eye on him, three-oh.' He pointed through the bridge windows to the sea. It sparkled in the morning sunshine as if delighted with itself. 'At least we've plenty of room,' he growled. Then, muttering about 'a bloody fishing boat. Bloody bollocks, I shouldn't wonder,' he left the bridge.

'You don't actually steer,' the third mate said, explaining the finer points of helmsmanship. 'You just keep bringing her back to her course if she wants to wander. But if you overdo it you'll start her swinging like a bloody roundabout. Remember — all you're doing is keeping her on course.'

After being relieved by Ginger at ten o'clock and a cup of tea in the messroom, I spent the rest of the watch cleaning up and washing down the deck with Southern and the bosun. What with one thing and another, by the time we reached Timaru several days later I fancied I had begun to acquire a nautical air.

Like that from Napier, our Timaru cargo was barrels of tallow, bundles of hides and bales of wool, all reeking of the meatworks and farms upon which New Zealand's considerable fortunes then rode. In Lyttelton the ship was filled to its hatch tops with more of the same.

It was growing dark when we dropped the pilot and cleared Godley Head. *Algonquin Park* turned north and headed for Cook Strait, through which she would head west across the Tasman to Newcastle, at the mouth of the Hunter River, north of Sydney.

Then would follow many weeks across the Indian Ocean to Durban and as many up the Atlantic to London.

All thanks to Old Blom, Mr Worsley and the fictional Mr Bill-bloody-Smith.

6

A . . . ship was my Yale and my Harvard.
Herman Melville

Each sea watch has its own quality. The four to eight is a time for optimism. It is the day's beginning, a time of dawn and sunrise. As the ship emerges into the flush of the new day, navigation lights are extinguished and the lookout stood down. Towards the end of the watch the bosun arrives on the bridge to receive the chief officer's orders for the day's work. The evening portion of the watch is a time for reflection, the day's end, sunset and dusk. The lookout is posted, the navigation lights switched on and the ship's features slowly dissolve as she sails into the gathering darkness.

The eight to twelve allows an afternoon sleep after the morning's work. Its evening portion is a time to review the day and savour the promise of a proper sleep during the night's quietest hours, from midnight until breakfast.

The twelve to four is melancholic. It sees neither sunrise nor sunset. From midnight is a time for pensiveness. Yesterday has gone and today is barely begun. From midday is a time of nothing. The morning is gone. The evening is too far away. It is the slack-water period of the day. Effort is desultory.

We were now in the twelve to four, the second mate's watch, once known as the 'graveyard' for its early morning hours. Everyone except for the deck and engineroom watches is turned in. It is a period when life is at its lowest ebb. Or so it seemed to the night's helmsman and lookout. The second mate's primary job was navigator. He spent most of his time alone in the chartroom so that the only animate object for the helmsman was the clicking gyrocompass. The lookout's was the loneliest post, especially if the weather was cold and overcast. The light of a distant ship gives rise to a pensiveness born of the knowledge that it could be the only other human gathering for thousands of miles around. But on a warm night with a clear sky and a million stars one's own company is enough. At least I always found it so.

Down below, day or night mattered little. Illuminated only by electric light, the firemen shovelled coal into the fires, cleared their hot ashes regularly and damped them down before hauling them to the deck and dumping them through the ash chute into the sea. For the trimmers in the hot, airless coal bunkers the pale electric light was dimmed by swirling, gritty dust as they wheelbarrowed the coal to bring it within reach of the firemen's shovels. But unlike the deck watch, at least they had company.

These days radar and satellite positioning have taken the edge off a landfall. But despite modern electronics today's mariners are still not convinced until they can see it for themselves. They still make visual landfall with the same satisfaction *Algonquin Park*'s gadget-less second mate sighted Australia.

After searching the horizon with his binoculars for some time he said, 'Ah, there it is.' He pointed to a faint smudge on the horizon. It could have been mistaken for a cloud.

'Australia,' he said.

Then he called down the voice-pipe to the captain.

'About bloody time, too,' the captain called back.

Neither should have been surprised. It would have been difficult to miss Australia. All they had to do was head west.

But I was exhilarated at the sight of my first new country as it rose slowly out of what had been a vacuum of sight, except for sea and sky and the occasional daylight smear of smoke on the horizon or a distant light at night.

Newcastle coal dust swirled everywhere in a gritty black cloud as cranes filled our bunkers. It breached every defence. Closed doors and portholes were of no avail and only made our cabins hot, dirty and disagreeable. To ensure we had enough coal to reach Africa, shore carpenters built huge boxes each side of two of the 'midships hatches and they were also filled. Across the Indian Ocean, as the firemen emptied the bunkers we would refill them from the boxes by wheelbarrow.

Ginger and I went to a Friday night dance. Within moments Ginger had himself a Judy, as his countrymen referred to girls.

'Come on, Kiwi, grab a Judy!' he called out as he swung by.

Ginger's Judy smiled over his shoulder. She pointed to her friend standing nearby. I made a tentative move. There was no obvious response. Still smarting from the mortification several weeks earlier after the Napier dance, I left the girl to herself.

Ginger and his Judy returned to her friend and beckoned me over.

'Kiwi, meet Valerie,' Ginger said, with a possessive arm around her shoulders. 'Valerie, meet Kiwi.'

'Hullo, Kiwi,' Valerie said. 'What's your proper name?'

'Peter,' I said.

'Peter. Yes, that's better,' she said. She indicated her friend.

'Peter, Bonnie. Bonnie, Peter.'

'How do you do?' we said and shook hands.

Ginger pulled a face. He considered formalities a waste of time under the circumstances. He steered the talk into matters better suited to assessing each girl's amatory potentials. After a few verbal jousts he rejected Bonnie as a prospect and returned his attentions to the more voluptuous Valerie.

Valerie, however, plainly wise to Men of the World, suddenly disengaged from Ginger and asked, taking my arm, 'D'ya dance?'

'Well . . . no, not really. Not very well, anyway.'

'OK. I'll show you.'

Ginger, being a lad whose self-complacency never deserted him, was able to endure rejection with indifference. He accepted his cavalier abandonment without demur and turned his attention to Bonnie.

Valerie guided me around the crowded floor. She was a willowy girl of about seventeen. Her brown hair swung around her shoulders like a velvet waterfall and her body rippled through her dress as she moved sinuously to the music.

Ginger ignored us as he and Bonnie swayed, chatting and laughing. He sure had a way with the Judies, and Bonnie, unlike the wiser Valerie, seemed more responsive to his talk and laughter.

But Bonnie winked at Valerie over Ginger's shoulder.

Valerie grinned and winked back.

'Fancies himself, your mate, doesn't he?' she said.

'Why?'

She tossed her head so that her hair tickled my chin.

'I just know he does,' she answered with the accrued female wisdom of centuries.

Ginger made several attempts to regain Valerie. But it was I who kissed her goodnight at her front door. Later in our cabin Ginger asked how I had got on. My enigmatic reply led him to believe I had 'got on' very well.

'Yeah, knew you'd be all right there,' he said.

'What about you?'

Ginger was equally enigmatic.

Southern turned restlessly in his bunk.

'For Christ's sake get your heads down and shut up,' he growled. 'Anyway, a real Judy'd have your bollocks for breakfast!' he added, almost happily.

Next day Valerie told me Bonnie went home in a taxi and Ginger had left the dance on his own.

Apart from Valerie and Bonnie there was little to discover in Newcastle. It was a dreary place, an industrial town of steel and coal. Its natives may as well have been New Zealanders with Aussie accents.

A few days later we sailed for South Africa.

An AB and the cabin boy had deserted the previous day. A deserter from another British ship had replaced the AB. He was brought aboard by two policemen and locked in the bosun's store until we sailed. The bosun and carpenter were blind drunk. The radio operator and chief steward were only marginally less so. The chief officer was in a swearing temper. He had spent part of the morning prising one of the chief steward's men out of jail. The

45

captain was angrier because the man still missed the ship. By several feet, in fact, when he fell from the wharf and was taken to hospital and left there half-drowned and still drunk.

⚓

In the Great Australian Bight the bridge wings rolled like a swimmer's arms as we were rocked from side to side by the long swells sweeping unhindered from the Southern Ocean. At times we slowed to a mere four knots, sometimes less, as the ship contested the outer breath of the Roaring Forties. She shouldered aside the seas in sheets of spray and shuddered as the thrashing propeller lifted out of the water with her pitching.

However, we still chipped rust, soogeed (washed with water and washing soda) paintwork or painted wherever rain, spray or wind was out of reach.

Late on Christmas Eve we left Cape Leeuwin's flashing lighthouse astern and as Australia sank beneath the horizon without trace, we began the long, landless trek across the Indian Ocean to South Africa.

Christmas Day came clear, warm and windless. The long, lazy swells were burnished like a mirror and *Algonquin Park* steamed at her full ten knots, her bow waves curling out in perfect symmetry on either side of her. Christmas dinner was what the cook called turkey, accompanied by what passed for trimmings, followed by doughy plum duff, tinned cream and a bottle of beer each for all hands.

Afterwards most of those off watch — white sailors and the engineroom and stokehold's Arabs, Indians and Africans from various countries including Zanzibar — lay on an after-hatch lazily recalling foreign ports and various misadventures. It was one of the few times the traditional antipathy between deck and engineroom, since oil and water don't mix, gave way to common community.

Much of the talk concerned bars, brawls, jail cells and policemen of different nationalities, severities and partiality to bribery.

And of course Judies of every age, shape, size, nationality, race, colour, carnal predilection and price range.

As much as her crew is a synopsis of its individuals' vices and virtues, so their ship is a synopsis of the vices and virtues of her designers and builders. Infinitely greater than the substance of her parts, she behaves as well or as badly as those who sail and understand or misunderstand her. Good, bad or ugly; a lady or a bitch; responsive to the right treatment, unforgiving of bad, she has a soul plain to those who live aboard her, who know her best.

And a ship's crew being individually and collectively as idiosyncratic as their ship, so *Algonquin Park*'s men encompassed socialists, communists, capitalists, atheists and every other possible 'ist'. They kneaded together with varying degrees of prejudice and tolerance, although there were sometimes headlong disagreements when ideas and opinions infringed national or racial boundaries beyond otherwise generally accepted limits. And with only a thin steel plate between them and disaster, ships' crews could scarcely fail to have ideas and opinions on any subject.

Southern, as if superior to life rather than part of it, took no interest in anything. He dozed and got sunburnt instead.

'Serves him right!' Ginger said with satisfaction. 'Bloody dozy prick! Probably can't even be bothered feeling sorry for himself.'

⚓

A ship is no place for xenophobes. *Algonquin Park*'s crew was a haphazardly cobbled together assembly from everywhere and anywhere, over forty men of differing race, colour, nationality, creed, age, size and temperament.

On the bridge were the captain and chief, second and third mates and radio operator. On deck were the bosun, carpenter and sailors, generally referred to as the 'crowd' — six able seamen, two senior ordinary seamen and one junior ordinary seaman (me). On the catering side were the chief steward, second steward, three stewards, cabin boy, chief cook, second cook and pantry boy. Down below were the chief, second and third engineers, donkeyman, greasers, wipers, firemen and coal trimmers.

Most of the men had been at sea through the war. In the 11-million tons of lost Allied ships, more than 40,000 merchant seamen had been killed — one in six compared with one in thirty-three in the combined armed services.

For the younger crew the beginnings of their lives at sea had therefore been dangerous and disagreeable — Ginger was a deck boy during the last year of it; his elder brother had been lost in an Atlantic convoy. For men such as the bosun and carpenter it had been an aberration in their otherwise normal seafaring lives. But no one was persuaded to talk much about any of it.

Their ancestors had sailed the seas since 1500 BC when it was likely the stones of Stonehenge were brought by boat from Wales to England, 500 years before the Phoenicians towed Lebanon's cedars to Tel Aviv for King Solomon's temple. By 55 BC, when Caesar's legions rowed across the Channel, the English were already voyaging on seas rougher than any Mediterranean water.

The ill-tempered, stocky captain fitted the pattern perfectly. The snappy chief officer, too. And the taciturn second mate. And the third mate, who always seemed to be falling foul of the captain. The leather-skinned, pipe-smoking, gold-earringed bosun could have travelled from his ancient lineage without a pause on the way. So could Southern, although he may have slept most of the time. Corny still had the Cornish swarthiness of his Celtic and foreign ancestors.

Few would have had a pleasant time during their ancestral journeyings. Ill-treated, badly fed crews sailing ill-found ships laid the foundations of hundreds of shipowners' mighty fortunes. So there was — still is — a legacy of antipathy between seamen and shipowners nurtured over hundreds of years.

Shakespeare opined that ships were 'but boards, sailors but men; there be land-rats and water-rats, land thieves and water-thieves.' Around the same time Robert Burton, in his *Anatomy of Melancholy*, posed the rhetorical question, 'What is a ship but a prison?' Samuel Johnson, a couple of hundred years later, also had a word or two on the subject. No man would be a sailor, he said, 'who has contrivance enough to get himself into jail; for being in a ship is being in a jail, with the chance of being drowned

. . . a man in jail has more room, better food and commonly better company.'

In Queen Anne's time the law required those tending the poor to send pauper boys to sea. It was a convenient means of relieving themselves of the care of unwanted lads. Many were as young as ten years old. They faced rotten salt meat and weevilly biscuits; captains and mates administering discipline with rope-ends and wooden marlin spikes; uninterested shipowners; lousy accommodation; poor or virtually no pay; ill-found and overloaded ships on voyages measured in years and in continual peril of storms, hostile shores and shipwreck.

In the 1890s New Zealand seamen, whose history and mores derived from their British counterparts, were allowed 72 cubic feet against 120 for passengers and 240 for workers ashore. Even heat and light in port had to be fought for. It needed the Prime Minister in the late 1940s to force the issue, saying 'everything possible will be done to install at the earliest possible date the necessary equipment for maintaining heat and light aboard ships full time when they are in port.' In the late 1960s the New Zealand Seaman's Union president said that 'every penny added to wages, every square foot of crew accommodation and every egg in the menu has had to be argued, haggled and fought for.'

At the beginning of the twentieth century a report on British ships said that:

At all times the forecastle was a foulsome and suffocating abode, and in bad weather the water and filth which washed around the deck among the chests and created the most intolerable and loathsome stench . . . here, however, these fourteen sailors and apprentices slept, washed, dressed and had their food . . . consisting almost entirely of inferior salted pork, unpalatable beef and brown biscuits, too often mouldy and full of maggots . . . the forecastle was full of rats which found their way into the hammocks in which the crew slept. In the West Indies that place was suffocatingly hot, and in winter, when approaching the English Channel, it was bitterly cold, no stoves or fires of any kind being allowed inward. No Siberian slaves suffered as much from the intensity of the cold as did those

49

sailors and apprentices, their damp clothes as they lay upon the chests or hung suspended from the beams being frequently frozen to such an extent that ice had to be beaten from them before they could be used again.

In the 1930s depression years, British ships' poor food, squalid accommodation and low pay were reckoned worse than any city slum. Even in 1938, when Britain had the world's largest merchant fleet — its 3000 ships equalled the combined totals of the next three nations, USA, Japan and Norway — seamen were 'among the most deprived and neglected of working men.' The death rate for crews was 47 per cent more than the national average, mainly through tuberculosis, cerebral haemorrhage and gastric or duodenal ulcers. The mortality rate below the age of 55 was twice as high among seamen as the rest of the male population.

Under those conditions during the Second World War, from the moment they took to lifeboats or life rafts or were left clinging to floating wreckage, or even just swimming, seamen were deemed unemployed. Many shipowners stopped their wages until they again shipped out. And while unemployed some did not have an easy time of it. In 1942 the British-manned oil tanker *Ohio*, badly damaged and her back broken, was brought into Malta lashed between two destroyers. But her surviving crew, which had twice abandoned and twice re-boarded their hopelessly crippled ship — a measure of the island's critical need for *Ohio*'s fuel cargo — was then classed as non-productive. This allowed them only bare minimum rations below the level of the civilian population.

But at least they had survived the bombs and torpedoes. One writer later said that 'lamentable lifejackets and lifeboats . . . were probably responsible for more British seamen's deaths than torpedo hits.'[1]

Lifejackets were made of cork blocks and sometimes broke their wearers' necks when they jumped into the water. They were later replaced with thick kapok-filled waistcoats that soaked up oil and sank within twenty-four hours. Lifeboats were of the same design as that rowed by Grace Darling and were difficult to get away from a sinking ship.

Even in the mid-twentieth century a chasm existed between the general populace and seamen no less wide than Sir Henry Fielding observed in 1776:

> When one goes to Rotherhithe or Wapping, which places are chiefly inhabited by sailors, but that somewhat of the same language is spoken, a man would be apt to suspect himself in another country. Their manner of living, speaking, acting, dressing and behaving are so peculiar to themselves.

It was a chasm well voiced when Lady Astor, Britain's first female Member of Parliament, suggested before the war that seamen returning from foreign voyages should wear yellow armbands signifying them as potential venereal disease carriers. *Algonquin Park*'s crew, every one of them, still regarded Lady Astor as an unholy, unhung bitch.

Many of the firemen and trimmers were also of a long seagoing lineage, such as the man from Zanzibar. The Arabs among them could have traced their voyagings long back into ancient times. One, an Iraqi, was nicknamed Sinbad.

Algonquin Park, a Liberty-type utility ship built in 1941 in Sorel, Canada, would also have had her times. Instead of lounging around on Christmas Day all hands would have had their lifejackets within immediate reach and her gunners would have been standing by their four-inch low angle guns and Oerlikons and Bofors.

On visits to Auckland during the war I had often spent time at the city wharves gazing at the ships. Their grey wartime paint, blocked-out names, life rafts rigged ready for immediate launching and the guns on their sterns plainly recited the realities of those days. As young as I was then, I already had a glimmering, aided of course by the movies, of the hazards the ships had faced voyaging to New Zealand. I sometimes wished I had been old enough to have been aboard one of them.

My fancies were therefore not entirely illusory as I lazed on the hatch top and gazed at the ocean, imagining our ship being stalked by an inquisitive periscope — one of her sisters, *Avondale Park*, was the last merchant ship sunk by a U-boat, U2336, off the east coast of Scotland shortly after Germany had surrendered. The excuse was that the German commander, Klusmeyer, had not received the signal to cease hostilities.

Algonquin Park and her crew therefore had all the elements of ancient and not so ancient maritime history woven within them. I suppose I did, too, my mother being an Englishwoman. But I still felt a bit removed from it.

⚓

At midnight on New Year's Eve the third mate rang the ship's bridge bell sixteen times in single strokes. The lookout answered by ringing the fo'c'sle bell continually for about a minute. A sailor presented the traditional lump of coal to the engineroom 'with the compliments of the deck department.'

Thus arrived the New Year.

Almost at the same time the captain resumed his general umbrage at life in general. He was the type of man unable to grant a grain of festive goodwill to all mankind at any one time. He had already distributed as much of his supply as he judged necessary.

As I stood at the wheel a cloud of small shapes skimmed across the calm Indian Ocean water. 'Flying fish,' the second mate announced as energetically as he had announced Australia. Squadrons of small gleaming bodies rose from the sea like silver ornaments, fanning out in long curves, their wide fins outstretched like wings. As their flight slowed their tail tips dipped back into the sea for another quick wriggle to propel them even further out of reach of the behemoth bearing down upon them. Flying fish can rise as high as 36 feet and glide for up to 200 yards.

Early next morning at the bow and lulled by the sounds normally accompanying the lookout hours — the soft resonance of the engine, the hull's creaks and groans, the bow wave, the silent thunder of shooting stars leaving their trails in the sky — I heard another sound. Although strangely in harmony with the others, it came from the sea itself. I looked over the side.

Dolphins rode the invisible pressure wave directly beneath and either side of the bow. Underwater they turned this way and that, trailing pathways of glowing phosphorescent light and cork-screwing their bodies in apparent sheer enjoyment. When they surfaced it was for a quick breath, the sound I had heard, and to surf on the crest of our bow wave before taking a curving dive back under the water. Sometimes they raced off into the darkness in trails of phosphorescence before returning like charging cavalry to continue their games.

They must have been there before. But it had been too cold and windy to lean over the bulwarks, so I would have missed them. This time they stayed perhaps half an hour before speeding off on dolphin business elsewhere.

For years after, every time I saw dolphins under a ship's bow I was reminded of that first time. It was then the profundity of the ocean first really impinged itself on my consciousness. This feeling was later fortified as albatrosses wheeled in our wake or occasionally glided silently alongside the ship close enough to establish eye contact. Usually they were alone, occasionally in pairs or, though rarely, threes.

There seemed to be no community between them. Their mid-ocean meetings were as if by sheer chance, their companionship accidental and only for a short time. With the whole of the Southern Ocean to roam in, it would have been a lonely life. But a supremely self-sufficient one, their only contact with the land being to breed.

Judging by messroom conversations, the same could have been said of some of the crew.

⚓

The low sweeping loom of a lighthouse signalled we had reached Africa. Gradually the lights of Durban became visible. They stretched along the horizon in little dots as if perforating the land from the sea. The best entry to a city is from the sea. It can be seen on a broad front. Approach by land is through the mess of its outskirts and back yards. But from the sea its broad front presents a mystery, and we can make a start on it as we should always make a start, from the beginning.

We had steamed 4300 miles from Australia and travelled for a month. New Zealand was 6000 miles and two months astern. The experiences spanning those two months were as if a lifetime had passed since leaving Russell — I also wondered if whoever had replaced me in the post office had solved both the postmaster and how to open the doors and hoist his bloody flag at the same time.

In the warm Friday dawn we passed between Durban's breakwaters behind a steam tug and tied up at the bluff for our coalbunkers to be refilled.

The first European to sight the place I had arrived at was Vasco da Gama. The Portuguese explorer had sailed along the coast in December 1497 while pioneering a route to the East. He named it Terra Natalis, or Natal, because it was Christmas Day. During the sixteenth and seventeeth centuries countless ships were wrecked north and south of Natal Bay, driven onto the forbidding and mysterious continent by violent seas and hidden reefs. In the early nineteenth century the bay was a refuge for Africans escaping the ruthless military reign of Shaka, the Zulu king.

It was about a century since the first determined settlers had crossed the bar of what was then the Rio de Natal, named because Europeans believed it was the mouth of a great river. European history began with the survivors becoming reluctant explorers as they struggled northwards towards Mozambique.

The sweating black men on the quayside handling our mooring ropes could have descended from those who would have been hostile to the newcomers and left most of the survivors to die of fever, starvation and exhaustion. As much as sheer fright.

Next morning Ginger and I took a ferry across the harbour to The Point and struck out into the surrounding city. Black people detoured around us to leave our way unobstructed. Nods or smiles, particularly at those of my own age, were met with a lowering of the head. It was my first encounter with the reality of race and it was difficult to understand, since there was no such division aboard our ship and its black and white crew.

Whether or not anyone smiled at me, however, I was absorbed by the fact I was thousands of miles in distance and ten hours in time from home.

We watched tall Zulu rickshaw pullers. Passengers sat like grand bwanas in the two-wheel, two-seater carriages. The brightly coloured pullers were dressed in huge, ornately beaded headdresses and tunics. They belted along the road balanced delicately on the arms of the conveyances. Their feet touched the ground with just sufficient high-kicking, prancing steps to maintain their surprising speed. Few of these colourful characters remain, and then only as tourist attractions. They have become victims of inflation and traffic regulations and, apparently, the notion that they represent one of the less savoury aspects of colonial Africa.

Ginger tried to get off with a department-store salesgirl. She had spoken in English to a customer ahead of us but rebuffed him in Afrikaans. This upset Ginger more than the rebuff. His reply in earthy Tyneside produced a torrent of Afrikaans.

'So y'understood me all right! Aye! Y'did that, y'cow,' he retorted angrily, his self-complacency vis-à-vis Judies for once disturbed.

Later on one of the beaches fronting the city and onto which the Indian Ocean waves curled in rolling processions, Ginger made no effort to pursue the possibilities when tanned bathing-suited girls responded positively to his libidinous gaze. Apart from leering at them he was right off South African Judies.

As we leaned over the rail with our mid-morning cups of tea, a welcome break from working on stages over the side in the sticky heat painting the ship's side, a ragged-clothed young African boy arrived at the gangway. He had a tray of small items for sale. He was invited aboard and given a cup of tea and some tabnabs. We bought something of everything — shoelaces, polish, envelopes, writing pads, postcards, cheap souvenirs.

The boy returned to the quayside and squatted on his haunches counting his money and rearranging his tray. He seemed not to notice a railway engine sidling past with more coal wagons. Leaning lazily on his cab windowsill, the driver looked up at us and grinned. Suddenly a piping-hot blast of steam burst from the bottom of his engine. As the swirl cleared the boy lay spread-eagled and crying, his bits and pieces scattered, some of them under the coal wagons.

Harry, a Hereford bull of a man you would not want near even indelicate china, swore and walked down the gangway. He helped the boy repack his tray, patted his head and wiped away his tears. Then he walked towards the locomotive.

'Going to have a word or two with the bastard,' he called back.

Everyone knew Harry as a man of few words.

'Christ,' someone said, 'now there'll be fuckin' trouble.'

There was. Harry dragged the driver from his cabin. A series of blows sent the man reeling before a signally vicious *whack!* slumped him to the ground. The boy looked on in astonishment and then limped away with his tray and proceeds.

During the fight — it wasn't really a fight, let alone a contest; there was nothing Homeric about it — the locomotive came to rest at the end of the quay where it harrumphed and hissed against the wooden stop as it tried to drive itself into the harbour. Harry dragged the driver back to his cab, lifted him bodily and shoved him back inside. It was several minutes before the befuddled man shut off the steam and disappeared with a staggering weave across the railyards.

Half an hour later a squad of policemen clumped up the gangway. They demanded to see the captain. Harry pointed to the bridge.

Ten minutes later the policemen stormed back to their cars. The captain followed them down the bridge ladder. He stopped halfway and stared at us as if awaiting homage after single-handedly seeing off a thousand dervishes on our behalf. When no one volunteered even a comment, he roared at us instead.

'You bloody-fuckin'-stupid fools! You nearly all got arrested!' But in a slightly softer voice, he added, 'Anyway, served the bastard right!'

Later he gave the bosun a bottle of beer to be passed to Harry with his compliments. Later still the chief officer told the bosun the captain had challenged the policemen to arrest the whole crew since he didn't know who had beaten up the engine driver, and wouldn't tell them if he did. Moreover, if his ship were held up he would complain to the newspapers that it was a Communist plot. And the authorities would not like that.

In later years as South African politics wended their inexorable way, I sometimes wondered what other indignities the boy endured. And what sort of man he became as a consequence. Hopefully he grew up with at least one corner in his heart reserved for a white man.

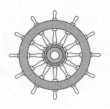

7

Push on — keep moving . . .
Thomas Morton

Just as there is an air of expectancy when a ship approaches land and arrives in port, so there is when she leaves. As she reaches the open sea the pilot swings against the hull as he clambers down the Jacob's ladder to the pilot tender. As he is carried back to the land he waves to the men on the bridge and the sailors pulling the ladder back aboard. The captain orders Full Ahead. It is signalled with double rings to tell the engineers that manoeuvring movements are finished and to work up to full speed. The ship trembles as her propeller boils and froths the water at her stern. As she sets her course her crew turns inward and resume their ordered places in the hierarchical community.

Thus is the land at last unshackled. We are at sea again. It is time to look forward.

And so as we left Durban behind a curtain of warm January rain, I shifted my gaze ahead — to the Cape of Good Hope and up the Atlantic to the Port of London, nearly 7000 miles away and nonstop unless we needed to refill our bunkers in Spain.

The waters along Durban's south coast are among the world's most dangerous and unpredictable, the combined result of sea bed topography and the Mozambique–Agulhas current flowing south. Waves running up from the Cape, known as Cape rollers, collide with the surge of the strong Agulhas current coming the opposite way.

The Admiralty's *South African Pilot*, given to few superfluous words and even fewer adjectives, says that 'under certain weather conditions abnormal waves of exceptional height occur off the SE coast of South Africa, causing severe damage to ships unfortunate to encounter them.' The guide goes on to describe such waves as 'extremely steep-fronted and preceded by very deep troughs. A ship . . . meeting such a trough will find her bows still dropping into the trough with increasing momentum when she encounters the steep-fronted face of the oncoming wave, which she heads straight into, the wave eventually breaking over the fore part of the ship with devastating force.' Another account tells it more graphically:

> *Waves hurled into uproar by this powerful collision . . .*
> *superimpose upon each other and thus frequently create a wave*
> *of extraordinary height and power at whose base lies a sudden*
> *deep gulf. A ship lurches into the gulf and then receives upon its*
> *back the terrifying immensity of water towering above.*[2]

This sudden deep gulf is quite literally a hole in the sea. In July 1909 a British ship, the Blue Anchor Line flagship liner *Waratah*, is thought to have been overwhelmed in this way during a southwesterly storm a day after leaving Durban. She was on the return leg of her maiden voyage from Britain to Australia with 112 crew and 109 passengers and a cargo of frozen meat and lead. No trace of her, not a single piece of debris, was ever found and she became the stuff of legend and myth — until July 1999 when she was found lying upright in 62 fathoms about six miles off East London.

During the Second World War the Royal Navy cruiser *Birmingham* toppled into such a chasm and the sea broke over the bridge, 60 feet above the water. The impact was so severe many of the crew below decks thought the ship had been torpedoed and went to their emergency stations.

In more recent times the 100,000-ton *Texanita* and the 45,000-ton *World Glory* were sunk. The British liner *City of*

Exeter was badly damaged and many of her passengers injured. In 1973 a new British cargo liner, *Bencruachan*, had her entire bow section bent 20 feet downward. The main beams became instantly white hot, so sudden was the moment of bending. The ship had to be towed stern first into Durban. A few weeks later the 12,000-ton container ship *Neptune Sapphire* had her bows broken off. Another more than twice her size, the Union Castle Line passenger ship *Edinburgh Castle*, suddenly fell forwards at an angle of over thirty degrees. A wall of water carried away deck fittings and flooded the passenger accommodation. In 1991 a Greek passenger ship, *Oceanos*, was similarly overwhelmed and sunk. Fortunately everyone was rescued.

Our passage was much more mundane, albeit uncomfortable.

The captain stood on the wing of the bridge like a waxwork emperor, his oil-skinned bulk hunched against the wind and streaming rain. He was always irritable near land, more so when it was hidden by the weather. At intervals he stomped into the wheelhouse and looked inquisitively at the compass. Then he returned outside and gazed intently towards the coast, as if willing it to appear through the muck.

Navigation in such weather was a matter of the officer of the watch's dead reckoning, the lookout's keen eyes and the helmsman's accurate steering.

'Keep an eye on her,' Southern warned me when I relieved him at ten o'clock, 'or the Old Man'll have your balls for breakfast.'

He did, several times. At the same time the third mate was rendered to an impotent rage since the captain first turned on him each time he caught me even slightly either side of the course.

'Watch it,' he hissed each time the captain had finished with both of us, 'or I'll have your guts for bloody garters!'

Between the pair of them I felt I was being gutted.

A messroom discussion about the black boy and the engine driver led to a decision, unanimous except for my dissenting vote, that being a newcomer to the game I should be taught a thing or two.

'Need to know how to look after yourself, Kiwi,' they said.

I was put into a fighting stance. A man at the back of me held my arms. Another stood in front and extended his fists.

'Now,' said the man holding my arms, 'when he goes to punch you, you do this,' pulling my hands up to cover my face, 'so you can protect yourself.'

As my opponent pretended to throw a punch my mentor shoved my right arm forward, 'and you cop him like . . . this . . . before he cops you . . .'

The ship suddenly pitched heavily and I received a hefty whack in the mouth.

'Shit! Sorry!'

After the messroom's inspection of my torn and bloody lip it was agreed I should go to the chief steward. I staggered along the wet, dark afterdeck with a handkerchief stemming the gushing blood.

'Bloody hell,' the chief steward said. 'You lot been fighting back there?'

I explained as best I could that they had been teaching me to box.

'Boxing, my arse. None of them could box a crate of bloody bananas. Brawling, more likely. Boxing? Bollocks!'

He fetched the second steward. Between them they agreed stitches were required. But it was a job more suitable for the captain.

The captain looked at me with weary disbelief.

'Well done!' he growled grumpily. 'At this time of bloody night! What happened? Fighting?'

'They were teaching him to box,' the chief steward explained with a doubting smirk.

'Boxing, you say? Bloody bollocks!' the captain exclaimed, echoing the chief steward's doubts that any of them could have been acquainted with the Noble Art. He opened his medical cabinet and threaded a curved needle while the chief steward bathed the long cut with stinging salted water.

'Right, lad,' the captain said, 'sit down and let's be having you.'

I sat bolt upright with the chief steward at the back of me holding me firmly by the shoulders. The captain stood in front of me with his legs apart to counter the rolling ship.

'It's all right,' he said as I shrank from the needle waving in my face, 'I've done hundreds. For God's sake, steward, keep him still so I can see what I'm doing.'

The pain provided its own anaesthetic and the needle and thread, apart from the first puncturing prick, contributed little to the total hurt.

I was not allowed on watch for four days. I read or sunbathed all day instead, and spent all night in my bunk and rose as late as I liked. It would have been luxurious except I could eat only soup through a straw, despite which my lip stung painfully if so much as a drop of the liquid touched it. On the fifth day the captain removed the stitches and I returned to the watches. But only to steer. I was not allowed on lookout for several more nights and the lip had to be dressed each day. Each occasion was followed by an admonition to keep clear of idiots wanting to teach me to box. The bosun cursed them, too. He had to take my place on the night watches.

After rounding the Cape, with Table Mountain and its cloud cap seen distantly through the haze, we headed northwest up the South Atlantic towards the western bulge of the African continent. The ship rolled lazily in the great Atlantic swells reaching up as remnants of Antarctic and Southern Ocean storms. Their slow undulations rose and fell like the earth's gently breathing lungs.

The Atlantic Ocean's nearly 32-million square miles is the second largest body of water after the Pacific. It formed some 150 million years ago, during the Jurassic period when a rift in the Gondwanaland supercontinent separated South America and Africa. Its name comes from Atlas, one of Greek mythology's Titans.

These were also the waters of the legendary *Flying Dutchman* whose captain, having blasphemously cursed the ocean, was condemned to sail about the Cape of Good Hope against the wind until Judgement Day. The phantom ship is supposed to bring calamity to any who see it. Sailing-ship sailors nailed horseshoes to the mast to protect themselves against an encounter. Another version has the ship sailing aimlessly while her captain plays dice, for his soul, with the devil. The legend was the basis of Richard Wagner's opera *Der Fliegende Holländer*.

Legend? Her ghost was reported by King George V when he was a midshipman aboard HMS *Bacchante* in 1881. His diary describes a 'strange red light . . . in the midst of which light the mast, spars and sails of a brig two hundred yards distant stood out in strong relief as she came up . . .' In 1959 a Dutch freighter also reported her heading for the ship and vanishing just as they were about to collide.

⚓

Each night the Southern Cross fell lower in the sky as we steamed up out of my own hemisphere and towards the other. There was an unmistakable change in the air as we neared the equatorial latitudes. The stars stretching from horizon to horizon scintillated upon the tropic sea like pinpoints of icy light. It was a setting in which the imagination could range until it strained beyond its capabilities. How can we properly comprehend an ocean night and its spaces? They are elements beyond sensible conjecture.

It's of course unlikely that I speculated in such fashion at that time. At least not coherently. Not until later, when the mind had weathered sufficiently to allow it to indulge more mature considerations. I need only observe others of my age at that time to realise this is probably so.

But if such thoughts did not formulate in the Atlantic Ocean off tropical Africa, they had their genesis there.

Ventilators were turned for'ard and improvised metal scoops thrust through cabin portholes to inhale the slim breeze of our passing. As we moved through the tropics the cabins became diabolical. It was worse with a following wind. It and the breeze of the ship's passage cancelled each other out. The funnel smoke then curled lazily upwards and acrid fumes and hot cinders fell from it and wafted around the decks.

In the windless doldrums and later the horse latitudes the air was hotter, stickier, muggier. It seemed too heavy to move.

Conditions were satanic for the firemen in the stokehold. Temperatures rose well above 130 degrees Fahrenheit. Perspiration streamed down the men's grimy black bodies. Their only relief was chewing their sweat rags and using them to clear eyes, noses and mouths clogged with coal dust made almost into mud by perspiration. Clouds of hot dust enveloped them when they raked out red-hot clinker. Then they were suffocated by steam when they wetted it before hoisting it up to the deck to be dumped overboard. It was even worse for the coal trimmers in the choking, ill-lit bunkers.

It was not surprising tempers sometimes flared down there.

A quarrel between two African firemen degenerated into threats of murder before the chief engineer intervened. No one, probably least of all the swearing, spanner- and shovel-wielding participants, knew the cause for such high drama. Its propellant was undoubtedly the inability to achieve even a pinch of relief from the conditions under which they laboured. I had already heard tales of stokehold animosity on some ships ending with a man murdered and disposed of in the fires.

Whatever the cause, the equally infuriated captain, gold-braided cap wedged firmly on his head to impress his authority on all concerned, stormed below to rescue his chief engineer from the imbecilic firemen. The four then stomped in a ranked procession along the hot steel deck to the bridge. The chief officer was called and further furious argument enveloped all five.

The firemen were logged — name, rank and misdemeanour entered in the ship's official log — and fined. The captain, chief engineer and chief officer then drank whisky. According to the captain's tiger (steward) this produced a dispute of its own.

Elsewhere around the sweltering ship frazzled tempers caused other passionate arguments and bloody mouths and noses. I was greatly alarmed by the raw aggression, despite everyone otherwise rendered dopey by heat-induced inertia.

Even Ginger and Southern almost came to blows until Harry the Hereford bull, himself in foul temper, threatened to severely injure the pair of them. It was a caveat to be conscientiously heeded after Harry's outstanding performance with the Durban engine driver.

'But you're still a big prick,' Ginger told Southern, less than sotto voce, when a reluctant peace was restored.

'And you're not even a *little* prick, y'Geordie bastard,' Southern snarled, fists still clenched in a tight ball. Southern's heated reply warmed Ginger for a moment but mindful of Harry, also a Geordie, both left it at that.

And boxing lessons notwithstanding, I was sensible enough to completely mind my own business the whole time.

The radio operator sometimes allowed me into his stuffy shack when I was off watch. Having learned Morse code in the Russell post office, I was able to read the dots and dashes coming through the static on his receiver. In much the same way as the railway-engine drivers had let me blow their whistles, he also sometimes let me call up another ship on his Morse key.

Ginger and even Southern had admired my ability to read the 'What ship?' Aldis lamp exchanges between the officer of the watch and passing ships. But when they learned of my visits to the radio operator they were severely disapproving. It was a moment of rare accord between them.

'We don't mix with those 'midships bastards,' they said. 'They are there. We are here. And here we stay — and there they stay.'

It worked in reverse, of course.

None of the 'midships bastards', not even the captain, unless in full uniform or on his official Sunday morning crew accommodation inspections trailed by the chief officer, chief engineer and chief steward, ventured into crew accommodation unless invited, and that would have been only for a very compelling reason, certainly not a social one. Neither side believed in egalitarianism. It was a blunt articulation of class-driven British social life.

But it was more than that. It was also a reminder of the reality of a ship. Shipboard life cannot allow for too much democracy. It has to surrender to an autocratic approach. For the sea itself is autocratic. It allows no debate and no space for the consideration of sensitivities. Just as it is in supreme charge of those who sail over it, those in charge of a ship must be supreme over those in their charge.

My visits to the radio operator would not have been out of place in earlier days. If qualified as 'wireless watchers', ordinary seamen were signed on as 'ordinary seaman and wireless watcher'. They kept watch in the radio room and fetched the operator when the ship was called or there was an alarm.

By now we were beginning to sight more ships than at any time so far. Their lines and general appearance echoed the national characteristics of their countries — Britain, Scandinavia, Italian, French, American — so that even from great distances the crew could generally tell their nationalities at a glance. In the case of British ships the men also knew their companies as much by their general appearance as their liveries. Some were familiar to New Zealand ports. I recognised *New Zealand Star* as a visitor to Napier. The big Blue Star Line ship steamed past at about fifteen knots. She glistened with paint fresh from her stay in London. Her passengers and crew lined the rails in the sunshine as she rose and dipped over the swells on her way south to the Cape of Good Hope.

I had always been filled with a profound sense of 'gone to sea' when watching ships leave Napier, their funnel smoke sniffing the horizon as they disappeared into the Pacific on their courses north or south to other New Zealand ports, or west to Panama. *New Zealand Star* had been one of them. As I watched her here on the other side of the world I sensed a fleeting homesickness. But it disappeared as rapidly as the ship grew smaller until she was no more.

As was the custom — now mostly consigned to a lower drawer marked Tradition — passing ships dipped their ensigns and blew a short whistled greeting to each other. I felt the stirring of a sense of brotherhood whenever I was given the job of dipping the flag. Spanking-smart Union Castle passenger liners on their regular runs to South African ports were tardy in acknowledging our courtesy. Some of the haughty bitches did not bother.

Understandable, I suppose. Their Blue Ensigns denoted their captains and a certain number of crew were Royal Naval Reserve. In such august presence and wearing only the red ensign, or Red Duster as it was usually known, we were only a tart, and a coarse one at that.

⚓

As a first-tripper I had to endure the Crossing the Line initiation. The ritual dates back to the ancient Greeks and Romans. The 'metes and bounds' delineating their seas and oceans were as mysterious and omnipotent as the gods themselves. Even a voyage beyond Gibraltar, the ancients' Pillars of Hercules, was an expedition beyond sanity. To appease their gods — the Romans' Neptune and Greeks' Poseidon — for their temerity, they believed that carefully worked out and rigorous tests, or rites, would help ease the way for those crossing the Line for the first time.

Those having already survived the gods' wrath were delegated to perform the rites on their behalf.

King Neptune's throne was a wooden box. His helmet was a galley pot adorned with rope ends. His beard was also of rope ends, this time covered with beer-bottle tops to represent barnacles. Wielding a wooden trident, King Neptune (Southern) was an intimidating figure. Queen Amphitrite, an African fireman in a rope-ends' wig and flowing flour sacks, sat demurely next to him. They were flanked by the Surgeon, Geordie the moustached AB, with a large jug of 'medicine', and the Barber, Harry, with a long wooden 'razor'.

Except for those on watch, all hands assembled on the hatch immediately abaft the bridge so the captain and officers could watch proceedings from a high vantage point. I was seized and dragged to King Neptune's court. Several pairs of rough hands pressed me to my knees.

'Whereas you, Kiwi Taylor, have for the first time entered my domain, you are required to undergo the initiation ceremony known as Crossing the Line. Surgeon, the medicine if you please. Queenie, ya' black bitch, give him a hand.'

Queenie's great black mutton hands forced my mouth open. The Surgeon's vinegar-laced rum burned down my gullet. The Barber smothered me with a mixture of syrup, eggs, paint, whitewash, cement and God knows what else. My face was lathered with soap and fish oil and ungently shaved with the wooden razor. A few snippets of hair were lopped off with scissors. I was then washed down with a fire hose and sent reeling around the deck to the cheers of the assembly.

The ceremony was a few hours premature. We were still some sixty miles south of the Line. It was not until seven o'clock that night that we crossed the equator and passed into the northern hemisphere.

That evening the BBC reported Mahatma Gandhi had been assassinated. I still felt as if I had, too. But I had no complaint. Instead I regarded with some pride the certificate handwritten on a page torn from a writing pad:

I hereby certify that, on God's good day, 28th January, 1948, at 1 p.m., Latitude 0° 0'0' Longitude 8°43' West, Mr Peter Lethbridge Taylor, was presented to my Court, and was duly cleansed and doctored in accordance with my rules. He was presented with this initiation paper which admits him to the Brotherhood of the Severn [sic] Seas, and makes him a member of the R.A. of W.W.W. [Royal Association of World Wide Wanderers]

Sig. James W. Southern
King Neptune

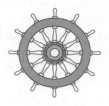

8

Unless God send his hail
Or blinding fire balls,
Sleet or stifling snow,
In some time, his good time
I shall arrive.

Elizabeth Barrett Browning

After passing up the Mauritanian and Spanish Saharan coasts we came upon the southernmost of the Canary Islands, which have been part of Spain since 1479. As we approached their tall volcanic peaks, Mt Teide the highest at 12,000 feet, rose from the horizon like inverted Vs. We steamed through the island group with towns and villages on each side of us and close enough sometimes to see breakers on the beaches. We were also somewhere near the point at which New Zealand lay directly below if I could follow a line straight through the centre of the earth.

The Canaries had nothing to do with canaries, Southern informed Ginger and me as we leaned over the rail barebacked in the sunshine with an end-of-watch cup of tea. The name came instead from the Latin *canis* — the first sailors there found the islands full of dogs.

Such erudition from Southern was impressive. Normally his conversation was restrained by what nature had given him, which it was generally agreed was not very much. However, it would have been presumptuous for me to agree with such a verdict. Southern may not have known much but he certainly knew more than me — one of the first things I learned during messroom discussion and argument was how little I knew about many things. And Southern having several times sneeringly called me to account for engaging in things I clearly knew nothing about, I had learned to keep quiet in his presence, especially after he said I was a 'fuckin' young Kiwi smartarse.'

'Yes, the big prick's a surprising bastard sometimes,' Ginger confirmed later, rather sorrowfully. While Southern may be sometimes right, in Ginger's opinion he was the wrong person to be right.

Some evenings earlier when I had relieved him on lookout, Southern had pointed out the Pole Star. This star, for all practical purposes, remains fixed above the North Pole. It is an infallible pointer to the north. Even the Phoenicians had known it. It was variously named Stella Maris, Star of the Sea, the Lodestar, Stella Nautica and the North Star.

'Now that we can see it, Kiwi,' Southern had said, 'it means you are leaving your half of the world behind you.' It was an unusually friendly remark, and an oddly understanding one. When he left I had stared at the star for many moments, suffused with a real sense of the 'romance of the sea.' And a glimmer of faith in Southern.

But the later disappearance of the Southern Cross, around 25 degrees north, filled me with an even more profound feeling — an awareness as acute as never before of the immensity of the distance I was from home. It was a sublime moment followed by an explosion of spirit. I had reached the edge of the horizon and the first page of a new atlas.

I had mentioned Southern's North Star comments to Ginger. He had been surprised.

'Yeah, I know all that. But how did you know?'

'Southern told me.'

'Huh! The bastard must've read it in a comic.'

As we rolled up the latitudes the watches began rigging the cargo derricks and coating their topping lifts and wire runners with protective fish oil. It was a messy job but the fish oil softened our hands to the extent that Ginger sometimes rubbed his together and said the first Judy he met would be subjected to a very soft feel indeed.

We had already painted the masts and derricks. The rigging had also been blackened down with a mixture of fish oil and Stockholm tar. From high above the deck in bosun chairs we lowered ourselves, applying the thick goo from buckets tied to our chairs. A dirty job but a pleasant one on an expanse of blue sea under the trade winds' towering white cumulus clouds and warm breezes, brief rain showers and sometimes brilliant rainbows shamelessly romantic in their intensity. We also continued chipping and painting so that the ship looked presentable for her arrival in London.

London! I still sometimes mouthed the word to myself, as I had done when I first saw it on our stern at the Napier wharf. The approaches to the great port had long been etched on my mind — Cape Finisterre at the southern end of the Bay of Biscay; Ushant at its northern end; the various landmarks up the English Channel — Lizard, Start Point, Beachy Head, Dungeness . . . the names stirred me every time I heard them mentioned.

Hard work, fine weather, a plenitude of food — a dietitian may have argued its qualities — hot sun and an absorbing interest in every new experience had begun filling out my bony frame and colouring its pale surface.

I had also learned to play cribbage and darts with some skill and enjoyed the regular messroom tournaments between watches and challenges between individuals, with piles of duty-free cigarettes at stake.

I no longer felt a stranger in the men's company. Nor, it seemed, were they in mine. I felt in complete concord, too, with a world in permanent motion as the ship responded to the never-motionless sea. During the watch below my fast-asleep body had long synchronised with the rhythms.

Nearing the wintry northern latitudes the world became little more than a monochromatic meeting of sea and sky. The air was chill and sombre. The sea was colourless and disorderly. The days grew shorter. The sun dwindled through murky skies to a yellowish, watery orb incapable of signifying much more than that it was daylight.

71

Stores began running low. Only sausages, eggs and toast were left out for our nightly end-of-watch suppers, which by now I could cook without cremating and for which, if he was particularly hungry, Southern occasionally complimented me.

Water was short and we washed in salt water with only a freshwater bucket rinse. No one greatly minded. The voyage was drawing to an end.

Toward the end of my lookout a low flashing loom appeared on our starboard side. I stared at it for a few moments to make sure. Earlier in the voyage I had sometimes reported a low star as a light. This time there was no mistake. It was a lighthouse. Cape Finisterre! I gave a whanging ring on the bell.

Finisterre on the starboard bow! The bell's clear, emphatic stroke signalled my excitement. We were about to cross the Bay of Biscay! *In the bay, in the bay, in the Bay of Biscay-O*, ran the old song.

Southern, Ginger and I ate our blackpan in the galley doorway out of the cold wind. We watched the light grow closer until its sweeping beams were plainly visible through the wintry murk.

⚓

All hands were by now suffering 'the channels'. This was a general stimulation induced by the nearness of home after a long voyage. It took the form of endless dhobying (clothes washing) and throwing overboard items no longer needed. Past enmities were dropped and tolerance grew to the point of fatuity. It was an unspoken response to the fact that no one was likely to sail again with any of his present 'Board of Trade companions'. Fortune threw them together; necessity made them live together. Beyond that few cared. For that reason seamen rarely formed friendships enduring beyond their present voyage.

Ginger's carnality was increasing in direct proportion to the decreasing miles. 'By Christ, Kiwi, I'm going to do some goosing, I can tell you!' he said, as we scoured green verdigris from the engineroom telegraphs on the bridge wings with a paste of bath brick and colza oil before rubbing them vigorously with brass polish. It was cold work and our fingers were almost numb. I imagined Ginger's would need to be greatly warmer before any female consented to even the hint of libidinous suggestion, let alone more robust exploration.

Early in the morning a faint flash far off the port bow signalled Start Point. It had been *Mayflower*'s last sight of home as she had set off to colonise America in 1620. For us it was our first English landfall. But we could see nothing of it. Only the flashing light signalled its presence.

Further up the Channel the air dripped in the patchy fogbanks whose towering, cliff-like walls rolled over us in a formless mass. Then, ensnared, we had to heave-to, with the steam whistle regularly sounding, others' answering blasts coming back as muted groans. The captain was greatly irritated when his ship was stranded in such anonymous confinement. He paced through the wheelhouse from one bridge wing to the other, stopping each time to stare at the compass and the helmsman who shivered in the cold, almost wet wind blowing through the open doors.

As the day began closing, Beachy Head's flashing light signalled our closest approach to the land so far. I gazed at the poet's green and pleasant land. He must have penned his words in summer. In midwinter, as much of it as could be seen was leaden and austere. Even the squabbling white herring gulls perched on the ship's vents appeared to be grey. They had been with us long before we had sighted land and had been the first intimation of its offing.

But of all the other places I had arrived at on my way here, the Beachy Head lighthouse and its backdrop of chalk cliffs signalled arrival with a capital A. Nothing accomplished in later life ever compared with the sense of satisfaction that beat inside me as we came abeam of the light and the fresh offshore breeze carrying the delicate fragrance of the land and its myriad bouquets.

The steel deck beat, too, with the engine's resonance as the misty lights of coastal England slid by. A ship's engine is her heart. It is heard or felt everywhere. Even at the top of the mast there is a slight pulse. Now it seemingly beat stronger, as if *Algonquin*

Park, too, inhaled the scent of the land, there to rest awhile after two years' voyaging.

Later in the evening the lights of Hastings shone through the gloom, and then Rye, the Cinque port from where Old Blom, who had helped fire my boldness to come this far, had himself come from so many years before. These were also the waters which had almost cost Mr Worsley his life.

Several times during the rest of the watch below I left my bunk and stood at the messroom doorway. With a cup of steaming co-coa for outer and inner warmth, I was enveloped by the thought that the next day I would have accomplished what I had set out to do. I would be in London.

We rounded South Foreland at dawn and passed Deal, where Julius Caesar had landed in 55 BC, then Ramsgate before rounding North Foreland and passing Margate.

In the Thames Estuary we threaded our way past sunken ships. Our wash swept in a mournful, watery dirge against masts and sometimes tops of funnels thrusting above the grey water in rust-ing testimony to the war that had ended only some thirty months earlier. It swept, too, against the tall steel legs of the Estuary's sea forts. The structures had housed anti-aircraft guns to reach the bombers on their way to continue London's Blitz. They were elo-quent statues to a nation's survival. Some had jagged holes in their superstructures from German air gunners' cannon shells.

We passed Southend's iron pier, over a mile long and built at the same time as the Eiffel Tower, and then Canvey Island, in King Alfred's day the base for Danish and Saxon pirates who raided the surrounding countryside.

Off Gravesend the pilot, picked up earlier off Dungeness dur-ing our watch below, was exchanged for a Thames 'mud pilot'. All hands were then called out to haul the mooring ropes from their lockers and coil them down on the fo'c'sle head and stern. Then we topped (raised) the derricks.

Interesting phrase, that, topped the derricks. Robert Derrick was a public hangman in Queen Elizabeth's reign. He was reck-oned 'an inventive craftsman' when he devised a spar with rigging enabling it to be raised to a predetermined angle to assist in the erection of the gallows. Thus were the felons 'topped'.

As we passed Greenhithe Ginger pointed out the famous old *Cutty Sark*. I had read all about her as a China tea clipper. Paintings had shown her as a beauty. Her figurehead had worn a short chemise, or 'cutty sark'. In her heyday the ship had carried twenty-eight sailors to handle the ten miles of rigging controlling her 32,000 square feet of canvas. Pushed only by the wind she had reached speeds far above *Algonquin Park*'s capability. After decades of anchored idleness, some of it as a training ship, *Cutty Sark* looked sad and disreputable, like an over-aged floozy. But unlike over-aged floozies she was capable of restoration. She now lies in her former youthful beauty in a concrete dry dock at the Greenwich National Maritime Museum.

Ships of all sizes and nationalities crammed the mud-coloured river. It was true. Every ship must come to the world's greatest port at some time during its voyagings. Indeed, some never left it, like the tugs, lighters and sailing barges crowding the busy waterway. As far back as 1796 nearly 8000 vessels and boats of all kinds at any one time occupied a space of four miles below and two miles above London Bridge. At night, river pirates attacked moored ships, night plunderers raided the lighters, and ratcatchers, mudlarks and warehousemen stole whatever could be stolen.

In Gallions Reach — what visions that old name conjured up — we were slowed and guided to starboard towards the entrance to the Royal Albert Dock by the Sun tugs at our bow and stern. They had joined us earlier downriver. The cold wind had a different tang down there. Not the bouquets of Cornwall, Dorset, Sussex or Kent, but instead the airborne mess and pollution of the world's greatest city. It had been enough when passing the Beckton gasworks, the world's largest such establishment until its closure in 1976, to grossly blotch and in some places raise cancerous blisters on much of the fresh white paint on the gasworks' side of our superstructure.

As they eased us through the lock into the crowded dock under a late English winter afternoon sky sagging like a grey roof, the tugs' acrid, cindery smoke eddied across the foredeck and stung our lungs.

We were pulled through the long length of the dock, lined both sides with ships bow to stern, many with lighters alongside, to our berth near the Connaught Street dock gates. As the last line was passed to the shore party the engineroom telegraph signalled 'Finished With Engines'. The signal was given and answered with three strident rings, which echoed from the bridge almost like a trumpet blast. The voyage has finally ended. The engines are finished with, lads. And so are you. Now you can go ashore and get as pissed as you like. Tomorrow morning you can pack your gear, collect your pay and go home. Until you're broke and sign on for your next voyage.

As we began walking from the fo'c'sle head the chief officer tapped me on the shoulder.

'Oi, Kiwi,' he said. 'Now tell me all about your fishing boat.'

'Fishing boat, sir?'

He grinned.

'And Mr Bill Smith.'

'Who, sir?'

He grinned again.

I grinned in return.

It was a gratifying moment. Made even more so when I thought of the Seaman's Union office swine in Wellington who had told me to bugger off.

I had. *And* I had landed butter-side up.

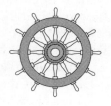

9

At length they all to merry London came . . .
Edmund Spenser

Most headed for warm English beer in the Connaught pub out-side the dock gates. Ginger had other ideas. With 'channel money', a three pounds' advance on wages due, in our pockets we walked in the chill air to Connaught Road and took a double-decker bus to the Plaistow underground station and the tube to Piccadilly.

My eyes and ears were tuned as never before. I was a testa-ment to James Howell's dictum that:

> *. . . among other people of the Earth, Islanders seem to stand in most need of Forraine Travell, for they being cut off (as it were) from the rest of the Citizens of the World, have not those obvious accesses, and contiguit of situation, and with other advantages of society, to mingle with those more refined Nations, whom Learning and Knowledge did first urbanise and polish.*[3]

Ginger had no need for learning and knowledge. Money burning his pocket like a flaming libido, within minutes he was bouncing down Wardour Street with the second girl who approached us. The first had been a bit much even for Ginger. He was not indis-criminately promiscuous.

'A right old scrubber,' he had said. 'Hell, man, she must be twenty-five! You'd have to be a real old prick like Southern to take her on!'

But it was unlikely Southern would have done so. Her bottle-blonde hair, tight skirt, teetering high heels, shallow smile and passionless voice matched his warning to me about old scrubbers. Southern's occasional advice was about the only virtue I ever observed in him. So I may as well mention it.

'Now then, Kiwi,' he had said at the dock gates, 'don't do everything that Geordie idiot does. London Judies are a right load of old scrubbers. You'll end up with the clap. Or worse. So bloody watch it!'

Old Blom and Mr Worsley had given similar advice although in more circumspect terms. But they had obviously rated women greater hazards than Cape Horn storms.

After Ginger disappeared felt I sharply alone, even more than when I first sat alone in *Algonquin Park*'s cabin in Napier. But I also felt fully self-contained. I had reached the top of my Mount Everest.

Big Ben chimed as I reached Westminster Bridge. I had heard it at home during the relayed short-wave BBC war news, so that our visual intimacy now was a mystical moment. I stared at the clock for several long moments. 'That's *Big Ben* . . . I'm *here* . . . I'm in *London*!' Had no one been around I might have shouted the fact. The first man on the moon could have felt no greater sense of occasion.

Along the Embankment I leaned over the riverbank wall under the winter-stripped trees. Lights' reflections danced on the muddy Thames water, their patterns regularly disturbed by rivercraft moving up and down in a liquid equivalent of Piccadilly Circus.

But eventually my body dulled. I had been awake more than a day. I was also very cold. Light snow was falling. I had to be sure, too, to catch the last train to Plaistow and the bus to the Royal Albert Dock. I had been surprised there was a last train and bus. I had thought London would be open day and night. Instead, it also closed down like New Zealand. Not as early, however.

⚓

78

Only Ginger's bunk was occupied. I dressed quietly but he stirred fretfully, disturbed by my bunk light.

'What's the time?' he grumbled irritably.

'Half-past six.'

'Jeez, Kiwi, there's no need to turn-to until we pay off.'

'Yes, I know. But I can't sleep.'

'For God's sake bugger off then.'

'Where's Southern and Corny?'

'Don't know and don't care,' he said. 'And turn the bloody light off!'

He burrowed further into his blankets.

'How did you get on?' I asked.

'Bloody great,' he said, suddenly roused. 'Ten bob — bit much for a short time, though. But a bloody good goose all the same!'

I left Ginger reliving the spasms of his ten bob's worth and went up on deck.

The early morning was weighted with the sullenness of winter and everything — dockside, warehouses, cranes, and the ships, in some cases up to three abreast, and lighters packed into the world's largest area of impounded dock water — was dusted with snow. But it was also lightened with the stimulating exhalation of the ocean and foreign lands and the docks' uniqueness of an odd, amphibious country between land and sea.

If I had then read it, I would have been reminded of a passage from Dickens' *The Uncommercial Traveller*: 'Down by the docks is a region I would choose as my point of embarkation aboard a ship if I were an emigrant. It would present my intentions to me in such a sensible light. It would show me so many things to run away from.' But for me it showed the many things I had run away *to*.

As I gazed from *Algonquin Park*'s deck it would have been impossible, ludicrous even, to have thought that one day the scene around me could vanish. But it did, in the early 1930s when the Royal Docks system — Victoria (opened in 1855), Albert (1880) and King George V (1921) — was closed. The last time I was there was in 1998. There was nothing left except the docks' expansive waters. No ships, no lighters, no cranes except for several preserved as museum pieces, no warehouses, no high dock walls. I went there on a conveyance also impossible to envisage from *Algonquin Park*'s deck — a driverless Dockland Light Railway train controlled by a computer in some other part of the city. Between our Royal Albert and the adjacent King George V dock, these years later there was now an airport for commuters — shades of Dickens' *The Uncommercial Traveller* — between London and European capitals. The only maritime activity on all of the Albert Dock's nearly mile-long length of waterway, once described as the hub of the British Empire, was a young woman on a rowing scull. On the Victoria Docks' water were a couple of windsurfers. All beyond belief. Beyond nostalgia even . . .

By eight o'clock, with still hardly a hint of dawn, dockers had taken over our ship. Dockside cranes rumbled and rattled as New Zealand wool, tallow and piles of stinking hides were hoisted from the holds to the quay and its big brick warehouses or into lighters on the other side of the ship.

I had never regarded my watchmates as representatives of England. They were seamen. They were of a much wider nationhood. But the dockers with their black boots, cloth caps, mufflers and rough clothes were a disappointing congress of the Yeomen of England who lived in the Land of Hope and Glory and who Never Never Will Be Slaves, etc. I felt an indefinable disappointment with my first sight of the English en masse.

After breakfast all hands were summoned to the officers' saloon to sign for our wages and discharge papers. Then we picked up our bags and walked down the gangway. As we neared the dock gates I looked back. Our ship lay passively captive to strangers who strode over her like jailers in hobnailed boots. Among the many others packed bow to stern in the grimy docks she looked like the tramp she was. Her superstructure was unkempt despite our chipping hammers and paintbrushes over the preceding weeks in the tropics. Rust streaked her sides despite our hard work painting them in Newcastle and touching them up in Durban. Yet she still possessed that indefinable femininity residing in all ships whatever their size, shape, age or purpose. Even a warship, a man-o-war, is still a She.

But tramp or not and scruffy as she was, like one's first real lover a man never forgets his first ship. In my case the ship came first.

At the dock gates I said goodbye to Ginger, Corny, Southern, Harry and the rest. Some returned to the dockland pubs; some to railway stations and the families they had left nearly two years before; some to seamen's missions which were their only homes until they were broke and shipped out again. I never saw any of them again. But however spendthrift, feckless, promiscuous, quarrelsome, prejudiced and sometimes intolerant they had been, they had been damned fine company.

⚓

A lifeless young twit from the company's office took me by car to Limehouse. He deposited me at the British Sailors' Society's Empire Memorial Hostel, a seamen's mission commonly known as the Stack o' Bricks, at 680 Commercial Road. He handed me 'this letter which requires you to report to the company's office promptly at 10.30 a.m. on the morrow, whereupon you will be informed of various matters concerning your maintenance and return to New Zealand.'

'When will that be?'

'No idea,' he said.

He didn't seem much interested either. He'd said little during the half-hour in the car. His behaviour suggested he would not regain his happiness until he was back in the safety of his Fenchurch Street office. He barely answered when I asked about some of the places we were passing through. He was bored when I tried to tell him something of the voyage.

My seaman's mission room had not changed much since it was built around the turn of the century. It was small and thin-walled. There was an iron bed with a skinny hair mattress, a small rickety wardrobe, a tiny table, a window and no heating of any sort. The only view through the dirty window was of grey roofs, sooty brick buildings and dingy chimneypots, all cloaked with a splattering of now slushy, dirty snow.

A 1920s writer described such establishments thus:

What lunatic architect designed a Merchant Seamen's Home to the exact likeness of a prison, and, constricted by the site boundary, formed the interior to resemble the forepeak of the Great Eastern? . . . A narrow iron bedstead supporting a hair mattress, clean sheets, a pillow, two thin blankets and a blue and white counterpane. The size of the room was about eight feet by five, but it was all a seaman really needed for two or three weeks before going broke and shipping out again . . .

I sat on my bed with the same feelings as on my hotel bed after arriving in Wellington and on my bunk when I joined *Algonquin Park*. It seemed each epoch in my life was to end sitting alone on a strange bed, as if each was an exclamation mark at the end of a long sentence.

Next day the marine superintendent told me 'the only need for further communication' was to keep him apprised of my whereabouts so that I received my monthly pay and an accommodation allowance equal to a seaman's mission three meals a day plus bed. 'And to receive your instructions concerning your return to New Zealand,' he said in a manner suggesting this was his major concern. 'Otherwise you can go where you like and do what you please.'

I was also entitled to cheap railway fares and ration coupons according to the Merchant Navy scale. This for some reason was more generous than the normal civilian scale, which was something of the order of 'one egg per week perhaps.'

'When will I be sent home?' I asked.

'As soon as possible.'

Instead he had me for some months.

Limehouse, so named because of the lime-burning works which served London's building trades since Edward III's reign and the last of which was closed in the mid-1930s, was a place where Thomas Burke found the 'scum of the world's worst countries.'

Another account tells of a 'ferocious metropolis of pubs, dancehalls, thieves, beggars, brothels and whores, some as young as twelve or thirteen; a reservoir of dirt, drunkenness and drabs, an integral part of Sailortown where many a seaman having survived the hazards of a long voyage was lured by harlots, slugged, robbed and sometimes murdered.'

The nineteenth-century roisterous, riotous, barbarous days were now replaced by mainly small Jewish shops, small cafés, pawnshops, street stalls. Yet most Limehouse habitués were still connected with the sea by trade or profession.

Dockers and seamen of all nationalities were the chief frequenters of the pubs. Some of the pubs were survivors from earlier days, like The Grapes in Shadwell and Charlie Brown's (the Railway Tavern to give it its proper name) outside the West India Docks, and in which were still sharks' backbones, ships in bottles and curios of every description from all over the world — Charlie himself had been a boxer and landlord of the pub since 1893. He died in 1932 and 16,000 people attended the funeral of the 'uncrowned king of Limehouse' at Bow Cemetery.

Further afield I explored the Tower of London; listened in St Paul's Whispering Gallery; leafed through book shops in Charing Cross Road; listened to light orchestras while I drank tea in Lyons Corner Houses; wandered through Westminster Abbey; slurped on some of Tubby Isaacs' jellied eels while rambling among the Sunday morning stalls and hawkers in the East End's Petticoat Lane, which in the 1500s was lined with 'fair hedgerows of elm trees' but was now a dingy thoroughfare except on Sundays. At the Windmill Theatre I gazed with libidinous interest at the long-legged, bare-breasted showgirls decorating the stage in various but unmoving poses.

If it was raining or snowing I bought a tuppenny ticket from Aldgate East and went to the end of each line and then switched to another. With much of the underground system above ground, I therefore saw great tracts of London for tuppence, emerging only at Tower Hill to buy another tuppenny ticket back to Aldgate East to catch a double-decker bus to Limehouse.

⚓

Pamir lay in Shadwell Basin at Wapping. She had arrived a month earlier. The past few months, however, had changed boyhood notions about going to sea. Two hours' lookout in bad weather could be miserable enough without the added prospects of swaying masts and yardarms in Cape Horn gales or Atlantic storms. Huddled against wind and spray and braced against *Algonquin Park*'s rolling and plunging, I had sometimes mentally converted her masts into *Pamir*'s infinitely higher ones. High above the deck in similar conditions and wrestling iron-hard, wet, whipping sails, some weighing as much as two tons, did not commend itself. The spare hours of a night watch in the warmth of the galley peeling potatoes or reading a book seemed a better if less noble prospect.

But I would still take the opportunity if offered.

Seamen greet each other in foreign ports thousands of miles from their last meeting as effusively as workers from adjacent offices at lunchtime in a city street. This accounted for the chief officer's lack of surprise when I knocked on his cabin door. I had expected at least a small measure of congratulation.

'Oh, hullo there. Young Taylor, isn't it? So you got here all right then? Thought you would,' was all he said.

We had come in opposite directions, he around Cape Horn, I the Cape of Good Hope; one blown around the world cleanly, sometimes at up to 14 knots, the other plodding along at around nine knots, trailing black smoke like some floating Yorkshire industrial town. But both had 'got here all right, then.' Apparently anything less would have surprised the chief officer.

After a brief conversation, mostly concerning London weather, he went to see the captain. 'Yes, if there's a job when we sail we'll probably sign you on,' he said when he returned a few moments later.

I first had to prove my affinity for heights.

'Right, up the mainmast and out onto a yard . . . let's see . . . the third one up.'

'The upper tops'l,' I said quickly. He looked at me with surprise.

'Yes,' he said. 'Right! Up! Quick as you can!'

The breeze, soughing on the maindeck, growled throatily as I went higher through the rigging. I clambered out along the yard-arm's footrope. At the end, far out over the water, I rested against the heavy steel spar and reflected on the contrasts between *Pamir* and *Algonquin Park*.

As I mused on climbing still higher I wondered how Ginger would find life aboard such a ship. Or Southern, or the bosun . . . I was interrupted by the chief officer's dimly heard 'something-or-other . . . and bloody quick as you can!'

Back on deck he asked if I minded heights.

'No, sir. I had thought of going to the top, until you called me down.'

'Really?'

I wasn't sure if he was commending my intention or implying that on his ship no one did any more, or less, than ordered.

'Anyway, you seem OK with heights. Here's our telephone number. Keep in touch.'

There were no jobs when *Pamir* sailed on what was to be her last voyage under the New Zealand flag. When she arrived in Lyttelton she was returned to her Finnish owner Gustav Erikson. After a couple of unprofitable voyages and being laid up as a hulk, the ship, built in 1905 and once part of the Laeisz Flying 'P' nitrate clipper fleet, was sold to a Belgian shipbroker. A Lübeck ship-owner bought her and restored her as a training ship. In September 1957, under yet again new ownership, she was overwhelmed by Hurricane Carrie off the Azores while on her way home from Buenos Aires with 2000 tons of Argentine barley. She took all but six of her 86 young German crew with her. Today all that remains of *Pamir* is a lifeboat in Lübeck mounted as a memorial to merchant seamen.

⚓

I should have liked to have spent more time in London. But I had also to see the Somerset villages and countryside my English mother

85

had talked of so often and whose eloquent descriptions had been part of my childhood.

For some weeks I stayed in Bristol with my aunt Francy. We visited relatives around the city and nearby villages. Every foray was by bus or in some cases long distances on foot. No one had cars.

When we ran out of relations I wandered around the drab city or sat inside in the cold, sometimes not even rising until midday. In the evenings we huddled around a coal fire listening to Tommy Handley on the wireless and drinking cocoa. God! What must it have been like when they were being bombed as well? My aunt said it had been slightly less a nuisance than food rationing.

Her husband disagreed. Bob was a small, wearied man whose bones almost rattled and, although he probably did not wear it to bed, at all other times wore a threadbare suit and bright tie.

'Don't talk such bloody nonsense, woman!' he said. 'Don't listen to her, lad. They were a real bloody nuisance at times!'

After being admonished for swearing he subsided again into brooding silence. Bob really roused himself only when we passed German prisoners of war on the Bristol streets. They were tall blonde Teutons in long greatcoats with POW stamped on the back.

'Bloody Huns! Look at them! Arrogant young buggers!' he growled.

Yet once when a German stood up to give him a seat on a bus he said, 'Thank you, lad. Very civil of you.' He didn't seem to notice the young man's slight bow and almost imperceptible click of the heels.

Mostly, however, Bob brooded in front of the fireplace with a cup of cocoa until it was time for bed.

To a youth an aunt of some forty years is elderly. Neither shares much in common. As well, with a morose and workless man-of-the-house who gave the impression of spending his life preparing for death but postponing it for as long as possible, life was in other ways constricted in the tiny flat at the top of a narrow dark stairway. The area itself, St Pauls, was a forlorn place; old working-class tenements pitted with bombsites, in some cases virtually uncleared, much like parts of London.

A female cousin of considerable elegance bearing an invitation to stay with her family was therefore greeted with relief. They lived in Pill, a small village on the Avon River near Avonmouth. I was sensible enough of family feelings to express some show of regret at leaving Bristol. My aunt, however, a kindly and when I came to know her better, an understanding soul, said I should go with Jacqueline. Besides, she had two brothers, Terry and Peter, around my own age.

My relations had some difficulty coming to terms with the oddity in their midst. They could not believe that New Zealanders ate pumpkins and turnips, which they regarded as cattle food. And her mother gave Jacqueline a sharp look when I mentioned that passionfruit grew around our house. It was the word passion which upset her. She was also suspicious of anyone from another village, and became disturbed whenever I ventured among 'they furriners'.

As spring arrived Jacqueline and I wandered over the hills and through the woods. I delighted in the English spring. 'If Winter comes, can Spring be far behind?' asked Shelley. A damned long way, it had sometimes seemed. It had not seemed possible England would ever emerge from the winter which had gripped it unremittingly.

We walked among the flowering fields and listened to skylarks high and melodiously invisible somewhere among the fluffy white clouds. Sometimes we lay in the warm grass and tried to spot them but we never saw one. Other times we all went for Sunday picnics among the greening woodlands, or crossed the Avon in a ferryboat rowed by a man with thick arms and a strong back, and walked to Shirehampton and Blaise Castle.

I also played darts or dominoes with the locals in the King's Head pub. The accompanying rough Somerset cider sometimes stranded me on the way home or caused me to lie in until late. Each occasion extracted another promise to my aunt Nellie and her husband Bert, as Zoomerzet a man as they ever come, never to go near the place again.

Later I visited a New Zealand relation, one of my father's cousins, and her English husband in a large house near Sonning Lock in Reading. It was an inauspicious visit, mainly because of a live-in girl who cleaned the house and looked after the family's young child.

For a few days she served me bacon and eggs in bed — the inconveniences of rationing seemed not to have hit the well-to-do household as it had my less-better-connected Somerset relations; it seemed each was living under a different government. The service ceased when it was thought to take longer than necessary. The family was far too well bred, of course, to enquire even indirectly if anything other than breakfast was afoot. But we were only talking about her hopes to emigrate to New Zealand one day. My undoing was asking permission to take her to the pictures on her one night a week off. Instead I was lectured by Himself on behaviour vis-à-vis servants.

I was directed to a leather armchair. Himself stood importantly at the fireplace. One arm was stretched along the mantelpiece. The other was thumb-hooked in his waistcoat in the manner of a man who does not justify his beliefs but announces them and moreover is always in agreement with himself. The maid, alas, had also told me he wore bright-coloured pyjamas and bedsocks to bed. The vision before me was therefore blurred by a mental reflection I could not be rid of.

'My deah boy,' he intoned in a well-bred voice and manner I imagine he believed was kindly, fatherly even, 'my deah boy, even if one is a sailor' — I felt satisfied to be so described but he emphasised the word with distaste as though facing a plate of jellied eels — 'I'm sure one understands that as a guest one is not over-familiar with one's host's servants. One understands, my deah boy, of course? Be respectful by all means' — his forefinger drummed among the mantelpiece silver in metronomic emphasis — 'and be kind, too. But one must remember they are servants. One has obviously been properly brought up. And so I am sure one understands, of course, my deah boy?'

One didn't. But one naturally said one did. And so while not favouring the prospect of being his deah boy, which being a sailor seemed unlikely anyway, one did one's best to at least ostensibly treat the maid as befitted her station.

I think my relative, somewhat younger than her husband, understood my interest in the girl. In deference to her position as the wife of an English gentleman, however, and mistress of the household, she offered no help. Except to say the girl was, of course, Irish. And to imply that her husband could sometimes be a pain in the arse.

⚓

After five months *Algonquin Park*'s managers still could not find me a working passage back to New Zealand. So they booked me a cabin on a P&O liner to Melbourne, a train to Sydney and a flying boat to Auckland.

Named after the Swiss town of Maloggia near St Moritz, the black and stone-coloured 21,000-ton *Maloja*, along with her sister, *Mooltan*, was built in 1923 for the Australian run. The ships each carried some 700 passengers. After reconversion from a Northern Patrol armed merchant cruiser and later a troopship, *Maloja* was undertaking a new job. Post-war British emigration was becoming a flood and she was on her first trip with over 1000 assisted migrants to Australia.

Of great note in her pre-war heyday — she was the first P&O passenger liner to displace over 20,000 tons — was that every cabin had a porthole. A contemporary newspaper enthused that:

> . . . the old inner cabins with their often oppressive stuffiness
> have completely disappeared. By a very clever piece of shipping
> architecture the sleeping accommodation has been designed so
> that all cabins, both first and second class, are porthole cabins.
>   Those desiring absolute luxury will find their needs provided
> for in special suites of rooms on the promenade deck. These
> suites are panelled in sycamore and furnished in Louis XVI
> style, while each suite has its own private bathroom . . .

Such refinements had gone. But six weeks to Australia as a passenger on a P&O liner would be cosy enough even if C deck cabins no longer extended to Louis XVI style.

As I stood at the stern watching our wake in the moonlight, Jean came out of the darkness and leaned on the rail. She cupped her head in her hands and was soon lost in a private quietude. The moonlight played over the contours of her face and her hair blew about in the breeze.

'Hullo,' I said eventually.

She straightened up and looked at me.

'Hullo,' she said. 'Are you going to Australia, too?'

'I'm going to New Zealand,' I said.

'But the ship is going to Australia,' she said.

'Yes.'

'So why are you going to New Zealand?'

After I explained myself she asked when would it get warmer.

'Couple of days, probably. Once we're clear of the bay, anyway.'

'The bay?'

'It's where we are now. The Bay of Biscay.'

'Oh,' she said, then asked what Australia was like. I told her it was, well, not like England. Or anywhere else for that matter, I supposed.

She brushed away a tear and I put a tentative arm around her. Over ensuing ocean nights and warm days our acquaintance stirred an emotional excitement rivalling that of Antony and Cleopatra. Her parents naturally enough were alive to the dangers attending a comely daughter on the high seas. When unable to do so themselves they detailed her siblings to keep their inquisitive eyes on us.

Maloja contained many nooks and crannies, however. Sibling attention was also easily diverted. Her parents, too, were prey to the same warm nights, the moon, the stars and all that jazz. They also liked to drink in the bar, play quoits and deck tennis, dance, attend fancy-dress competitions and have time to themselves.

Despite the intimacy of the nooks, however, the friendship remained chaste apart from much kissing and some inexpert and tentative fumbling. Her parents had assured us, or more particularly me, that 'if you do anything, anything, *anything*, we'll know about it straightaway.' We did not doubt it for one moment.

All the same, after cavorting in the swimming pool and seeking a secluded spot, ostensibly to dry off in the sun, there were occasions when our excitement was difficult to contain as we lay in intimate contact in our wet bathing suits.

The passengers crowded the rails as we arrived off Fremantle. The land was flat, sandy and seemingly barren. The port appeared wilder than the Wild West, its inhabitants only marginally less so. Of the nearby city, Perth, nothing could be seen. And above stretched the huge sky of a flat country.

As much as their convict countrymen who had preceded them nearly a hundred years before — the country's first convict settlers had arrived here in 1850 — they could have imagined nowhere less like the country they had left. Australia was much too vast a land to encompass in one coherent thought. Their own would have been lost in the bottom left-hand corner of it. Our next port, Adelaide, Jean's destination, was a week away across the Great Australian Bight and still only about halfway across the continent. Sydney was the same distance again. Had they travelled from their own country the equivalent distance from Fremantle to Sydney, they would have gone beyond Moscow or just about reached Timbuktu. Which was probably where some of them thought they had arrived.

The remaining days to Adelaide and Jean's departure were exquisitely miserable. The last I saw of her was her tall figure standing quietly alone in the shade of a wharf shed at the Outer Harbour.

We waved and called as the big ship pulled away to continue her voyage, in which my main interest had now concluded. We wrote intensively for several months. But promises undertaken in the starry darkness on *Maloja*'s decks faded with the passing months. It's the fate of most shipboard romances. I'm told so, anyway. I never had another one.

The Tasman Empire Airways flying boat trembled as its mighty engines drove it slowly from Rose Bay into Sydney Harbour. Then all roared in unison and as the aircraft gathered speed her bow wave reached high above the cabin windows in sheets of green water. Suddenly the buffeting ceased and she rose into the air with long trails of water streaming from her pontoons. Eight hours

later a spraying glide onto the Auckland harbour ended a luxurious finale to my first adventure.

As the Russell bus passed over the dirt road I had pedalled on
my way to the sea all those months before, I ruminated on my
adventures so far and wondered what sort of reception I would
get at home.

My brothers and sisters stared. My father shook my hand and
offered me a beer. The cat rubbed my leg. He stretched his neck
and began to purr as I tickled him under the chin.

'Hullo cat,' I said. 'You'll never guess where I've been.'

My mother gave me a hug and said, 'And just *where* do you
think you've been?' She had asked the same question whenever I
had tarried too long with Old Blom or Mr Worsley.

'Out,' I said.

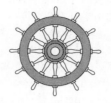

10

How much a dunce that has been sent to roam
Excels a dunce that has been kept at home
William Cowper

Some people said good on you. A few said it was a pity others hadn't shown similar enterprise. One said I should be still at school. The postmaster renewed his prediction of my dismal future. His staff remained silent in the face of his lofty proclamation. The grocer offered me a temporary job. But I had outgrown being a delivery boy. I was now seventeen, dammit.

My friends listened in wonder as I related my various adventures, magnified or not according to their credulity. With Old Blom and Mr Worsley I was sensible enough to be more accurate.

I returned to Napier. But in mid-winter cargoes and therefore ships were scarce. I joined the Forest Service planting pine trees on the scrubby Rangataiki Plains near Taupo. We lived in single-man corrugated-iron camp huts with a camp bed, a small table and some coat hangers serving as a wardrobe. A rudimentary fireplace was meant to provide heat but, depending on the wind's direction, all the heat went up the chimney or the hut filled with smoke.

After porridge and mutton chops we were trucked into the scrub before sunrise. A gang ahead slashed paths through the bracken. Behind them we took four paces, dug a slit, shoved a seedling into it, heeled it in, took another four paces, dug a slit, etc. We worked Monday to Saturday. Sunday was usually spent in bed or playing cards or arguing and quarrelling in the dining hall. I quickly tired of working in the cold and wet and living in the miserable hut. The foreman took me to the main road and left me in the rain to await the Auckland bus.

I shared a room in a city boarding house with a prison warder. He was a heavy, hard-featured man with close-cropped hair and a pencil-thin moustache. During the evening meal he regaled the table in detail with the exploits of his charges. The few he liked he called My Inmates. He dismissed the rest as Guests of The Majesty.

He held an arcane admiration for burglars. Sometimes he spent the evening in our room telling me the tricks of their trade while I tried to listen to the Hit Parade.

Once I asked, if burglars were all that clever, why were so many in jail?

He launched into a detailed discourse on how burglars could avoid subsequent guardianship by himself on behalf of The Majesty. His profound understanding of burglary would have made him a proficient burglar. Or, since his knowledge of them would have made him better able to catch them, a passable policeman. Yet perhaps neither, which was why he had settled as a prison warder, a sort of middleman.

A tram conductor sometimes reflected over our roast mutton and fatty gravy that had some of his practices towards the felons been practised on the population-at-large, the warder himself should have been a permanent Guest of The Majesty. The warder usually retorted that if the tram conductor was ever himself a Guest, comments like that would earn him a pretty tough time of it, mate. The tram conductor then usually told the warder to get stuffed and left the table. But not until he had finished his pudding.

I got tired of them both. I was also unable to find a ship. And so I returned to Napier and my previous lodgings.

⚓

'Well, well!' said a girl in one shipping agent's office. 'It's you again!'
'Sure is,' I said cheerfully.

I took her out several times and had a number of outstanding pashes at her front gate. But she later decided there was no future in such carry-ons since I was sure to leave in the end.

For several weeks I crawled under woolsheds and farmhouses squirting poisonous liquid into borer holes in their wooden foundations. In overalls and cotton masks it was hot, dirty, smelly work. We usually slept in the shearers' quarters. Breakfast was mutton chops and porridge. Lunch was mutton stew and bread. Dinner was roast mutton, potatoes, cabbage and gravy. If New Zealand had not been exporting most of its mutton we would have suffocated under a mountain of the stuff.

For a month I worked in a fish factory. I also supplied the landlady regularly with cheap fresh fish until the boarders complained at the surfeit of fried, boiled, baked and grilled fish, raw fish salads and fish pies. They begged for roast mutton instead.

Next I worked in a nursery until a fertiliser cockup killed several hundred petunias. Regarded much as an assassin who had not been properly executed and moreover had escaped, I decided it was wise to leave immediately.

The next several weeks were in a meat works until eight hours a day of blood, guts, warm flesh and cold gumboots became intolerable. I gave up and remained a vegetarian for several days.

In the hospital maintenance gang I helped erect stone walls until a newly built wall fell down in heavy rain. Apparently the concrete plaster had not been mixed correctly although I still say it was done, like the petunias' fertiliser, to the foreman's instructions. Anyway, the rain washed it all out. The stones tumbled down across the doctors' car park like the Wall of Jericho. A loud trumpeting followed the event.

Unable to find another job and the search for a ship so far unsuccessful, life was becoming complicated. But I was about to face a far greater complication.

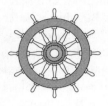

11

Sigh no more, ladies, sigh no more,
Men were deceivers ever,
One foot in sea and one on shore,
To one thing constant never.
Shakespeare, *Much Ado About Nothing*

Lillian was sixteen. The swing of her long legs, the toss of her shiny black hair, the flash of her dark eyes, her beguiling smile and the impudence of her infectious laugh held me in some sort of thraldom. We did everything done by those suffering adolescent love.

We talked about Causes and Meanings as we walked arm-in-arm but arrived at no Conclusions. We entwined fingers at the movies. We listened intently to jukebox love songs while contemplating each other over frothy milkshakes. We declared our love softly at the movies, urgently at the front door, furtively at family gatherings and passionately in the park where we nibbled each other's necks and ears and kissed almost to the point of exhaustion. We dreamed about each other at night. She, usually about living happily ever after. I usually the same, although her long legs were often focal features of the happy future.

We skirted sex with long, erotic bodily contact whenever safely away from discovery. We explored buttons and zips and the soft, warmly intimate flesh as far as the top of the thighs. Sometimes for an electrifying second or two we reached for the spaces in between. But female virginity was a property rarely surrendered, and then not lightly. Anyway, her mother, like Jean's, regularly warned us she would know if we 'did anything silly.' Our coursing blood sometimes made it difficult not to. It left us flushed and out of breath and my sustained arousal was at times physically tormenting and left me feeling emasculated.

I suffered another torment, however. Any mention of ships brought a response difficult to counter without sailing headlong into a verbal quagmire. It was the one passion we did not totally share. Visits to ships and shipping agents had to remain secret.

'Yes, I need a jos,' *Leicester*'s chief officer said. 'Have you been to sea before?'

My discharge paper from *Algonquin Park* was as good as a passport.

'Fine. Be at the shipping office two o'clock this afternoon. We're sailing tomorrow evening so you needn't turn-to until midday tomorrow.'

I returned to the boarding house and lay on my bed. My thoughts were mixed. I tried to reconcile the two greatest passions of my life. It was impossible. They were irreconcilable. I tried to sleep but could not. And so I made a cup of tea and telephoned Lillian at work. She was silent for a long moment.

Then she said, 'I knew you would one day. But why?'

I explained, truthfully, that I had walked down to the port because I had nothing else to do. While sitting on a bollard in the sun I had heard by chance that the ship was short of an ordinary seaman. And so I had gone aboard and seen the chief officer. Lillian's long silence intimated it was a shoddy explanation.

'Where are you going?' she asked eventually.

'London.'

'When?'

'Tomorrow night.'

'So we can still see each other tonight?'

'Yes, of course. Can I walk home with you after work?'

'Yes. Come home for tea. I'll ring Mum. And then perhaps we can go to the pictures.'

'OK.'

97

After a long silence she said, 'I'll have to go . . . there's a customer waiting . . .' The flatness in her voice suggested there was no customer. She was going to the staffroom and would be there for some while.

The evening meal with her family was a dismal event. We didn't enjoy the movie, either. We left before it finished and went to the beach.

'I hate the sea,' Lillian said, staring moodily across it. 'I do. I hate it.'

She shed wet, salty tears and her body trembled. I looked out to sea and shed a tear or two myself. It remains one of the least complacent moments of my life. We watched the horned moon rise above the horizon. Its yellow light shone palely across the water. The soft breeze ruffling her hair and the tinkling euphony of the wavelets on the shore added to the pathos of the night.

We made passionate declarations of love and faithfulness and promised ourselves, when we were older, a life together. Our affirmations were genuine and heartfelt. Not even the ultimate intimacy of sex could have affirmed them more strongly, although on the cold, sharp-pebbled beach the experience might have been less than memorable.

We took the long way back to her place. It was well after midnight. For me every step was like a penance. It was alleviated only by frequent stops for embraces, which smothered us as if we were trying to infuse our souls.

Her mother brought us a cup of tea in the sitting room and told her daughter she really shouldn't stay up much longer because she had to go to work in the morning. I was given scant attention, however — even less than the rest of her family had given me earlier.

Napier's lights dropped astern as we set out next evening and were enveloped in the ocean night. We were heading southwards for Cook Strait. There we would turn west across the Tasman Sea, Bass Strait, the Great Australian Bight and then northwest to Aden, the Red Sea, Suez Canal, Genoa and London. With *Leicester* lifting to the swell, I submerged beneath the moment.

I would have been happier, however, had it not been for Lillian's tall, accusing figure on the wharf. I could still taste her lipstick and smell her perfume. As the moon rose on our port beam I relived every minute on the beach when we had watched the same moon. After I came off watch I put her photograph on the shelf above my bunk. Her smiling face seemed tinged with a wistfulness I had not seen before.

We exchanged long letters over the ensuing months. I explained each time why I had gone back to sea. But it was too complicated for an 18-year-old to properly explain, or for a 16-year-old even to begin to understand. Enough, however. She eventually married someone else and had six children, after which her husband died of a heart attack.

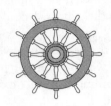

12

I have been here before.
Dante Rossetti, *Sudden Light*

The Federal Steam Navigation Company's *Leicester* was another Liberty ship but of different design to *Algonquin Park*. Her original name was *Samesk*. She was built in Baltimore in 1944 to an adapted pre-war British design of Ocean class tramp steamers. Nearly 3000 of the ships were built in the United States, sixty of them before that country entered the war. The first were completed in 257 days. Then they began to be built with increasing rapidity. One, in November 1942, was launched less than five days after her keel was laid, although much of her had been prefabricated elsewhere.

The ships were the backbone of Allied convoys. They were later described as 'the type of vessel which, in its hundreds, is accredited with saving not only Britain, not only the Allied cause, but the whole world from disaster . . .'[4]

Samesk was employed first in the Mediterranean and then the North Atlantic. The war ended while on her way to take part in operations against Japan. Diverted to Singapore, she was the first supply ship there after the Japanese surrender. Later in Hong Kong 1400 Japanese prisoners were packed into her holds and taken back to Japan. She was then released for commercial service.

Many British companies bought the ships until they had replaced their wartime losses. Along with *Samkey*, from the same Kaiser shipyards, her present owners bought *Samesk* and renamed her *Leicester* in line with the rest of the county-named Federal Line fleet. Peace proved more dangerous than war for both ships.

In 1948 *Samkey* and her crew vanished somewhere in the Atlantic en route from London to Cuba. It was no isolated incident. Less than half her kind had survived the war. Most had been sunk by the enemy, while others, like *Samkey*, simply disappeared, earning their class the nickname Disappearing Sams.

The same year *Leicester* almost did the same. In doing so she figured in one of the most remarkable ocean sagas of modern times.

A month after *Samkey* was lost, *Leicester* made an uneventful voyage to New Zealand. On her next she sailed for New York loaded with 1500 tons of sand and gravel ballast dredged from the River Thames.

Investigations of *Samkey*'s disappearance showed that when in ballast, as she had been, the material was carried 'tween decks instead of deep in the lower holds. This made the ships less stiff and easier to handle. But, the investigators suggested, if the ballast suddenly shifted it would throw an immense weight to one side. The effects on the ship's stability would be immediate. She would capsize.

While it was uncertain *Samkey* had disappeared in this way, *Leicester* was fitted with shifting boards forming a solid wooden barrier along the midline of every hold to prevent the otherwise unrestrained ballast from shifting.

Ten days after leaving London, *Leicester* was battling for her life in winds over 140 miles an hour. Even before the height of the hurricane her captain had been swept from the bridge by a gigantic wave. A following wave carried him back to the boatdeck thirty feet away. He had been lucky on another count. He should have been *Samkey*'s captain when she disappeared. Instead he had been at home in bed with pneumonia.

As *Leicester* fought for her life a deep rumbling sounded throughout her hull. Much of the ballast, because of the huge forces set up by the ship's violent movements, had broken the newly fitted shifting boards and slithered to one side. She listed 50 degrees and water poured into every opening and flooded the engine room, rendering her completely out of control. Four sailors were lost in the seas rampaging across her almost submerged decks. Two more were lost during the later rescue 500 miles southwest of Cape Race, the rescue itself an epic feat since the hurricane, although now passed, still left the fierce conditions of a severe storm.

The abandoned, heavily listing ship drifted 600 miles through more storms until found by two Newfoundland salvage tugs. They towed her 800 miles through more storms to Bermuda. After temporary repairs, *Leicester* was driven ashore in another hurricane and holed on the coral reefs along with one of rescuers. The other had left earlier to rescue another Liberty ship, *Oscar Chappell*, damaged and adrift off the Azores.

Patched with concrete, *Leicester* eventually left under tow for New York. More severe weather began working her patches and water rose in her holds and engineroom. Eventually the sinking ship was dragged into Baltimore. Long suffering but infinitely enduring, she was pumped out and repaired. Her captain and some of her surviving crew sailed her to New York where, 105 days after leaving London, she began loading for New Zealand.[5]

I had joined her in Napier halfway during her next voyage.

⚓

Leicester was an oil burner so, unlike *Algonquin Park,* there was not a continual stream of cindery coal smoke trailing behind her. Our food, too, was very different. Menus did not depend on which day it was. There was fresh milk until it ran out it and was replaced with powdered milk. There was fruit and freshly baked bread every day.

Fire and lifeboat drills, or Board of Trade Sports, were held every Friday. *Algonquin Park*'s safety exercises had been few and erratic. And the captain and deck officers, unlike *Algonquin Park*, conducted their noon sextant sun-sights in their best uniforms and in ranked order. It was almost a ceremony.

The differences illustrated the fact that *Algonquin Park*'s managers — the Aviation & Shipping Company, although God knows what aeroplanes had to do with it — was a small tramp enterprise cobbled together to take advantage of the immediate post-war trading boom. With little history of its own it relied on Merchant Navy traditions to maintain its seafaring Britishness. The Federal Line, however, was a long-established company with its own traditions and practices superimposed on those of British seafaring.

Leicester's crew was also greatly different. Most were regular company men from London or the Hebrides. They were a mixture of ages. The older men had been seamen all their lives. Some of the young were escaping their two years' compulsory National Service. Six years in the Merchant Navy was an alternative to two years in the army, much of which would have been spent chasing communists in Malayan jungles.

A few had already done so. One had a photograph of himself grinning and holding a severed communist head. The senior ordinary seaman impressed few. Most regarded him as a swashbuckler who under any sort of pressure would doubtless buckle more than swash. Sceptics believed the communist head had more likely been handed around for everyone to have their photograph taken with it. Some didn't know what to believe. Others didn't want to know. Those who had also been in Malaya hinted that tales should not be told out of school.

After nearly a month from Napier we passed between Socotra and the Horn of Africa, and arrived at Steamer Point in Aden to replenish our oil bunkers. The anchorage was crammed with ships of all sizes and nations, including the French liner *Pasteur* with reputedly the biggest funnel in the world. A clamour of small craft buzzed between every ship and the shore. Behind the busy scene glowered a harsh backdrop of stark, volcanic peaks burnished by eons of red-hot Arabian sun and dust storms.

Bumboats arranged themselves around us like flies around a carcass. All hands parried and haggled with their beseeching but hard-nosed Arab traders for every type of merchandise. Nothing had an absolute value. Value depended on how well buyers and sellers sized each other up. The means of exchange was duty-free cigarettes. When trading was deemed to be at an end someone dropped a piece of pork into one of the bumboats. The effect was like a hand grenade going off in a goldfish bowl.

From Aden we passed through the narrow Straits of Bab el Mandeb, Arabic for 'gate of tears' because of navigation hazards and swift currents.

The Red Sea, one of the world's oldest trade routes, old even before European history, was like a gigantic moving port, a continual procession of ships; freighters and tankers of all flags but predominantly British; big Empire-class troopers going to or returning from India and the Far East; patrolling Royal Navy warships; Blue Funnel, P&O, Bibby Line, British India and foreign passenger liners. Arab dhows weaved among the throng. At night many carried no lights. Often the only sign of them was moon- or starlight reflecting from their sails.

Each morning the sun rose as if the very guts of the earth had torn loose. The molten explosion hung a few moments over the scorched bare mountains of Africa on our port side. For the rest of the day it blazed across the sky until dropping like a fireball beneath the high escarpments and deserts of Arabia on our starboard side. In that biblical sea and through the Straits of Jubal into the Gulf of Suez the air was warm even inside the lungs.

At Port Suez a large searchlight was lashed to the bow for the night portion of the canal transit. A canal boat was hung from a derrick and lashed to the ship's rail, for its crew to ferry our ropes ashore if it was necessary to stop at any time during the passage.

Along the canal banks the British Army was well in evidence. Seven years later the whole Imperial picture would change and the canal itself be the pivot for one of the last gasps of Empire. When it reopened several years later it would be Egyptians who administered it and piloted the ships. But then it was inconceivable that Egyptians could take over, let alone successfully run, such an enterprise.

Yet they had done it before. A long time before, certainly.

A lock was begun in 1310 BC by Siti I and completed by Rameses the Great. During the twenty-sixth dynasty around 600 BC Necho II started a 50-odd miles long waterway from the Nile to the Red Sea. It was completed by Darius I. Over the centuries it was restored by Ptolemy II, Philadelphus, Trajan and Hadrian.

In the 1790s Napoleon Bonaparte was ordered by the French Directory to 'cut a canal through the isthmus of Suez, and to take all necessary steps to ensure the free and exclusive use of the Red Sea by French vessels [and] to expel the British from all their possessions in the East, wherever they may be.'

The French failed, torn by revolution and opposed politically by the British. Other French calculations were badly astray, too. They believed Mediterranean and Red Sea levels differed by thirty feet and that locks would be needed.

Nelson scuttled the whole idea, anyway. At the battle of the Nile he sank most of the French fleet, stranding Napoleon and his army into the bargain. He then returned to Naples and became infatuated with Lady Hamilton.

It was another Frenchman, Ferdinand de Lesseps, who succeeded in building the 101-mile-long canal through the desert. Shortly after its opening in 1869 the French lost control of it through British political and financial chicanery. Earlier, in 1885, the French Academy had told de Lesseps he had created:

> . . . *a serious embarrassment. Not merely does the canal connect two inland seas, but it will also serve as a communicating passage to all the oceans of the globe. In case of a maritime war it will be of supreme importance, and everyone will be striving at top speed to occupy it. You have marked out a great battlefield for the future.*

With similar prescience, Germany's Bismarck later described it as 'the British Empire's spinal column.'

The canal's long closure after the 1956 Suez Crisis conflict disrupted trading patterns and led to the virtual replacement of large passenger liners by aeroplanes. It also created tankers too big — the first was the 104,000-ton *Universe Apollo* built in 1959 — for the canal but carrying sufficient oil that it was economic to instead travel from the Persian Gulf around the Cape of Good Hope.

But we passed through a peaceful scene. British soldiers at their canal posts acknowledged our waves and shouts. Picturesque feluccas sailed close to its banks in the light desert breeze.

White-robed Egyptians and their laden donkeys plodded across the hot yellow sands.

Shouting and waving their arms in a seemingly continuous quarrel, Arab and African dockers began discharging our Port Said cargo into lighters. All hands in the meantime parried with a circus of bumboat hawkers of every description in small boats alongside. Some found their way aboard.

In an oversized kilt, carrying a bagpipe and sporting a Rolex Oyster watch and introducing himself as the 'son of my father Jock McGregor from Greenock och aye mon,' one promised what he assured us would be 'an egg-zee-bee-shun of splendid music-ship on my father's bagpipe. Och aye mon! Gor' blimey mate!' and so on until he judged he had accounted colloquially for all those present.

The money we paid was worth the vision of a skinny, bandy-legged, barefooted, kilted Arab wearing a fez, claiming to be the son of a Scotsman and playing a bagpipe splendidly badly on the hot steel deck. Even the Hebrideans were impressed.

Others touted the charms of sisters, cousins, nieces, some even of mothers, aunts or brothers. The ensuing bargaining processes were conducted within the same basic limits:

'All virgins, mister. Very clean. Very cheap. You come in my boat and I take you in two minutes in my father's taxi. You have good time for one hour. You come back, mister . . . so very much refreshed!'

'How much?'

'Only one pound.'

'A fuckin' *quid*?'

'OK. Fifteen shilling. But only for you.'

'Still too much, ya' thievin' git.'

'OK. For you, mister, ten shilling. You my friend.'

'Dirty bastard!'

'I beg of you mister. OK. You still my friend. Five shilling. Just for you, mister.'

'Yeah! Five bob's worth of pox!'

'My friend! I beg of you! I very honest man. All virgins. Very clean. Very cheap. Best virgins . . . oh, so very clean.'

'Lying bastard!'

'Please, mister. I beg of you. All virgins, very . . .'

'Yeah, clean. Fuck off!'

'OK. So maybe you want jig-a-jig postcard instead? Maybe jig-a-jig book?'

The postcards and books were badly printed and illustrated activities in which, in my certain if unpractised opinion, any movement would have caused the participants severe dislocation at the very least.

There were also equally suspect items such as watches, camelskin bags, beads, jewellery and a hundred and one other things to be haggled and argued over. I had seen none of this on the voyage aboard *Maloja*. Instead I had visited the Simon Artz department store with Jean and her ever-vigilant parents.

We arrived in Genoa six days after leaving Port Said. Most of the Italian coast had been out of sight except for mountaintops and the setting sun striking the top of Vesuvius near Naples.

Our berth was near the old Molo Vecchio. It had been built in 1257 and extended in 1553 and again in 1642. Genoa is one of the world's oldest ports and was already a trading post in 6 BC. Its original Ligurian inhabitants had established contact with the earliest known Mediterranean sailors, the Phoenicians and Greeks. The ancient city was also the birthplace of Christopher Columbus.

It was the place, too, where another of my life's markers involved a bed.

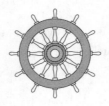

13

There are worse occupations in the world than feeling a woman's pulse.

Laurence Stern, *A Sentimental Journey*

With the other two members of our watch I set out on an exploratory walk. We gazed at churches and cathedrals and other fine old buildings before turning right along the Via Garibaldi to the Piazza Corvetto and then down the Via Venticinque Aprile. Sightseeing was thirsty work. Somewhere along the way we entered a small bar.

Three girls at a small table beckoned us through the tobacco smoke.

One was of medium height and lusty build which here and there was beginning to liquefy into mere fleshiness. Another was of only slightly more slender form. Both demonstrated a brisk interest in my two companions, Mitchell and Watson. Having had a surfeit of culture, they soon bargained their way into more seamanlike endeavours. They left within minutes.

The remaining girl brought her chair next to mine. An uncertain participant in the former proceedings, I had been at a loss at her voluble encouragement to her friends to clear off with my companions while she devoted her attentions to me.

William Hazlitt expressed the opinion that Italian women:

. . . so far as I have seen hitherto are detestably ugly. They are not even dark and swarthy, but a mixture of brown and red,

coarse, marked with the smallpox, with pug features, awkward,
ill-made, fierce, dirty, lazy, neither attempting nor hoping to
please. Italian beauty (if there is, as I am credibly informed,
such a thing) is retired, conventual, denied to the common gaze.
It was and it remains to me, a vision of the brain![6]

Balls! This Italian was dark, beautifully made, unfierce, certainly
attempting and plainly hoping to please, and was nothing if not
real.

She had about her a surreptitious incandescence. Her high
cheekboned, olive-skinned teenage face had no makeup except
ruby-red lipstick. A seductive aroma of light-scented womanhood
wafted subtly yet insistently from her. She moved closer and ran
her slim fingers up and down my arm as if tuning a violin —
Paganini, like Columbus, had also been Genoese.

Directing her challenging Latin eyes at me from beneath thick,
curving eyebrows, she asked my name. I told her. She repeated it
then regarded me gravely for some moments. She moved even
closer, until her thigh touched mine. Its intimacy was like a bolt of
electricity.

'Firsta time, no?'

It was clearly more of a statement than a question. I stirred
uncomfortably.

'First time? Well . . .'

She italicised her question.

'*You notta before hadda da girl? No?*'

'Well, no,' I agreed. 'But,' I added, as if to acquit such a serious
defect, 'I have a girlfriend.'

'Girla-friend? Huh! Pouf!' she pouted, raising an eyebrow so
that her Roman nose twitched. She looked at me quizzically for a
few moments. 'So! You love-a youra girla-friend?'

'Yes,' I said, the forlorn figure on the Napier wharf suddenly
etched sharply in my mind.

The girl tickled the lobe of my ear. The sensuousness of her
lightly probing finger and the continued intimacy of her firm warm
thigh began addling my brain and stirring my blood to the turbu-
lence of a waterfall. Lillian had sometimes done the same and

produced the same upheavals. To that extent she and this unknown girl were sisters under the skin.

'But you notta before hadda da girl? No?'

'Well, no. Not actually.'

'Whatta you mean, notta actually?' she demanded with a teasing smile. 'You justa *playa* witha youra girla-friend?'

I lapsed into disconcerted silence. She was right. Of course she was. She knew it, too. But she was a kind girl. She squeezed my arm gently.

'*Si*. I am-a . . . how you say? Sorry? Si, I am-a sorry. OK? So, you love-a youra girla-friend. *Si*! I un'erstand. For that you are a gooda boy. But you gotta be a *bad*-a boy! Thena you become *man*! So, you come-a my house? *Si*?'

'Your house?'

She smiled with an almost liquid expression.

'*Si*. My house. I make-a you man in-a my house! *Si*! Thena youra girla-friend, she love-a you more better!'

I felt bashful about being thus made-a into a man, and dubious about Lillian loving me more for it. Anyway, it was all very well for Mitchell and Watson. Their wages were twice mine. The price they had arrived at was more than I had for our whole time in Genoa. Despite financial restraints, however, it was expecting too much of the essential male not to rise under such immediate inducement.

'*Quanta costa?*'

Mitchell and Watson had used the term frequently. It had made the bargaining process almost ritualistic.

The girl cogitated a moment or two while her finger traced a light path around and inside my ear and her thigh continued pressing against mine. Her actions were goading me into a vortex of forces becoming impossible to resist. Whatever their *quanta* bloody *costa*.

She seemed to be making up her mind about something. I half-hoped she was about to give up, although I was unsure if I would feel relief or regret.

'So, firsta time, *si*?' she asked again.

'Well, yes,' I said.

She regarded me a few further moments. Then she squeezed my arm, smiled, stood up and smoothed her dress. Each pass of her hands snuggled it around the outline of her body. Its every curving inch testified to raw, irresistible concupiscence. Her slender legs, slightly apart, I thought suggestively but perhaps only to stand more comfortably, added to the impossibility of refusal whatever the price tag.

She mentioned a price.

I recalculated my lira urgently. Damn! Even though appreciably below the price of her two friends, she was still beyond my means. Damn! Damn-BLOODY-damn!

'Too much *quanta costa*. Look, not enough money.'

She counted the bundle of notes in my hand and pursed her lips slightly.

'*Si* . . . maybe notta mucha money!'

She leaned down and rested her hand lightly on my knee, then moved it slowly and sensuously up my thigh. She lingered near the top and blew her warm breath lightly into my ear. If it had been possible my interest would have risen even higher. She counted the notes again.

'OK,' she said softly. 'For me, no money. Justa little for Mama anda Papa? *Si?*'

'Well . . .'

'*Si*. You come-a with me. OK?'

She was one determined signorina.

'Sure! You come! I give-a you gooda time for firsta time. Firsta time — ooh! You make-a me *vairy* happy. I make-a you a man. Thata make-a me *vairy* happy! Justa smalla money for Mama anda Papa. *Si?* For me, I give-a you fuck for love.'

The word hit me like a bomb. I had not heard a girl use it before. It was the ultimate aphrodisiac. I could but let her lead me through the Old Town's back streets.

The tall tenements leaned agedly towards each other across the narrow *carugi*, in some places only about twelve feet wide, until they almost blocked out the sun. All around was the vibrancy and pulse of ghetto life as the inhabitants of the canyons strode about their business, sat or lounged in doorways or leaned out of windows in earnest and animated conversations with each other and passers-by.

As we threaded through the throng the girl responded in voluble and rapid Italian to others who greeted her. Her ripostes and continuing firm grip seemed to indicate she had found a prize of some sort.

We entered a low, arched doorway and crossed a tiny marble courtyard to ascend a narrow stairway to another door.

A man whose vest and braces arced from his neck to his belt with notable curvature, his threadbare wife and several even more threadbare children sat on stools at a wooden table cutting up vegetables.

The girl bade me sit with them while she poured a couple of glasses of sour red wine. The *bambinos* stared and giggled. Papa showed no interest except to grunt when I said hello. Mama's smile did not reach her eyes.

'You gotta some money?' the girl said. 'Justa for Papa anda Mama? Like-a I promise? Anda maybe little for *bambinos*? *Si*? For me, nothing. OK? I give-a you for love like-a I promise . . . ooh! Youra firsta time . . . you make-a me vairy happy!'

I fished out a handful of lira and looked on anxiously as she counted some notes. Mama recounted them then looked enquiringly at her daughter. With an intensive verbal and hand discourse the girl conducted what must have been an explanation. At its conclusion Mama subsided, looked at me and nodded with a smile, which this time seemed a little more genuine.

'*Grazie, signore*,' she said and gestured to her daughter to give me another glass of wine. The girl smiled at her mother, returned the rest of my money and led me and my wine through the door one of the *bambinos* had opened in readiness.

She closed the door and gave a slight genuflection to the Virgin Mary hanging over the dressing table. As she stood upright she crossed herself and indicated the bed.

God may have been in her mind but the Devil was in her hands. She told me to continue with my wine while she began the preliminaries with an eroticism which, being a very accomplished girl, left my wine unfinished, but several times nearly spilled, and my interest raised to an urgent and almost intolerable extent . . .

After we disentangled ourselves she murmured through half-closed eyes, 'Ooh! I am-a happy! You? You are-a happy? *Si?*'

No! I was surprised at being slightly unhappy. The earth was obviously unmoved. Neither did bells ring nor birds sing. And the Virgin Mary cast a bemused countenance over what must have been a foolish scene; me in my shirt and socks, she with her thin dress pulled high above her jutting alabaster-white breasts. I stroked the warm wetness at the top of her thighs.

'*Si*,' I lied.

She rubbed the smouldering silkiness of her leg against me in an intimate gesture. Her foot played with mine while she propped herself up on one elbow. She looked at me solemnly. She was a sagacious girl.

'Notta mind,' she said quietly as she delicately tapped the end of my nose with her finger. 'Firsta time maybe notta always so good. Too quick. Nexta time, longer. Mucha better!'

She straightened my shirt.

'*Si*, nexta time longer! Ah! *Si*! *Mucha* better!'

'*Si*,' I said.

'*Si*!' she agreed. 'Because-a you notta boy no more. I make-a you *man*! *Si?*'

She rose and smiled down at me. She smoothed her dress, combed her hair and left the room. She returned with a bowl of warm water, soap, a couple of small clean towels and two glasses of wine.

'We wash,' she said, 'thena *vino*.'

She touched my glass with hers and we drank.

We left the bedroom holding hands. Mama continued peeling vegetables. The *bambinos* jabbed fingers into each other's sides. Papa grunted when I said *arrivederci*. On the way back through the canyons I bought us each a cake and she kissed me on the cheek.

As she went into a bar the nameless girl gave me a backward look and friendly wave, munching her cake as she went in search of more profitable custom.

'*Arrivederci*,' she called. 'You notta forgeta me? No?'

'No,' I called back. 'I'll not forget you.'

How could I? She was one of those people and it was one of those occasions a man does not forget. And as the minutes wore on I began to feel like a man of the world. *Si*! I also thought I heard a faint peal of bells. Maybe I was humming to myself. Anyway, by the time I reached the ship I already had the beginnings of a jaunty step, despite the muscular ache radiating from newly exercised regions.

A week later I turned nineteen, in a Bay of Biscay early-winter storm, a tempest which struck me, having now been made into a man, like a wet, wild stimulus of a new life. When we reached London I would join the National Union of Seamen and the British Shipping Federation's 'pool' and be issued with a blue British Seaman's Identity Card and a Certificate of Discharge book into which particulars of all future voyages would be entered.

I would be a bona fide seafarer.

In all respects. *Si*!

And my share of the National Debt could have tripled for all I cared.

⚓

As we pushed through the grey English Channel I noted the various seamarks — Start Point, Beachy Head, Dungeness etc — with an effected air of *déjà vu*. But my excitement was harder to contain once in the Thames Estuary. As we sailed up the river and made fast to our tugs before entering the grimy, ship-crammed Royal Victoria dock, I felt an almost profound sense of homecoming.

I based my renewed explorations of London on the relatively salubrious Red Ensign Club in Dock Street. My window looked out on similar grey roofs, sooty bricks and dingy chimneypots as from the Stack o' Bricks. But I could also see the top of the Tower of London to one side and St Paul's Cathedral the other. The Royal Mint was also not far away.

The establishment was opened in 1830 and was reputedly the first of its kind in the world. Joseph Conrad once stayed there. Its food and accommodation were better than the Stack o' Bricks and its management and residents alike much less tolerant of drunkenness and rowdiness. This discouraged the bums who found the cheaper and more Spartan Stack o' Bricks significantly more to their tastes — for the same reasons they also avoided signing aboard better found and so better disciplined ships.

The Red Ensign's padre was at the Battle of Jutland during the Great War. He was a slender, slightly stooped black-clothed man with a wooden leg. Having lived among seamen all his life he was not easily scandalised on the Lord's behalf.

I spent some evenings bent over the bar listening to his Royal Navy tales and how, when a shell landed near enough to alarm him into crying 'God Almighty!' he was seized with the vow to work on God's behalf for a living provided the shells continued to miss him. One didn't, and took off his leg. But since it might also have killed him, he assumed losing his leg instead of his life constituted a powerful memorandum from above.

'Then again, my boy,' he said gravely into a glass of warm Carrington, 'I might have been just damned lucky.'

Like all good members of the ministry he was also well acquainted with the real world.

The Red Ensign's Dock, Leaman and Cable Street environs were once part of the infamous Ratcliff Highway. Along it 'all the dregs and offscourings of male and female humanity swarmed in the foul and filthy dens of the Highway, ready to prey on the lusts, the follies and the trustfulness of the sailor.' Charles Dickens called the Highway a 'reservoir of dirt, drunkenness and drabs, thieves, oysters, baked potatoes and pickled salmon.' Another account tells of a 'warren of alleys running northwards from the Ratcliff Highway to Cable St in which bawds offer insalubrious lodgings to seamen too drink-sodden to care where they fornicate.'

Between the Highway and Cable Street was once Tiger Bay, 'an evil district [in whose] dancehalls girls of fourteen years old — old in the ways of vice before they had left the years of childhood behind — danced the cancan with drunken sailors of all nationalities.'[7]

The area was now quieter. Indians, Jamaicans, Africans, Arabs, Singhalese, Greeks, Turks, Lebanese, Chinese, English, Irish,

Welsh, Scots, Jews of all nationalities; all lived if not in equality, at least in varying degrees of peace.

Several times a week, however, the accord was disrupted by injurious and bloody fights in and around the nearby Blue Anchor and Brown Bear pubs, both of them renowned in the clipper-ship days — in one version of the old sea shanty 'Blow the Man Down' are the words 'I hailed her in English, she answered me clear, I'm from the Blue Anchor, bound to the Brown Bear.'

There were other fracas and squabbles in the backstreets. Most were satisfactorily ended by a couple of big policemen, sometimes three if the odds were more than about a dozen-to-one. Few of the disagreements were because of the racial mix. It was some years before the Race Relations Act made people more aware of race relations and so made race relations worse. The fights were instead usually over shapeless, powdered harlots who would have done the earlier Tiger Bay or Ratcliff Highway proud.

Small, dimly lit, smoky, low-ceilinged cafés abounded in the area's old brick buildings. An Indian who stirred hot curries over kerosene burners on the floor owned one. His plump, colourfully saried wife sat on a stool in a dark corner preparing ingredients. She sat in silence except when her husband called to her. They then engaged in a round of high-pitched noise that appeared more of a row than an exchange of intelligence. When it finished she again scuttled into silence. What they spoke of I never knew. But my curry was delivered with smiling politeness or unsmiling acerbity depending, it seemed, upon the volume of the previous proceedings.

Others were a Lebanese who served round bread and spicy shish kebabs, a Greek who delivered London's best bangers and mash and a Turk who turned out the mushiest mushy peas in the entire kingdom.

All the time the November weather was its usual dreadfulness. God knows why everyone in the British Isles hadn't migrated a thousand years ago. Or since they chose to stay, why they built and lived in the hemisphere's coldest buildings. At least they could have built verandahs along the shop-front pavements to keep off the rain as we did in New Zealand. Our early colonists had been

English, Scots, Welsh and Irish. It must therefore have been they who first built them. It must have been to keep off the antipodean sun.

Eventually I received a telegram to rejoin *Leicester*.

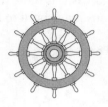

14

I think I'd like to be a witch.
I'd churn the sea, I'd tether the winds,
As suited my fancy best.
I'd wreck great ships, if they crossed my path
With all the souls on board.

Old Cornish Song

November's English Channel is bad enough, grey, coldly miserable, unpredictable and dangerous. November's Atlantic can be profoundly worse.

The barometer began dropping rapidly and radio messages began apparently telling of something afoot — 'apparently' because generally the only way of knowing what was happening was by the helmsman relaying remarks between captain and officers, or by what was told officially to the bosun who may or may not then tell his men.

Confirmation that the worsening weather was the outrider of something considerably greater came when the captain ordered rope lifelines rigged both sides of the main deck from bow to stern. The watches below were turned out to place steel storm battens across the hatch tarpaulins and check and tighten the wooden wedges that held the tarpaulins against the holds' coamings. Hold ventilators were turned off the wind and thick canvas covers tied tightly across their cavernous circular mouths to prevent the entry of any water. Thick steel cabin porthole deadlights were lowered and screwed home.

All the while the ripped black clouds thickened and lowered. The rain fell heavier. The wind blew fiercer. The seas rose higher until their collapsing tops were blown away like misty smoke so that the division between ocean and atmosphere became indistinguishable.

We were finally enveloped in the primeval uproar of a North Atlantic winter storm.

The ship laboured up each curling-crested wave. At the top it paused briefly amidst the spume of the breaking water. As the wave passed beneath, her forward length was left suspended above the following trough. Then, no longer supported and sometimes with a speed that momentarily made a human body feel almost weightless, her 8000 tons fell down the other side and crashed to a standstill with such breakneck power the hull trembled and the steel masts jerked and pulsated like trees in an earthquake.

With each tumble the stern angled high out of the sea. The propeller thrashed the air and shook every plate and rivet. The engineers struggled to reduce revolutions until the stern was again thrust deep until, throwing her bow clear, *Leicester* climbed the next moving hill. Water streamed from her decks like a surfacing submarine as she reared sometimes high enough to almost bury her stern.

Despite the helmsman's efforts to keep her shoulder to the seas, *Leicester* was regularly and derisively thrust aside to slide sideways down their lengths. Then she was engulfed from bow to stern, the 'midships superstructure in which we lived little more than a steel tidal rock. She strained at every seam as she struggled to emerge, water cataracting over her sides in furious torrents.

High on the wave tops, their tumbling crests disintegrating in flying spume and driving spray, the spectacle was awesome; immense valleys and endless rows of almost vertical hills, rank upon rank of liquid hordes charging from the horizon like a teeming cavalry in an undisciplined onslaught.

The cooks were ordered to abandon regular meals. Despite steel bars across the stove tops to keep a semblance of order among wildly jumping, sliding, clattering pots and pans, nothing needing liquid could be cooked. It was enough for the galley hands to avoid being thrown against the hot stoves without the added danger of burns or scalds from spilled hot liquids.

Bacon, steak, tea, toast and tabnabs were the order of the day for some time. We could not eat at the tables, despite tablecloths soaked with water to stop things sliding across the table surfaces that were themselves divided by wooden 'fiddles'. Instead, we stood wide-legged and pressed against the messroom bulkheads, plates flattened into our chests as we fought to keep upright. Sometimes we were knocked completely off our feet.

Off watch we lay wedged in our bunks amid the wet-dog smell of damp clothing, continually shocked awake as the ship rolled far to one side and slid down the wall of a wave, or a huge sea rampaged across the deck and smashed against our accommodation, rolling us so far over that oilskins on their coathooks streamed out almost horizontally and any loose objects hurled like projectiles. The more violent occasions were the stuff nightmares are made of. Green water crashing many feet deep against our portholes made their protective steel deadlights seem thin indeed.

At the height of the storm the seas reared so high, sometimes nearly 100 feet, that the wind could not reach us in their sometimes quarter-mile or longer troughs. But it scourged us with a ripping shriek as we topped their cliff-like tumbling summits. It was beyond belief the air we breathed could move with such speed.

The bosun and carpenter and several of the most experienced ABs later struggled on the boatdeck taking off the lifeboats' canvas covers. Then they refilled freshwater tanks, added blankets and extra stores and ensured the davits were greased and rope-falls in readiness. And, although the lifeboats' survival, never mind our own, in such conditions would have been unlikely, the captain had the mast cargo lights kept burning at night.

'Just in case,' he told the bosun matter-of-factly. 'You never know what might happen.'

The lights turned the night-time scene into something out of hell. Each breaking sea came spuming out of the darkness and into the pale illumination as a singular, clamorous messenger from the demons. In daylight no wave assumed an entity of its own unless of extraordinary size. It was just one of countless monsters.

'Old Blom' on his ketch *Rye* in Russell.

Algonquin Park at Lyttelton. Like most British tramps, she was run to minimum Board of Trade requirements.

Algonquin Park's bosun — the sort of man painters paint and writers write about.

St Paul's Cathedral, London, surrounded by evidence of the wartime blitz.

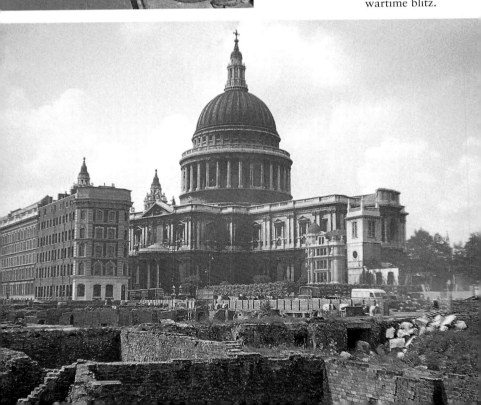

P&O liner *Maloja* entering Fremantle harbour (photographed several years after Peter's voyage).

Leicester in naval drydock at Devonport, Auckland, under extensive repair after the severe Atlantic storm.

Peter aboard *Gitano*, passing Gibraltar on the way to Turkey.

Immediate

Originators Instructions (Indication of Priority Intercept Group, etc.)		Codress/Plaindress	No. of Groups
TO:		FROM:	
	C in C Plym (R) Adenty		
	My 260120 B		5
	Have now obtained perfect	10
	Echo sounds trace of submarine	15
	am attacking to destruction	20
		25
	260201 B	30
		35
		40

Message from HMS *Affleck* to the Admiralty about the sinking of a German submarine.

A West African cargo surf boat, about to collect cargo from *Lagos Palm*.

The first photograph Peter developed and printed from his Box Brownie camera — *Lagos Palm* on the Benin River en route to Sapele, Nigeria.

Port Fairy in Fremantle, dressed for Queen Elizabeth's coronation. Peter joined the ship in Canada after a first-class trip on a BOAC flight.

Snowbound in Yugoslavia on the way from London to Baghdad, Peter and his companions lived with local families for almost a week.

Peter travelling in the Arabian desert, with his Scotland Yard-sanctioned pistol at his hip.

During a transit of the Suez Canal, aboard the tug *Champion*, with a canal workboat slung from the ship's derrick.

Matthew Finders at Port Said en route to Brisbane — a brand new ship which later became a luxury cruiser around the Pacific.

But such extraordinarily sized individuals could be seen in the distance. There was time to prepare for their towering inevitability as best we could. In the darkness, however, each was an individual with no hint of the stature of its follower until it fell with indifferent savagery, as if intent on forcing the ship to the ocean bottom.

On lookout, crouching alone and clinging to the binnacle behind the dodgers on the monkey island above the wheelhouse, events seemed even more climacteric. We seemed to be the only sentient living things in a consummation of chaos.

The screaming wind; rain driving like ice splinters; seas thundering unseen until they came in their spuming fury into the lights' weak periphery; the violent rolling, climbing and precipitate falls; the creaking, groaning, straining, stretching hull, all combined to elevate a sense of impending calamity.

It gave meaning to the words I had sung with such feeling in church not many years before. I felt truly in peril on the sea and utterly unhappy. But I could not fail to be impressed by the sheer natural brutality around me. There was a monumental honesty about the savageness of something with neither brain nor soul and so insensible in the exercise of its power.

Along with the hymn another childhood event had buried itself deep in my cognition. It resurfaced over the years whenever I felt a momentary and foolish intimacy with the sea. It may have been what kept me from fantasising about it. I knew it was a barbarian.

In the morning I had been playing in the wavelets and building castles in the sand. In the late afternoon I sat silent and shivering in a storm wind near a drowned man whose boat had been overwhelmed in the breakers. My father and several others tried to resuscitate the cold blue body. They gave up as the sun set. They pulled the dead man beyond the waves' grasp, wiped his face and closed his eyes and covered him with someone's overcoat, then sat with him until a policeman took him away on the back of a lorry.

My relief at the end of a lookout missed his footing climbing to the monkey island. At the same moment a vicious roll swung him wide from the ladder. He lost his grip and crashed to the bridge deck. He rolled around momentarily stunned and in danger of sliding through the rail into the sea.

I looked in disbelief then clambered down to rescue him. He was a heavy man and another massive roll slid us against the rail with our legs protruding through it. It was only with a great effort that I was able to drag him back and prop him up out of harm's way.

When he regained his sensibility he shook his head, shivered, coughed and opened his eyes.

'Fuck,' he said. 'What happened?'

I cleared my eyes and mouth of spray and told him.

'Fuck,' he said, as he stood up and resumed his way to the monkey island.

I reported the event and the captain ordered the man below and me to continue on lookout on the lee bridge wing. Its weather side was too dangerous because of the seas sometimes reaching it. Maintaining a lookout was impossible, anyway. Eyes slitted against the miscegenation of wind, rain and spray could see nothing through elements bent on slicing heads from shoulders.

The captain spent much of his time on the bridge. A tall, ascetic man, despite his studied calm, Captain Andrews was plainly not happy. Sometimes he uttered a slow and well-enunciated 'Oh, shit!' when the ship fell unusually heavily off a wave and the next came rolling down the deck or over the side in a solid wall burying the hatches and deck housings before bursting against the bridge.

In intimate contest with a wholly hostile force it is difficult not to dwell on the chances of survival. I felt for my life. It was a deep, almost primeval fright. It permeated every part of me, body and consciousness, and severely dented the customary youthful belief that unlike everyone else I would live forever. I had begun to believe the future could be predicted only in increments of about ten minutes. It shortened to five minutes each time the captain said, 'Oh, shit!'

Everyone was also mindful that in similar circumstances, only a couple of voyages before, the captain's predecessor had been hurled from this same bridge into the sea. Only by a promiscuous stroke of chance had he been carried back by the following wave. A similar event now was unlikely to have the same result. As seamen rarely lose their deep-rooted suspicion of the sea, when Captain Andrews swore it was with a considered and measured passion which seemed to come from deep within him.

Survival lay in his capabilities and the merits of the shipbuilders and enginemakers. And since each had their fallibilities, one also had to trust to luck. Or as some might have it, God. On the other hand, since presumably He was responsible for the tempest in the first place, trust in such a tyrant could have been entirely misplaced.

The unconcealed unease of the most hardened and experienced men, normally taciturn Hebrideans who had been at sea all their lives, sharpened the misgivings of the less experienced. An occasional remark showed their full awareness that in similar weather *Leicester* had lost six men and had narrowly escaped being totally lost herself. And there was *Samkey*, too, her sister who had disappeared without trace along with all her crew, some of our crew's relatives among them.

The ship's increasing reluctance to resume an even keel indicated something amiss among the cargo. The chief officer and bosun fought their way along the deck to the holds. Fortunately, Liberty ships' hold-access was by ladder through deckhouses at the base of the masts. On many other ships it was necessary to lift exposed hatch-covers.

The two men found hundreds of bags of basic slag in the No 2 hold broken free of their dunnage restraints and sliding across the sheet steel cargo, on top of which they had been loaded in Antwerp. They were fetching up on one side of the ship and causing her to list. It was a dangerous state of affairs.

All hands were turned-to. Wearing life jackets we were sent in relays to drag as many back into place as we could. We worked in the gloom of cargo light clusters lowered into the holds. We were continually thrown off our feet and into each other as the seas echoed around us, smashing against our thin steel sides and sweeping across the hatches above us.

We worked twenty minutes at a time before being relieved. Then, signalled by Aldis lamp from the bridge when it was judged safe to do so, we raced in pairs down the deck, clinging for our lives to the lifelines and sometimes reaching safety by seconds.

Eventually the elements ran out of energy. They left a rolling, confused surface as though great submarine creatures had just finished fighting. The sun began showing occasionally from behind the slowly dispersing clouds. Still with a considerable list from the shifted cargo, we resumed course for Willemstad in the Dutch Antilles island of Curaçao in the Caribbean. The weather finally calmed and we made good time through a sparkling tropical sea to Sombrero Islet and the Anegada Passage between the Virgin and Leeward Islands.

Willemstad's tiled roofs, gables and baroque facades of its eighteenth-century Dutch architecture were a welcome sight as we passed behind an assisting tug up the narrow St Anna Bay Channel, to come to rest well inside the Schottegat. Europeans first visited Curaçao in 1499 and by 1527 it had been settled by the Spaniards, after deporting the entire Indian population to Hispaniola in 1515. The Dutch took over in 1634. They needed Caribbean salt for herring preservation. The English took the island off them for a while during the Napoleonic Wars but returned it under the Treaty of Paris in 1815. The Dutch found oil in Lake Maracaibo in Venezuela in 1914. Because the lake was too small for ocean-going ships, Royal Dutch Shell built refineries on the island and brought the oil from Maracaibo by small 'mosquito' tankers for refining and transhipment.

Our cargo was restowed and some deck damage repaired and we were moved to nearby Caracas Bay where, overlooked by a stone fort established by Captain Morgan, one of the Caribbean's more notorious pirates, our oil bunkers were refilled. We may have stayed had the captain known the real state of his ship following the Atlantic storm. But he didn't. And so we set off for the Panama Canal.

⚓

In the sixteenth century the Spaniards had ideas of building a canal through the Panama Isthmus. A local Spanish official suggested a route close to that of the present canal. Later several other plans were suggested, but no action was taken. And then in 1880 along came Suez's Ferdinand de Lesseps.

'I maintain that Panama will be easier to make, easier to complete, and easier to keep up than Suez,' a confident de Lesseps said.

He planned a sea-level canal similar to the Suez Canal and began the job with a symbolic blow from a pick-axe wielded by his small daughter Ferdinande. But for the next nine years malaria and yellow fever decimated the diggers. Some 20,000 died. De Lesseps, by then a publicly maligned man, died in 1894 at the age of 89.

In 1904 the Americans, although haunted by de Lesseps' failure and French graft, extravagance and swindling, began anew. Their efforts were also unsuccessful until 1907 when President Teddy Roosevelt handed the job to the US army under the charge of an engineer, Major George Washington Goethals. The redesigned canal and its locks were opened in August 1914. It had been the most costly single effort ever undertaken anywhere in the world.

Today some 15,000 ships pass through the canal each year. They are lifted 85 feet by locks at one end and dropped at the other, on the way sailing through the mountainous spine of the Isthmus of Panama. Each time the locks are used around 50 million gallons of water are pumped in and then flushed out to sea. Most of the water comes from the artificially created Lake Gatun and nearby Lake Madden, formed in 1935 for extra water.

When *Leicester* passed through, much of the route was through rainforest covering 1300 square miles of the watershed. Most of the time it rained in steamy tropical downpours. By then, 20 per cent of the original forest had been cut.

About 70 per cent of the forest has now gone. This is bringing less rain to fill the lakes. As well, half a million tons of soil are washing from the denuded hills into Lake Madden each year and reducing the amount of water it will hold. Lake Gatun is suffering the same environmental damage.

In the early 1960s the canal was already too small for some of the larger ships then being built. Nuclear bomb builders exhibited an alarming enthusiasm for another bigger canal using their 'devices' to burst apart the mountains of Darien.

And their predecessors had reckoned de Lesseps was mad!

⚓

Except for a couple of strategically posted engineers to pass orders from the pilot to the engineroom should the bridge telegraphs fail, the canal transit was an idle time for most of us. Canal authorities provided helmsmen and men to handle the lines attached to the 'mules', small locomotives that pulled us in and out of the locks.

There was also an armed guard in the wheelhouse. Some said he was there to prevent anyone attempting to take over the ship and block the canal. Others said it was proof of Americans' preoccupation with guns. Sceptics said it was to provide ex-soldiers with jobs. Most professed no interest. It was enough to lean over the rails with mugs of tea and be idle spectators of proceedings for a change.

The voyage from Panama to New Zealand was generally pleasant. The ship rubbed her cheeks fondly against the Pacific's long, lazy swells as if having forgotten their Atlantic brothers' earlier conduct.

We were traversing the world's largest and deepest ocean. It is immense, more than twice the size of the Atlantic, 64 million square miles covering more than a third of the earth's surface and holding more than half its free water.

We passed few other ships and no land except one or two tropical islands in the hazy distance. Life ran its normal tempo in which the sounds of a ship at sea become so regular as to be accepted as silence, her movements so continuous as to be stillness.

Outward bound ships on the Britain–New Zealand–Australia run were generally cleaned and cargo working gear overhauled. In the coastal ports the hull was painted. Homeward bound the masts, derricks and superstructures were painted. Apart from the usual watchkeeping jobs of steering and night lookouts, our work during the three weeks across the Pacific to Wellington was mostly soogeying paintwork, chipping rust, repairing or replacing cargo-handling wires and ropework and odd painting jobs.

Rounding Cape Kidnappers on the way north from Welling-ton to Auckland we crossed *Leicester*'s track from the previous voyage from Napier. At that point I had been around the world.

In Auckland, while being readied to load wool for New York and Philadelphia, the bottoms of the holds were found to be buckled. Marine surveyors discovered even greater structural damage. The Atlantic storm had badly deformed our hull. Divers found heavy steel hull plates indented several inches between the frames. In some cases the frames themselves were badly distorted.

We were towed to the Devonport naval drydock where *Leicester* underwent New Zealand's biggest-ever and most intricate ship-repair job. Damaged steel was replaced. Frames were straight-ened. Some 700 intercostal plates were fitted to the double bottom to provide extra stiffening fore-and-aft. Extra girders were installed beneath the main deck to strengthen the hull full length.

As a wartime utility-built ship, the ship was welded instead of riveted using a shipbuilding technology not then anywhere near its prime. It was later believed not all Liberty ships disappeared during the war because of enemy action but in many cases be-cause their hulls broke apart when welded seams failed in heavy weather or extreme cold. Fortunately, *Leicester*'s owners had struc-turally strengthened and riveted her more vulnerable points. She would not otherwise have survived her Atlantic battering.

After all, as Joseph Conrad wrote about the *Titanic* enquiry, 'there is not much mystery about a ship. She is a tank . . . ribbed, joisted, stayed . . . and for the hazards I should think about as strong as a Huntley and Palmer biscuit tin . . . well, perhaps not quite as strong. Just look at the side of such a tin and think of . . . a ship and try to imagine what the thickness of her plates should be to approach anywhere near the relative solidity of that biscuit tin.'

If kicked by a mule, Conrad went on, the tin 'would come back to earth smiling, with only a sort of dimple on one of its cheeks. A proportionately severe blow would have burst the side of . . . any triumph of modern naval architecture like brown paper — I am willing to bet.'

The homeward voyage was uneventful. Anyway, 'events' were something we could do without. The company thought so, too. Before we reached London the ship had been sold to the Nassau Maritime Company in the Bahamas. She was renamed *Inagua*. She was sold again and renamed *Serafin Topic* and later again *Jela Topic*.

Several years later, as *Viking Liberty*, she ran aground off Trinidad on her way to New York. She was refloated and towed to New Orleans. But she was beyond repair and in 1966 was broken up in Santander on Spain's Bay of Biscay coast.

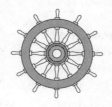

15

A man must serve his time to every trade.
George Byron

The Federal Line's *Durham* was the last ship built by Workman, Clark and Co before their Belfast yards closed in 1934. A diesel-engined, twin-screwed refrigerated cargo liner, she was the epitome of solid and stolid British design and seaworthiness. Her forest of samson posts and derricks marked her as a workhorse. Every morning we scrubbed her wooden decks from her straight-stemmed bow to cruiser stern. Once a week we barbarised them with sand. Every piece of brass, every piece, was polished regularly.

Durham was lucky to have survived the war, unlike nineteen of her company. In July 1941 she was in a small Malta convoy heavily and repeatedly attacked but she was only superficially damaged, and survived more attacks in Malta. The day after leaving, a mine blew a large hole in her No 1 hold. The paravane streamed as a mine-protection device was also blown into the hole, with another mine entangled in it. The ship's carpenter cut it loose with a hammer and chisel.

He was decorated for it. He should have received the top-order George Cross instead of the bottom-order British Empire Medal.

Two days later in Gibraltar an Italian two-man submarine attacked the badly damaged ship. A propeller was blown off and the engineroom and after-holds flooded. After a struggle the ship was beached. It was four months before she was repaired enough to be refloated.

She languished for another eight months until she was towed back to Britain by the Admiralty tug *Bustler*, one of the most powerful in the world. It was a remarkable feat to tow a ship 1000 miles at nearly seven knots, rudderless, 52 feet down by the stern and veering uncontrollably. Even more remarkable was that both escaped the attentions of the Luftwaffe and U-boats.

For many years the ship had been the company's cadet training ship. Our spacious accommodation at her after end had been cadets' cabins, messrooms and classrooms.

As well as crewing the ship, aspiring officers were tutored in the classroom, now our recreation room, in navigation, marine architecture and ship handling. All the while they were reminded of the carved wooden motto above the accommodation entrance — THE SHIP IS MIGHTIER THAN THE CREW. Undoubtedly so. The sea is mightier still. So *Durham*'s cadets would or should have learned that whatever the individual status of its component parts, a ship's crew really is at the arse end of the order of things.

That's why seamen, most of them, anyway, are among the world's greatest sceptics. Or if you like, pragmatists — few can swim very well. And that may have been what cost Captain Cook his life. After being attacked on the Hawaiian beach he fell into the water — had he been able to swim he may have made it to a nearby boat.

Falmouth, Newport, Cardiff and Glasgow all dripped morosely in October's rain. It was dour, persistent, irritating stuff. When it ceased it was only in an inconclusive sort of way. In Liverpool a cold, grey, soggy fog deepened the general melancholia of Merseyside's colourless, indifferent landscape. The dank atmosphere, made danker by the thousands of household coal fires on either side of the Mersey, produced a gloom like a mournful Victorian novel. It was not a place to cheer a man. Nothing could be seen beyond the adjacent ship, itself little more than an amorphous shape, and little heard beyond the doleful wails of ship and shore foghorns, including a grunting monster at the end of our Gladstone

Dock berth. It seemed impossible we could sail from this place to one where there was sunshine.

The sprawling seaport, then second only to London, was originally colonised in the eighth century by Norsemen. Its name is said to derive from the Norse Hlitharpollr, 'pool of the slopes.' In the twelfth century King John established Liverpool as a base from which to further his scheme to conquer Ireland. Later it was the home port of the slave ships to Africa. As Britain's chief emigration port it was the starting point for the Australian Gold Rush. In 1847 the *Illustrated London News* described Liverpool and its across-the-river neighbour Birkenhead as 'the finest examples on record of the brilliant results of unfettered British enterprise.'

Liverpool reputedly had Britain's, and possibly the world's, first lifeboat station, at Formby in 1777. Indeed, Liverpool was a town of many world firsts — among others the first wet commercial dock, opened in 1715, in Queen Anne's time; the first provincial newspaper, *The Liverpool Courant*, in the same year; the first school for the blind (1791), the first school for the deaf and dumb (1825), the first society for the prevention of cruelty to animals (1841), the first slum clearance project (1864) followed by the first municipal housing (1869). Liverpool was also where Meccano sets, Dinky toys and Hornby model trains were invented and manufactured.

Gladstone Dock in which we were berthed was opened in 1927 to hold the largest trans-Atlantic passenger liners. Going ashore we trod the same cobblestones on which powerful Clydesdale horses had once drawn loads of 'up to ten tons each over surfaces hard and durable with low tractive resistances and good foothold for the horses.'

The war-weary city seemed to have done little more than clear away much of its bomb rubble into heaps while awaiting better days. But Scousers still pointed with pride to the twin Edwardian bird statues atop the Liver Building (with the world's biggest clock faces) at Pier Head from whose Princes Landing Stage the big Atlantic liners arrived and departed. The Germans had continually boasted they would smash the birds from their perches. They always failed. And so long as the birds remained, well, what the hell! Eventually they were removed for their own safety.

The Admiralty's Atlantic headquarters from 1941, Liverpool was the focal point of the Battle of the Atlantic. It was also a major naval escort base and by the end of the war more than 2500 convoys, around 13,000 ships a year, had sailed to and from it. Not that it provided a necessarily safe haven. By the end of April 1941 there had already been sixty-eight air raids. A month later fifty-seven vessels from lighters to 12,000-ton ships were sunk in the docks and adjacent river. Thousands were killed and tens of thousands made homeless. In one raid a ship loaded with ammunition blew up and parts of it were found up to nearly three miles away.

But then Liverpool, where Hitler's sister-in-law Brigid once lived and with whom Hitler reputedly stayed for several months in 1913, was an easily found target, one which Hitler himself had identified as being of 'decisive importance'. The German pilots flew along the Irish Sea using unblacked-out Eire as a beacon. The U-boats hammering the convoys also refuelled in quiet bays in Southern Ireland.

Durham had sailed in the convoys. So had some of her present crew. But their only interest in Liverpool now was its dockside pubs.

As a cargo liner and with a hugely bigger crew, even a butcher and a baker, than either *Algonquin Park* or *Leicester*, there was a greater rigidity in the hierarchical nature of shipboard community.

Still only a junior ordinary seaman, I and others of similar proletarian rank spent one week a month as 'peggy'. We looked after the sailors' messroom, toilets, shower rooms, recreation room and accommodation alleyways, almost as skivvies. We polished and scrubbed out, made the tea, fetched the meal kits from the galley, laid the tables and washed the dishes. We were roundly abused if things went wrong. Which occasionally they did.

But being at the bottom of the societal heap was not the problem. It was being treated as such. The inevitable outcome of such treatment is that there are times when in one's considered judgement society can get stuffed. Society rarely agrees with being stuffed, however. History is littered with bloody noses as a result.

Not to mention the collapse of nations.

Notwithstanding history, early one Saturday afternoon I was growing increasingly irritated waiting for some of the ABs to return from the Caradoc pub, a rip-roaring establishment outside the dock gates and notorious (and still existing but now a virtual tourist venue) across all the seven seas.

Eventually I thought 'Stuff them. I want to go ashore, too.' And so I tipped the remainder of the midday meal into the gash bucket and washed up.

Dammit, the fruits of having been made a man had been well ripened by now and I had a date to keep. But blonde-haired Joan, a passionate, leggy nymph from Aigburth, was unlikely to wait around in the fog while I waited to catch an Overhead Railway train to meet her at Pier Head.

I was about to leave the messroom when the men returned. They stared at the unlaid tables and washed-up kits before becoming a stumbling, swearing, babble of bellicosity.

'Jesus, where's our fuckin' grub?' someone finally demanded. Oh dear!

'It's in the gash bucket.'

'The fuckin' *gash* bucket?' His tone implied he thought he must have suddenly become hard of hearing.

'Who put it there?' someone else asked, in a similar tone. 'The fuckin' Man from Liverpool, I suppose?'

The Man from Liverpool was a mythical character aboard every ship who was responsible for all inexplicable happenings. Such as a meal in the gash bucket.

'No,' I said. 'I did.'

My passionless statement was greeted by an enormous silence like that which comes at the end of some tumultuous era.

Ted detached drunkenly from the angry men and advanced towards me. He was a beefy Londoner whose prognathous jaw showed his nature to be a bastard was as much as it was the nature of water to run downhill. As a baby he probably chewed the ends off bricks and as a schoolboy probably thought Magna Carta was King John's wife. Eyes slitted, mouth snarling, fists tightly clenched, Ted stared at me as if I was an alternative food source.

'Gash bucket? Our grub? Jesus, kiddo! In the fuckin' *gash* bucket?'

His breath wafted around me like a beer cask gone off.

'What'aya gotto say fo'ya'fuckin'self?' he slurred drunkenly.

My daylong anticipation of a repeat of the previous night's excitement with the sensual Joan prompted a bravado strong enough for me to face him squarely.

'As a matter of fact, Ted, to you, fuck all,' I said evenly.

Emboldened by his look of astonishment, my bravado rose to an idiotic pitch.

'In fact, *absolutely* fuck all . . .' I looked around the group, 'to any of you!'

Their looks of astonishment drove me even further.

'I'm entitled to go ashore, too, you know. I'm not waiting around all day for you fuckin' lot. I'd have put the kits in the warmer if someone'd told me you'd be back. But nobody did. So I thought you were eating ashore.'

'Is that fuckin' so?'

By now my confidence had propelled me beyond any sensible consideration of consequences.

'As a matter of fact, Ted, yes, it fuckin'-bloody-well is.'

Ted hesitated. He had clearly expected a physical response. A verbal one, more importantly a defiant one, even more importantly, an apparently calm one, was unexpected. Perhaps he inferred it as 'do whatever you like, you Cockney bastard — but your dinner's still in the gash bucket!' He inferred wrongly. Of course he did. My composure was becoming less and less by the second.

Ted looked around the group as if seeking an answer. There was none until someone allowed his head to lead. This showed him to be more sensible than most.

'Well, Ted,' the man said, 'it's in the gash bucket. And there's fuck all we can do about it.'

Ted gave a drunken shrug.

'Fuck off ashore then, if you're going. But by Christ, Kiwi, do it again and I'll have your balls for a necklace!'

Truth aboard a ship was seldom transmitted with a subtlety beyond that necessary to live together in comparative peace. In the light of Ted's undoubtedly sincere if not factually accurate statement, it would therefore have been rash of me to prolong dignity, let alone defiance. One must recognise the point at which courage becomes stupidity.

'No, Ted, I won't.'

Ted sat down heavily in a chair. He put his head in his hands and said, several times, 'No bloody grub! Jesus-bloody-Christ! And it was bloody oxtail, too!'

The man who had rescued me said quietly, 'Dangerous thing to do, Kiwi — at sea you assume nothing.'

I had enough experience already to know he referred to more than tipping assumed unwanted food into a gash bucket.

'I know,' I said.

'But at least you stuck up for yourself,' he went on. 'All the same, Ted can be a right dangerous bastard when he's pissed.'

Back in the Caradoc the grub-less Ted laughed himself silly, although whether his drunken mirth was because of my supposed courage or the loss of his oxtails was unclear.

Nevertheless, for the rest of the voyage those likely to be late back aboard always mentioned it. It was not so much out of respect for us, but the employment of seamen's inherent commonsense. Whatever they did to the peggy-for-the-week, it wouldn't resurrect their dinner from the gash bucket.

⚓

As the fully laden ship felt her way down the still fogbound Mersey, invisible ships answered her regular whistle-blowing. Others occasionally appeared through the gloom like phantoms of wartime convoy ships returning to Merseyside.

One week a month as messroom peggy was not overly onerous. There was plenty of time for cribbage, much of the afternoon off and all night turned-in until 5.30 the next morning. But back on watch-keeping it seemed the only two kinds of people in the world were chipping hammer manufacturers and paint companies. As junior ordinary seamen we were seldom allowed to do proper sailorising jobs. They were the preserves of the ABs. And with the ship on automatic steering during daytime there was not even the peace of a couple of hours at the wheel away from the interminable chipping rust, soogeying and painting.

More unsettling was the realisation that round voyages between New Zealand and Britain were no way to see the world. A day in Curaçao while our oil bunkers were replenished, a few drinks in Colon's dingy bars, a few more in Balboa after the Panama Canal transit and many weeks tied up in New Zealand or Australian ports hardly constituted foreign travel.

And so although the ship had a good library, meals were ample and well-cooked, fresh bread was baked every day, a swimming pool was erected on the after-deck after we left Panama and even Ted, provided his oxtails were not interfered with, proved companionable, it was as if I was back at the Russell post office.

⚓

Nearly three months were spent in Wellington during the 1951 New Zealand watersiders' strike. When it was plain the strike would be prolonged — it lasted more than five months and degenerated into almost a national disaster — all hands were set free until cargo operations resumed. The only requirement was that the ship be kept operating normally. The necessary skeleton crew shared the duties among themselves. The rest, and the others when not on duty, took jobs in the city.

One of the officers cleaned shoes in the early mornings at a big Wellington hotel, one became an expert barman, another a night porter. Engineers and engineroom hands shared jobs in an engineering works. Several of my friends and I shared a job in a factory making wooden butter boxes. Others mounted night-time pillaging forays into the holds. The goods, mostly Irish linen sheets and pillowcases, were disposed of next evening in the pubs. Despite the old seafaring dictum 'more days more dollars', with such a long period of uncertainty ahead of them most also generally bitched, boozed, bickered and got into trouble of one sort or another.

But for those of us afflicted by the rising sap it was a happy hunting time and we competed in the numbers of girlfriends on call at any one time. It was a time of cheerful chauvinism whose parameters both sexes understood and rarely challenged with any élan.

Sam was the most successful. He was a Kentish lad. He bore no resemblance to even an indifferent oil painting. Nor was he of any particular physical stature. And he certainly knew nothing of the finer points of seduction, as we thought we knew them.

Yet for reasons known only to themselves, girls fell apart when confronted by his easy-going, personable nature. Sam had an unerring instinct for picking the better prospects among his admirers. After some amiable chitchat he would, being a lad not suffering from premature articulation, pose the short but always courteously delivered and in most cases apparently quite reasonable question — 'D'ya fuck?'

It must have been the ultimate aphrodisiac, despite its blunt brevity. About one time in five he received an immediate Yes, sometimes even a Yes Please. He rated this an acceptable strike rate. It meant he 'didn't have to piss around too much, mate. Cheaper, too.' Rejection was usually with a look of astonishment, although sometimes softened with an implied Well, At Least Not Until I Get to Know You Better. In which case Sam followed the getting-to-know-you routine if it seemed unlikely to need too much time, money or effort. He was also able to judge the intrinsic worth of even the most apparently determined rejections. On one occasion a hefty clout was accompanied by the threat of 'a kick in the knackers, ya' Pommy bastard.' Celebration of Sam's defeat was premature. Before the evening was out she took him back to her bed from which he did not arise until sometime the following week.

We studied Sam's technique intensively. But it was plainly unique to him. Our only recourse was the long-winded expenditure of time, money and effort. And more to the point, the successful identification of those in whom to make the investment.

Sam could not understand our expensive labours.

'It's easy enough,' was his only advice. 'All ya' gotta do is fuckin' ask.'

* * *

The 151-day waterfront strike was a bitter affair. Police were everywhere. Seamen could not leave or re-enter the wharf gates without passes.

Politicians on all sides talked in circles. Truth was a tricky hand to play in a game that confused their own interests with the public interest.

The National Government said the country was threatened by communists and it was going to ensure 'the food of this country be not destroyed . . . Great Britain be not starved . . . that the national security and defence was assured.'

The Opposition charged the Government with 'acting the same way as others around the world which had later turned into dictatorships.'

The Government declared a state of emergency. It used regulations which four years earlier it had roundly condemned the then Labour Government for supporting, thundering then that the regulations it was now invoking contained 'all the elements of a Communistic system, of totalitarianism and dictatorship.'

As the strike lengthened the watersiders' union was deregistered. Strike leaders accused the Government of a frontal attack on the wages and conditions of all workers. The post office was authorised to open mail suspected of containing material supporting the strike. The police were ordered to arrest anyone helping the strikers or their families in any way. And so newspapers refused to publish statements or letters supporting the strikers. One editor urged that police be armed and to shoot in the face of defiance. The strikers then accused the Government of violating the Declaration of Human Rights and appealed to the United Nations.

Homes were searched for printing presses and so the strikers did their printing in cars while driving around the streets. Anyone caught distributing the pamphlets was arrested. Compulsory military training was suspended. Soldiers and airmen worked as watersiders or coalminers. New Zealand seamen then struck and ships loaded by the armed services were crewed by naval ratings.

Plots were hatched. Someone tried to blow up a railway bridge to stop trains carrying coal mined by soldiers. There was a riot or two around the country. Many shouted and a few were injured.

The strike ended with victory for the Government. But the cost was high. Coal had not been mined, 70,000 tons of cement not produced, 31 million pounds' worth of wool not sold, 600,000 cases of fruit had rotted on trees or in packing sheds.

Shipowners were unbothered by it all. To make up for the more than 3000 shipworking days lost they slapped a 50 per cent surcharge on cargoes to or from New Zealand until they recovered their losses.

Politicians weren't vexed, either. They called an early election and were re-elected with their power base firmly cemented for some years to come. Principles were one thing. The ballot box was another.

On our return to London I had the three years' sea-time necessary to ship out as able seaman. The certifying stamp in my discharge book secured both personal sovereignty and the ability to live below the level of worry. My own wellbeing was my only concern. I earned enough to keep my teeth in good repair, my body warm and my feet well shod, but was otherwise supported only by good health and confidence. I possessed only what I could carry. It was not much and so was not a burden. I was a certified member of the world's largest merchant fleet. The ships went everywhere and so I could go anywhere. And I had nowhere to go but all over the place.

I had reached the moment of which Samuel Johnson said, 'When men come to like a sea-life, they are not fit to live on land.'

And although I had no way of knowing it, I was also nearing the halfway point in the period of a man's greatest freedom — the interval between leaving his mother and getting married.

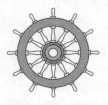

16

I got used to not caring a damn, just to
walking and staying put when I had walked far
enough . . . to letting myself drift . . .
Graham Greene, *Journey Without Maps*

In Poplar's Board of Trade shipping office a man sat on a tall chair behind a wooden counter. A smooth-faced man with the untroubled countenance of a Brahmin, with hair in his ears but little on his head. His eyebrows curled up like horns. His rotundness strained his waistcoat buttons each time he moved. Not that he moved much. Leather patches on the elbows of his fading suit eased the wear of leaning on the counter across which he conducted his official life as if engaged in some sense of weary purpose. Otherwise he presented a figure of harmony, in tune with his contented curves.

At his back hung a very good painting of a sailing ship, slightly askew as if also weary of its purpose. Yet it was not incongruous. Its portrayal of sea, wind and ship belied the ambient atmosphere. The musty, Dickensian office would once have been crowded with the crews of such ships.

Poplar itself had been the cradle of Britain's maritime greatness. But why Poplar? There were no poplars in Poplar any more than there was hay in Haymarket or friars in Blackfriars or Swiss in Swiss Cottage and certainly no elephants or castles in Elephant and Castle.

The King's ships had been built there, like *Royal Oak* in 1661 in the Blackwall Yard, which existed from 1612 to 1907. Henry VII's *Mary Rose* had been fitted out in a specially built 'dykinge and castyne' dock. The world's then-largest merchant ship, *Himalaya*, was launched at Blackwall in 1853. It was still in service with the Admiralty until sunk by German bombers in World War II off Portland. The Royal Navy's first ironclad warship, HMS *Warrior*, was launched there in 1860. So was Brunel's *Great Eastern*, in 1857. Clipper ships such as *Thermopylæ* and *Cutty Sark* unloaded China tea in the nearby East and West India Docks, whose clinkered brick warehouses were once reckoned some of the finest functional architecture in Europe. William Booth in 1865 opened a mission in Whitechapel that later became the Salvation Army, with its first hostel a converted warehouse by the West India Docks. Sir Walter Raleigh lived in Poplar. His house remained until the Blackwall Tunnel was built.

The sailors crowding the office would have been a superstitious lot. They would have hated sailing on a Friday, the day of the Crucifixion. Or the first Monday in April, since it was supposed to be both Cain's birthday and the day Abel was killed. Or the second Monday in August because it was believed to be the day of Sodom and Gomorrah's destruction. December 31 was another bad day, being the day Judas Iscariot hanged himself.

But otherwise they would have professed little interest in religion, although they would have prayed with immense passion when their ships were in peril.

Scratching his inner ear with the top of his fountain pen, the man looked at my Merchant Navy identity card and discharge book.

'New Zealander, eh?'

'Yes.'

'Another foreigner, then.'

'Foreigner? I'm not foreign!'

'Colonial, then.'

'Don't know about that, either.'

'Oh, well, don't suppose it really matters. At least you're one of us.'

'How's that?'

'Well, you're white and talk the same language. And I suppose being a New Zealander at least you're related.'

'Well, my mother is English.'

'There you are then.'

'Where?'

'On the right side, son, on the right side,' he said, still scratching his inner ear. 'We'll be overrun one of these days by foreigners. Jamaicans, Indians, Africans, Arabs. The lot,' he said, with the air of a man who is absolutely certain about things he is certain about.

It was a time when Britain was short of labour and the government was allowing in people from colonial countries like the West Indies and West Africa to fill jobs in London Transport, the National Health Service, the railways and major firms. The rush had started when an ex-troopship, *Empire Windrush*, arrived at Tilbury in 1948 with nearly five hundred West Indians 'exercising their legal right to move freely within the British Empire.' The flow increased when the United States later erected barriers against immigration.

'There'll be trouble one day,' he went on after a moment's reflection. 'Damned politicians filling us up with foreigners. There'll be big trouble! Mark my words! Democracy is sometimes its own worst enemy. Sometimes I wonder what we're coming to,' he said, as if the world was rocking dangerously on its axis.

But he was right on both counts. Paki-bashing, Notting Hill Gate, Toxteth, the National Front; all lay waiting to ambush the future. Race relations was then a cryptic term, seldom heard. But a portly elderly man dealing across his counter with seamen from all over the world, he knew what race relations were all about. They swirled, flowed and argued across his counter all day.

'Just made AB, eh?' he said, finishing with my documents and finally his ear. 'Well, I've just the job for a first-trip AB. *Gitano*. She's down at the East India Dock. Old ship but belongs to a good company. Ellerman Wilson. But the mate's a bit of a hardcase from what I can gather. Just sacked an AB who signed on the other day. One of your countrymen as it happens. He was hopeless, according to the mate.'

* * *

Gitano was a coal-burning 3000-tonner of the Ellerman Wilson Line and registered in Hull. Built in 1929, her ramrod-straight stem, tall, thin upright funnel and box-like superstructure rendered her a deep-sea version of Masefield's classic 'dirty British coaster, with a salt-caked smokestack, bucking through the Channel in the mad March days.'

I picked my way across the dunnage-cluttered decks and dodged the cargo swinging out of the holds to the quayside. I climbed the bridge ladder to the chief officer's cabin. He looked at my documents.

'Good God, another bloody Kiwi? First-trip AB, too! What's that bloody man doing to me? Not a pisshead, are you?'

'No,' I said.

'Better not be. Just sacked one of your countrymen. Only aboard two days. Boozed the whole time. Hopeless bugger!'

'So I heard,' I said.

'So be warned,' he said, as he handed back my discharge book. 'Shipping office tomorrow morning. Nine o'clock. On the dot, mind you!'

The chief officer was a man plainly not given to euphemisms. He was also an intuitive man-management expert. He would have given short shrift to anyone blathering on about 'human-resource management' or 'industrial relations.' His expertise lay in well-honed experience and common sense. His crew was therefore a conglomerate of ages, temperaments, experience and abilities able to rub alongside each other like the ingredients of well-baked bread. They were typical of the generally tolerant, pragmatic nature of British Merchant Navy crews.

After drydocking in Antwerp for her bottom to be scrubbed and painted and the rest of her generally smartened up, *Gitano* loaded in various Continental ports and set out for the Mediterranean.

After we dropped the pilot off Flushing I leaned over the rail and looked forward to the new voyage. It would be quite unlike the round-the-world treks to New Zealand. Such excursions seemed in retrospect to be pilgrimages into the almost drugging peacefulness of the monotony of a seagoing routine limbo where nothing happened, was ever likely to happen, or had ever happened.

Gitano's longest passage was nine days from Gibraltar — before which we had passed Tarifa and beyond which lay the Gitano mountains, or cordillera — across the Mediterranean to Mersin at the foot of Turkey's Taurus Mountains and once a Neolithic settlement.

Being the middle of the week it was only possible to walk around the dock area after the day's work. It was pleasant enough among the waterfront palms and trees and eucalyptus' and hibiscus' bouquets filling the air.

Having become mildly interested in the peripherals of history, I would like to have caught a bus to nearby Tarsus where St Paul was born and to where Cleopatra, under a gold awning and dressed as Venus surrounded by cupids, sailed up the River Cydnus to meet Marc Antony, master of Roman Asia but dressed as Bacchus for the occasion.

From Mersin a short run took us across to Iskenderun, originally Alexandretta and founded by Alexander after routing the Persians at Issus. It was once the port for trade from India and Persia. Jonah was reputedly cast on its beach after 'the Lord spake unto the fish, and it vomited Jonah upon the dry land.' Behind the high Amanos mountains at its rear lies Antioch.

Korea-bound Turkish soldiers unloaded crates into lighters that were then hauled by tugs to the ships about to take the soldiers and their supplies to war. The Turks were in sharp contrast to the Guards I had watched on parade in London. Against the Guards' upright bearing, disciplined, precisely measured marching and smart, pressed uniforms, the nondescript, badly shod Turks appeared a rabble. They would have been the despair of a Guards' regimental sergeant-major.

But in the opinion of some of *Gitano*'s younger men who had served their two years' National Service, a bawling, ramrod-backed, red-faced British regimental sergeant-major would not have impressed the Turks. They might have thought he was a joke and died laughing.

During idle moments the soldiers sat around the deck sharpening knives. They tested the razored edges on pieces of rope.

'My God, I wouldn't like to meet one of you little buggers in the dark!' someone said.

A soldier smiled cordially, acknowledging the tenor of the comment if not the words themselves.

'Communeest,' he said. He grinned and drew his weapon across an imaginary throat. 'Communeest! Ahh!' He rolled his eyes and made a throaty gurgle. 'Communeest!' he said. 'Cut, yes?'

The question may not have covered one of the larger problems of the time. But nor was it trivial.

'Je-SUS! Stuff you, mate — but thank God you're on our side!' said one of the sailors.

The only Jews I had so far met, or had known were Jews, had been in London's East End. Many were descended from European and Russian grandparents who fled the pogroms in the 1800s, people who according to one writer, 'know no work on Sunday and no rest on weekday.' My acquaintances had been in some business or other; tailors, café owners, pawnbrokers and the like. So it was a surprise in Haifa to see Jews digging ditches and labouring at similar menial tasks. As it was to see Arabs in long white cotton robes working alongside them, and an even bigger surprise to see Arabs selling Jews cups of coffee in small cafés.

Haifa was an important fortification during the Crusades. Mount Carmel, at whose foot it lay, had overseen all the fortunes of history the city had endured in its long life. Saladin destroyed it in 1191. Napoleon Bonaparte captured it and then lost it to Ibrahim Pasha in 1839. Carmel itself had also suffered. Survivors of the old Aleppo pines that once clothed it stood forlornly as ancient remnants of former glories.

Wrecked buildings were reminders of the enmities still bubbling within the metropolis. Some of the damage had been the work of the Haggana and Stern Gangs against the British, some the work of Arab against Jew and vice versa.

One of my watchmates knew all about it. John had been in the Palestine Police Force for a couple of years before giving up in despair and going back to sea.

'Pack o' bastards, mate,' the ex-policeman said. 'I tell you!

Jews! Wogs! The whole bloody lot! A right pack o' bastards!'

He would have had good reason for believing so, he and his fellows being targets for both sides. Being an even-handed man as befits a good policeman, however, he would not elaborate, beyond once explaining that the rough, red scar on his shoulder was from a bullet.

'Didn't even know where it came from, let alone whose it was,' he said.

We had seen the scar before, when we showered or worked bare-backed in the sun. But even in the face of direct enquiry he would volunteer no information about it except that it had been 'bloody sore at the time, mate, I can tell you.' So we concluded he had been in a knife fight somewhere, although most of us believed that would have been surprising. He was a man who not only avoided trouble but also completely minded his own business, a man as quiet as a shelf-load of books. It was only returning to the vicinity of his experience that caused him to explain the scar and voice what were obviously deep-seated feelings. But he seemed to do so almost against his will.

At Tel Aviv–Jaffa we anchored offshore and loaded thousands of cases of oranges from large boats rowed by Arabs. The twin-city metropolis is Israel's largest and the country's cultural centre. Jaffa itself is an ancient port stretching back around 4000 years. The Tel Aviv part is comparatively new. Zionists founded it to the north of Jaffa in 1909. Israel's independence was proclaimed in Tel Aviv in 1948 and Jaffa became part of the city two years later.

We sometimes went ashore in the boats and poked around Tel Aviv and its ancient neighbour. Each displayed the same amount of recent ruins as Haifa. During our trips ashore the ex-Palestine policeman usually had a scowl on his face. He nevertheless reckoned Jaffa oranges the best in the world.

⚓

'Twenty-one today, eh, Kiwi?' the chief officer asked as I relieved the wheel at the beginning of the morning four to eight watch in the Ionian Sea on the way to Naples.

146

'Yes,' I said, surprised at his remark. 'But how did you know? I didn't realise it myself until I happened to look at the calendar in the messroom just now as we were turning-to.'

'I was looking at the Articles last night and noticed it,' he said. 'Got the key of the door now, eh?'

'Yes, suppose I have.'

'Bollocks,' he said. 'You've had it since you left home. I noticed your first trip was at sixteen. Anything you can now do legally you must already have done a thousand times illegally!'

I had been surprised myself that reaching my majority had conferred no sense of sudden freedom.

'Anyway, tell you what,' he went on, 'if you want to get pissed you can have the afternoon off when we arrive.'

I thanked him for his permission to get officially drunk. But since we were arriving at daybreak, what about the whole day off?

'Christ, man, I didn't mean a holiday. I only meant to get pissed. Still . . . yeah, OK, once we've tied up you can have the rest of the day off. I'll tell the bosun.'

As the sun rose over the starboard bow, the ship slowed and my two watchmates rigged the boatrope and rope ladder for the Naples pilot. I was still at the wheel as we entered the port. I looked forward to my day off.

Naples, like most Old World cities, has a long and turbulent history. It was founded by Greeks around 600 BC and captured by the Romans some 300 years later. It then became the favoured residence of emperors such as Nero, Titus, Hadrian and Aurelius. Sicilians, Spaniards, Austrians and French later occupied it, and the Germans, until bombed out of it by the Allies.

In between times unrest, revolution, epidemic and earthquake rocked the city of churches, castles and palaces, in one of which, at the end of the Via Chiaia, Sir William Hamilton entertained Lord Nelson, who later ran off with Sir's wife. Naples' music schools spawned musicians like Scarlatti, Donizzeti and Bellini. Enrico Caruso began his singing there.

'And how did you like Nar-pullee?' the chief officer asked later.

He was on deck overseeing cargo operations and practising his Italian on Italians wanting to practise their English on Englishmen.

'Quite interesting,' I said.

'Ah, Nar-pull-ee . . . *Bella*!' He rolled his eyes and spread his hands like an Italian. 'But you didn't get pissed?'

'No. Anyway, I told you in London I wasn't a pisshead.'

'In that case, you ought to go to Pompeii tomorrow. You might find it interesting. Like to go there myself when I can. I'll lend you a guidebook if you like.'

Sometimes the chief officer surprised his men. But not greatly so on this occasion. Tomorrow was Saturday and his generosity cost him only the loan of a guidebook.

⚓

The morning train from the Corso Garibaldi passed through the city's outskirts and into a countryside of olive groves and vineyards. Then it skirted the foot of Mount Vesuvius to arrive at the railway station from where I took a horse-carriage to the ancient city's Nolan Gate.

There were few at Pompeii that day, the odd tourist and some workmen. With the guidebook I wandered around trying to visualise the inhabitants and their lives until Vesuvius overwhelmed them in 79 AD.

I didn't really 'see' Pompeii, however, and had begun regretting not being with the rest of the lads among Naples' vino and signorinas, until I met a man on the bottom steps of the amphitheatre in one corner of the silent stone city. He was taking measurements and writing in a notebook. Might be interesting to talk to an archaeologist. Provided he could speak English.

Drawing nearer I recognised him as one of our Liverpool firemen.

'Hullo there, Scouse,' I said, surprised.

He grunted monosyllabically.

Smallish, sinewy and middle-aged, Scouse seemed to have shared little of the good life. His face was pinched from years of hard living in ships' stokeholds. His back was bent from shovelling coal into their fires, his hands rough and coarse and arthritic from handling the shovels, rakes and slices.

I think he regarded me as an intrusion until he saw the guide-book. It implied at least some interest in the place. But all he said was, 'you'll get fook all outa that fookin' thing.'

True. I had not gained much from it so far and had begun to regard Pompeii as little more than a collection of obviously very old stone houses and scattered pillars. It barely mentioned the amphitheatre, for instance, except its dimensions. It didn't say it once seated 50,000 people. The only tangible reality around the place was the quietly smoking Vesuvius in the background.

'What are you doing?' I asked.

'Measuring.'

'What for?'

'Y'fookin' blind or something? Me fookin' notebook, of course.'

'Sorry, mate, yes, I can see that. But why?'

The question unacknowledged in any way, I began to walk away. Stuff you then, you miserable old sod. I would return to Naples and find the lads and get among the signorinas.

'Oi!' he called after me, 'if you want to be fookin' useful come and fookin' help instead of asking doomb-fookin' questions.'

I was glad I helped him and his fookin' notebook. My assistance opened a floodgate. Gold nuggets reside in, and with care can be mined from, the depths of the most unlikely people. Their station in life is little guide. Nor their place of residence, in Scouse's case Liverpool's rough and tumble dockland area of Bootle.

I remembered passing through the Canary Islands and Southern's brief mention of the derivation of the islands' name. A surprising bastard sometimes, Ginger had said. He might have said the same of Scouse. But since Scouse was probably not such a prick as Southern, it may have been with some admiration.

Scouse's free use of expletives made the things he talked of no less valid. A lifetime in stokeholds and coming from a place like Bootle was cause enough for a man to swear continually. Being a fookin' fireman from fookin' Bootle, however, was not necessarily a recipe for a bloonted-fookin'-intellect. QE-fookin'-D.

* * *

Years later aboard a large modern container ship from Wellington to Fremantle on a publisher's freelance writing and photographic commission, I was reminded of Scouse and others like him. Their differing backgrounds, experiences and resulting characters were all bound up in the persona of Bert, an AB from Tilbury.

Bert went to sea when he was fifteen. Among other things, including 'a few excitements' during the war which he left mostly unexplained, he had been penniless in Canada, incarcerated in a South American jail, partied with a Middle Eastern potentate, escaped several determined marriage bids, got the clap from a woman who would otherwise have succeeded and was later caught by a girl he had known at school.

Bert was a knowledgeable man. He read widely and indiscriminately. He had a more than passing knowledge, too, of many of the world's religions. He had briefly embraced several of them while trying to decide who or what to believe. But eventually, being essentially a logical man, he became an agnostic.

He paid no attention to any aesthetic qualities in his tales. He spun the fine gold of his life in a steady monotone without elaboration. A listener could not have failed to appreciate that the weathering years had produced a personality with a firm grasp on life and its sometimes bitter truths. He was not necessarily happy. But he was content. It was a condition that allowed men like him to follow their individual clocks with little care for the chronology of the rest of the world. Insouciant to the world around them, they remained aloof to the rat race to success. Iconoclasts to the last man, they measured success differently, in the logical belief that only rats won the race, anyway. Success at sea could be equated with the intuitive dexterity of a good piano player or a trained hunting dog (some men, of course, never get the hang of it, just as some dogs never know what to do).

At the time I was involved with people who had reached or were reaching the pinnacles of their professions. Bert's company over several beers renewed my opinion that many of them should have spent some of their formative years in a ship.

The buffetings from its rough-as-guts Southerns, Berts and

Scouses would have forced home some real-life perspectives and led some of them to avoid becoming the sorts of people who ended up fools in all but their own specialties.

'Wonderful fookin' place, this, Kiwi,' Scouse went on. 'First came by accident. Caught the fookin' wrong train. Boozed of course and a right silly fooker in those days. But I was fookin' sober by the time I got here and I got interested in the fookin' place,' he said, waving his arm in a wide gesture of encompassment.

'Why?'

'Fooked if I know, really. Probably because I'd always fancied exploring Egyptian fookin' pyramids. But when I went to a pyramid it wasn't very fookin' interesting. It was only for dead fookers. This place had living fookers in it . . . and if you listen . . . all these stones fookin' talk, you know.'

He was silent a moment or two as he drifted back through the centuries.

'People actually sat where we are sitting now, watching the gladiators,' he mused. 'During the excavations they even found some gladiators who had been chained up to stop them escaping or knocking themselves off. Mind you, everyone in the whole place was probably fookin' mad. Aren't we all?'

He was again silent for a few moments while he struggled back to the present.

'What was the war all about? Madness on all fookin' sides. I tell you that for free, mate. I was in it, you know. Got the hammer a couple of times. First was a torpedo up the arse. Second was a fookin' mine. Fixed my system good and proper, I can fookin' tell you!

'Anyway, that's what happened here. Blood'n'fookin' guts. Right here, right where we are sitting. And the place would have been packed. They had a riot once and the senate closed it down for ten years. Over there, that's where the gladiators came in. A bit like a Spanish fookin' bullfight, I suppose, except both sides here were reasonably equal. Went to a fookin' bullfight once, y'know. Disgoostin' fookin' carry on. All I wanted to see was a bull running his horns through a fookin' matador!'

He continued in similar vein as we measured and he filled his notebook.

'For a place in London,' he said when asked again why he was doing it.

'What place?'

He didn't tell me. He pocketed his notebook instead and said, 'I'll show you something of Pompeii if you're interested. We've enough fookin' time.'

For the rest of the afternoon we tramped around the city. Its obdurate silence would have been palpable except for my guide's Arcadian investment of life into the ancient scene. It was as if he was directing a play on a stage from which the actors had fled.

On the Via Stabiana he explained the stone blocks straddling the street were for citizens to step across when heavy rain ran down the street. They were spaced at such distances that horses' legs and carts' wheels could pass between them. He showed me the indentations worn by generations of Pompeiian feet and the ruts from cart wheels in the spaces between.

We visited the House of Vettii, the home of rich merchants with explicit sexual frescoes around the walls, and the House of the Fruit Orchard, not then completely excavated. Along the Via dei Sepolcri he showed me the tomb of Marcus Umbricius Scaurua, a fish-sauce merchant, public benefactor and provider of gladiatorial games. He described the shops along the Via dell' Abbondanza and the taverns where wine was kept cool in clay jars under marble counters.

He interpreted the great houses' wall paintings, ornamental motifs and other decorative compositions with an added fluency since he had by now ceased describing everything as fookin'-this-that-or-the-fookin'-other.

We were the last to leave Pompeii. Vesuvius stood innocently benign in the late afternoon sun as the custodian shut the gates behind us. We walked to the station and returned by train around the mountain to Naples.

We had a bowl of spaghetti and a couple of glasses of cheap red vino in a back-alley café. We talked for a while and I asked if he was married.

'Aye,' he said.

'Any kids?'

'Aye,' he said, 'a whole fookin' tribe.'

Then we walked back through the city to our ship. He lent me a copy of Pliny the Younger's account of Pompeii's destruction before going below to wield his shovels and slices in the heat and sweat of the stokehold.

'Yes, an interesting character, old Scouse,' the chief officer said when I returned his guidebook the next morning. 'Only goes ashore in Naples. I think the chief engineer gives him as much time off here as he can. Bumped into him in Pompeii myself last trip. The old bugger's quite a scholar. Especially for a fireman.'

Praise indeed from the chief officer, normally the sort of man who if you saved his life may offer to buy you a drink.

'Aye, a surprising old bugger,' he went on. 'Does stuff on Pompeii for the British Museum, you know. Got a medal of some sort during the war, too. Something to do with a torpedo up his arse.'

Scouse had not mentioned that 'work for a place in London' meant archaeological research for the British Museum. Nor had he mentioned anything about a medal.

At breakfast a group of small ragged children and an elderly nun grouped silently around the messroom door. The children stared at our heaped plates from the sanctuary of her arms stretched protectively around as many as she could encompass. For some moments both sides looked at one another.

'What's up, missus?' Brum, an AB, finally said. 'Want some grub?'

'*Grazie, signor.*'

'Come on in, then. No good pissing around out there.'

We winced but the nun, whether or not she understood his coarse remark, smiled and guided the children through the door.

'*Grazie,*' she said. 'Only for the *bambinos*, you understand.'

We shuffled our chairs for the children to come between us. Someone made more toast, another refilled the teapots. Brum sent the deck boy to the galley for more porridge and bacon and eggs 'and quick about it, kiddo.'

The boy returned and said the cook had told him to get stuffed.

Brum swore and went to the galley himself. When he returned he told the deck boy to go back and pick up the extra bacon and eggs.

Few of the children were higher than the messroom table and some of the men sat the littler ones on their knees. Brum was a man as rough and unsympathetic as his native Birmingham and normally indifferent to anyone not English. But he attended his two tiny *bambinos* almost tenderly, jiggling them gently on his knee as he helped them with their food.

'Poor little bastards,' he said.

'No, *signore*. They all orphans,' the nun refuted him, quietly. Brum didn't reply.

'Jeez, Brum, you look like a real daddy,' someone said. 'Got kids y'self?'

'No, mate,' Brum said, wiping his charge's small upturned face and overfilled mouth. 'Wife's barren.'

When the children had eaten their fill the nun gathered them up and shepherded them back to the deck. As they were about to walk down the gangway, Brum said, 'Poor little bastards. Look after them, lady.'

The little nun stood on tiptoe, smiled and kissed him on his stubbly cheek.

'*Si*, my friend,' she said. Her smile came from her eyes and made their corners crinkle. '*Grazie*.'

As the group reassembled on the quayside the nun waved and Brum waved back.

'Beat that,' he said roughly, almost dismissively, as he turned away. 'Kissed by a fuckin' nun!'

Everyone has his way of saying things. The important thing is what really lies behind the words. Give them our own habitual values and we are sure to misunderstand them. But on this occasion it was plain that Brum had been touched by the elderly nun's kiss. And probably vexed at not being a father.

I mentioned the episode to Scouse a couple of days later.

'Aye,' he said. 'Not fookin' surprised. Aye, a soft fooker is Brum. Helps out at an orphanage sometimes. Told him once that if he was that fond of fookin' kids he could have some of my fookin' tribe.'

After steaming down the French coast past the Gulf of Lyon and along the Spanish coast past the Balearic Islands, Cartagena and Almeria, we arrived in Gibraltar. I wandered around Main Street and Casemates Square, climbed to the old Moorish castle, had a couple of beers and bought several cheap postcards of Spanish flamenco dancers with dresses embroidered in delicate Spanish needlework.

If anywhere has been a 'key' to geopolitics, it has been Gibraltar. William Pitt called it 'the most inestimable jewel in the British Crown.' Thackeray thought of it as 'the very wax of an enormous lion, crouched between the Atlantic and the Mediterranean, and set there to guard the passage for its British mistress.' Scylax called it the end of the world beyond which no ships could pass. Spain's Queen Isabella 500 years ago called it the Key to Spain. As shipping and commerce increased others called it the Key to the Mediterranean.

Great have been the collisions at its site, a crossroads of cultures, continents, climates and seas. Neanderthal man crossed the Straits from Africa on his way to Europe. In 1942 allied armies crossed the opposite way to North Africa.

Successive rising and falling sea levels have scarred the Rock's face with caves up to 800 feet above the present sea level. Sabretoothed tigers' teeth have been found in some of them. Apes driven by ice from Northern Europe found their last refuge in Gibraltar. It is said that when they disappear so will the British. In 1943 there were seven left. Churchill arranged for seven more to be brought from Africa. Britain's fortunes then turned for the better.

Gibraltarians are an amalgamation of peoples rather than a race. When Britain occupied the Rock in 1704 almost every Spanish inhabitant left. Others took their places. Many came from northern Italy, particularly Genoa. Moors and Jews came from Africa. Portuguese, Maltese and Balaeric Islanders also came. To this conglomerate were added British soldiers and sailors who had served their time and had no wish to return to their native islands.

I asked Scouse if he knew much about Gibraltar.

'Fook all,' he said. 'Prick of a place. Haven't even been ashore since God knows when. Nothing to see. Nothing to do. Strange buggers, anyway, Gibraltarians. Even if they are like us.'

'Like us?'

'Fookin' British, mate.'

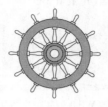

17

Let us have Wine and Women, Mirth and Laughter
Sermons and Soda Water the day after.

Byron, *Don Juan*

An over-sexed Christmas with a succession of girlfriends of diverse reputes culminated — for reasons I was never sure of — in a night beneath a grimy brick-arched railway bridge and several others in the equivalent of an earlier-century almshouse.

I had also been entangled in an altercation with a policeman. I was marched off to the nick with his baton prodding the small of my back each time I protested that those he should have arrested had taken flight before I had realised what was happening. I had been only a bystander to someone else's fight. An almost somnolent one, which was why I had been so easily arrested. But my protests did no good and I shared the rest of the cold night in an odoriferous cell with a snoring drunk and another who kept shouting that he would 'do him in, the noisy bastard.' Two others in the next cell began swearing at each other. Eventually they ran out of swear words and began fighting until a very large policeman unlocked their door. The sound of falling bodies was followed by a peace that reigned for at least an hour. The process was repeated throughout the night. In between times I slept a turbulent sleep of nightmares and dreams.

In the morning I was released and given a cup of tea and a bowl of cold water to wash in. I thanked the desk sergeant.

'As well you might, me ol' china,' he said. 'And don't be so bloomin' silly in future. Or it'll be the bloomin' Ol' Bailey for you, no mistake.'

'What about the other lot?' I enquired.

'Friends of yours?' he asked.

'No. Never seen any of them before.'

'Well, you wouldn't want to see them again, either. Stupid buggers . . . the two you were with are brought in at least once a week and get fined a fiver each time.' He gave me back my watch and wallet. 'Anyway, it's nothing to do with you whatever happens to them, and I wish it had nothing to do with me, either . . . so just bugger off. And remember what I said.'

Prospects of more insalubrious nights with drunks, deadbeats, the homeless, the hopeless, the quarrelsome, the down-and-out, the generally psychotic, and the desk sergeant's advice, dictated a return to sensibility and profitability as early as possible. More importantly, I also needed a measure of recuperative celibacy to recover from what had been the best Christmas since I started shaving. By any other measure it had been the worst.

The man at the Poplar shipping office was still in his tall chair, leaning like a bent statue over his counter. I handed him my discharge book.

'Good Christmas?' he asked.

'Yes thanks,' I said. 'Mostly, anyway. Yours?'

'Not as good as yours by the look of you. Anyway, we gave up celebrating a long time ago apart from cream with the plum duff.'

He must have reached the age, although at twenty-one I could not imagine what it might be, at which food was more important than sex and sex itself was a welcome chance for a lie down.

'Still, never mind Christmas. It's all over, thank goodness. So, where to this time?'

'Don't really mind, so long as I can sign on as soon as possible,' I said.

'Are you sure? You don't look all that fit to me. You look as though you should be in bed.'

I told him I had had enough of bed for the time being. He required no further explanation. He shuffled his papers. West

Indies? Caribbean? Mediterranean? Baltic? America? Canada? South America? India? Continent? It was enough to cause indigestion from choice. But because of a continuing interest in one of the Christmas girlfriends I did not wish at least for a while to venture too far. It was unnecessary to retire one's libido altogether. One needed to be sensible about these things.

'The continent would do for a while.'

He shuffled his papers again.

'Here you are, then,' he said. '*Jackonia*. Walford Line. Regents Canal and Dagenham to continental ports twice a week. You know, the usual places — Ghent, Bremerhaven, Rotterdam, Antwerp and the rest. Carries captain, chief officer and second mate, two engineers, three ABs. Watches two on four off. Home trade articles so the ABs take turn about as cook. Quite a democratic little society. If it works properly.'

I really would have been better spending several days in bed. But I had no money for one, not even in the Stack o' Bricks. A ship could be my only refuge.

Many deep-water men are at first seasick aboard much smaller ships. It is because of the entirely differing motions of the two. In keeping with most, and I am nothing if not average, my stomach inwardly collapsed during *Jackonia*'s cork-screwing Channel crossing.

When it was my turn to be cook, the fumes of fatty chops and frying eggs in the tiny, claustrophobic galley made me even more nauseous. The cramped and airless confines of my narrow bunk offered no remission, either. The only relief was on watch.

'Never mind, Kiwi, most deep-sea men get seasick the first trip,' Budget said. He was one of the other ABs and a Welshman. His nickname stood for something I never really understood since I couldn't always understand the other when he attempted to enlighten me. His broad Yorkshire village dialect was a foreign language. The most I could deduce was the nickname had something to do with the complications of a wife and mortgage.

'Poor old Budget,' Yorky had said. 'Hasn't really got the stomach for such things.'

159

But given my abilities as a cook, Budget was obviously a man whose stomach could soar above all other prejudices.

'Then they get seasick again when they return to the big ships,' Budget went on. 'Did a trip to Australia once with P&O. *Arcadia*. Completely bollocksed for the first few days. But ginger biscuits fixed me. Buy some when we get to Bremerhaven.'

I did. Whatever their magic constituent or constituents were, on the return voyage to the Thames they rendered the ship's corkscrewing and the galley's fatty fumes at least endurable.

Jackonia's captain was an irascible old fellow. He had little faith in modern aids. But he had one hell of a nose.

'Don't need no bloody fancy modern gadgets, Kiwi,' he said. 'God gave me a nose and by Christ I know how to use it, be-Jesus.'

An odd mixture of profanity, but hell, he sure could use his nose. He had learned as a young man on Thames sailing barges to smell his way around.

Since the Chinese are believed to have discovered the directive abilities of a magnet while his kith and kin were still in the Stone Age and even the old Thames barges had foghorns of a sort, compasses and foghorns fell outside the captain's definition of fancy modern gadgets. His nose, compass and other ships' foghorns were the only instruments to guide him down the crowded, fog-bound Thames into the thick midwinter Channel weather and through rain, sleet and snow up the great rivers to the European ports.

The chief officer had to admit that his electronic plots and the Old Man's dead-reckoning via his nose and the compass invariably tallied. That was provided the captain did not have a cold. Which he seldom did because he ate lots of garlic despite Plato, Pliny and Plutarch all maintaining that garlic destroyed a compass' attractive powers.

Time in port was our own except for whose turn it was to be cook. Wintry European seaport cities, however, were no places to wander around. Much of the time we lay in our bunks reading or catching up on sleep.

We sometimes made friends with the families into whose great river barges our cargo was generally unloaded for onward carriage into the heart of Europe. Some of them invited us aboard for a drink and meal.

When we ventured ashore it was generally only to wander from the warmth of one small pub to another through streets cold and wet with grey, slushy, midwinter snow. Otherwise we left continental ports mostly to themselves. Anyway, the need for a warm room made continental girls expensive in winter. Five bob's worth in the slushy grey snow was not worth tuppence.

⚓

One afternoon, bored with bunks and pubs, Budget and I went aboard a derelict British warship tied up astern of us in Antwerp. She had been stripped in readiness for the wreckers. But whoever had stripped HMS *Affleck*, a Captain-class destroyer escort, one of seventy-eight built by the Americans in 1943 and leased to the Royal Navy, of almost everything else had not bothered overmuch with her radio office except for its equipment.

Papers were crammed into half-open drawers. Others flapped forlornly around the room in the puffs of cold wind that occasionally found their way through the broken doors. I scooped up a shirtful as we left.

Leafing through them later in my bunk I found I had enough to compose a snapshot of *Affleck*'s life and times, although it was several years before I pieced it together more fully.

'Anyone who nowadays wants to find out what the military realities were which governed the Second World War could do worse than study the history of the submarine,' wrote Michael Salewski, a German historian. Every submarine mirrored at once both the greater strategy of war and its everyday horror, he said.

'Anyone who at that time was confronted with the submarine phenomenon was afforded an insight into the very essence and aberration of the entire war, if only he had the will to see. For what he witnessed was a monstrous process of inconceivable events and metaphysical horror, a mixture of unutterable banality and indescribable uniqueness.'

Statistics[8] support Salewski's sentiments. Of 40,900 German U-boat crews, nearly 26,000 were killed and 5000 captured, a 76 per cent loss rate. Of the 1162 U-boats built, 784 were lost, 220 were scuttled rather than surrender, 156 surrendered and a couple hightailed it to Argentina. By 1943 U-boats were to all intents and purposes technically and tactically obsolete and relatively easy prey for Allied escort ships and aircraft. In 1944 alone 220 were destroyed, twenty-three of them in the Bay of Biscay area. Four of those were between June and November.

Among the papers was the record of the death of one of the four. HMS *Affleck* detected her off Ushant at the northern entrance to the Bay of Biscay, on Saturday 15 July 1944.

The ensuing hunt at the end of a long summer's day was with good cause. By war's end U-boats had sunk nearly 2900 Allied ships and damaged more than 260 others. Crews had died in blazing oil or exploding petrol; in freezing Arctic seas; in tropic oceans; in Atlantic storms; anywhere within aiming distance. The first British death in World War I was a merchant seaman killed in the North Atlantic by gunfire from a German submarine, the first in World War II was a merchant seaman aboard his ship sunk by a German submarine within the first hour of war.

Affleck had already helped sink several U-boats. Fifteen days before, she and HMS *Balfour* had sunk U-1191. Five months earlier, in February, she had sunk U-91. A month later, in March, she helped dispatch U-392. The same month, she destroyed U-358 after a relentless 38-hour-long search during which the submarine was at times as deep as 1000 feet. It proved to have been the longest hunt for any submarine during the entire war.

The record later pieced together from various sources chronicles *Affleck*'s previous victims' numbers and commanding officers' names. But for some reason it does not list this U-boat's details. So no one knows who was in the 200-foot-long, 20-foot-diameter cylindrical steel hull when the warship came upon her.

Whoever they were, they would have been very young, barely trained and even less experienced. By then the minimum age for U-boat commanders was 21 and 20 for chief engineers. Many ratings were teenagers.

By then, too, the average U-boat undertook only two voyages before being sunk. This one may have been keeping within the average. It may have beaten the odds and been on its third. It may have been on its first. It was certainly on its last.

The reason for *Affleck*'s readiness for the breaker's yard was plain enough. Five months after sinking the unknown U-boat, her stern had been completely wrecked when struck by an acoustic torpedo from U-486. The submarine was being pursued after sinking the 11,500-ton troopship *Leopoldville*, a former Belgian ex-luxury liner, five-and-a-half miles off Cherbourg. The ship was carrying 2200 American troops and a British crew. Seven hundred and eighty-five troops and 16 crew were killed or missing. U-486 was herself lost with all hands in April 1945 when she was torpedoed off Bergen by a British submarine, HMS *Tapir*.

Many of the signals were routine — U-boats' suspected whereabouts and probable patrol areas. Messroom conjecture came nowhere near guessing how the Admiralty could have known where U-boats might be lurking. Budget reckoned it was guesswork. Yorky's speculations were unintelligible. The reason became apparent only some years later when the activities of the wartime Bletchley Park code-cracking teams were revealed. Among the collection, however, were five centrepiece relics of high drama.

The first was a message sent at 3.05 p.m. on July 15 1944:

Immediate: To C in C Plymouth (R) Admiralty from EG1:
Followed weak oil slick for five miles to its source [the submarine obviously having already been found and depth-charged]. *Obtained asdic contact in this position and have attacked it, producing fresh oil. Consider in contact with bottomed U-boat. My position 48 degrees 56 minutes N, 04 degrees 31 minutes W. Remaining until enemy destroyed.*

The time of the next message is illegible:

Immediate: To C in C Plymouth (R) Admiralty. Have now obtained perfect echo-sounder trace of submarine. Am attacking to destruction.

At 6.08 p.m.:

> *Immediate: To C in C Plymouth (R) Admiralty from EG1.*
> *Have carried out two accurate attacks dropping delayed action*
> *depth charges on and around e/s trace. Oil is bubbling up and*
> *splintered wood is in the vicinity. Some pieces and an oil sample*
> *have been retrieved. Consider enemy destroyed. Request*
> *instructions as to patrol area.*

But the Admiralty asked for more details to eliminate any doubt
before entering the warship and her submarine into the record.
And so in measured terms *Affleck* explained, around sunset, that:

> *The initial oil slick ran 053 degrees for two miles, then turned*
> *gradually and distinctly to starboard to 232 degrees and ran*
> *two miles to its source where light oil was rising. Initial asdic*
> *contact was obtained here and target moved 600 yards. After*
> *first deliberate attack there was no further movement. On*
> *completion, an area one mile wide and many miles long was*
> *thickly covered with oil.*

The last signal was sent at 10.14 p.m. in response to continued
Admiralty curiosity:

> *Specimens were collected by [HMS] Bentley who confirms that*
> *oil has diesel characteristics. One piece of wood, possibly teak,*
> *is much soaked with the oil, has no shiny nails in it, and is*
> *slightly curved and bevelled, being 4½ inches by 1¼ inches*
> *thick. The other bits appear to come from gratings and are soft*
> *wood but not rotten or waterlogged.*

In such a manner was the death of the unknown German submarine and its anonymous crew conducted, measured and confirmed
to within one quarter of an inch.

Reflecting over my photographs of *Affleck*'s gutted bridge as I
pieced the story together some years later, it was not difficult to
imagine the high drama and tumult methodically conducted and
witnessed from that now silent, stagnant spot.

Understanding it was another matter.

But *Gitano*'s Scouse fireman would have understood well enough. It was just such a U-boat that had sent a fookin' torpedo up his arse, dammit.

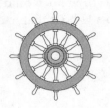

18

There is always something new out of Africa.
Pliny, the Elder

The post-Christmas London girlfriend suggested we elope. Presumably at my expense. As there is a time to start and a time to stop, so there is also a time to change direction. And so since sex and common sense rarely share the same bed, I abandoned her and the rigours of the northern winter.

I asked the Poplar shipping office man for a ship bound 'anywhere warmer than this.' He regarded the light snowflakes still on my hair and the shoulders of my overcoat.

He rifled through his papers.

'How about the West African Coast? Warmer than here. But rain and mosquitoes and things, too. Anyway, *Lagos Palm*, if you're interested. She's at the West India Dock. Shed C. Signing on tomorrow morning and sailing in a couple of days.'

Lagos Palm belonged to the Palm Line, the shipping subsidiary of the United Africa Company and part of the Lever empire. We loaded in several continental ports with which I was familiar. But Hamburg, 70 miles up the picturesque town- and village-lined River Elbe, was a new experience.

The city had been heavily battered during the war. What I had read of the heavy fire-bombing (the British code-named it Operation Gomorrah) that ignited Hamburg's air to 1000°C and caused 120-mile-an-hour hurricanes of flame, had conveyed little of its reality. Hamburg had been a triumph of destruction, like Carthage,

166

destroyed by the Romans in the Third Punic War and its ruins spread with salt as a gesture of supreme contempt. The city was a reminder that Germany was the sort of country which could create more history than it could handle without destroying itself.

Unlike Britain, sunk in the soup of post-war fatigue, despite the Festival of Britain doing its best to revive national pride, Germany was already reviving if Hamburg was any measure. Ruined buildings still standing had been cleared of debris and their remains stood tidily while bomb sites were cleared for rebuilding. Some had started.

In some areas, however, huge tracts of ground lay bare. Not even a blade of grass grew there. A solitary, twisted tram line ran across one of them. There was no suggestion there had ever been a street. I tried picturing the night-time bombers over this city of Brahms and Mendelssohn and Charlemagne. A bird singing atop a pile of rubble ruined my imaginative effort.

'Surely to God you don't feel sorry for the bastards,' an AB said when we were discussing the solitary tram line later in the messroom.

'Well, not really, I suppose,' I said, a little uncertainly in the face of his obvious feeling.

'Well, there's no need to, mate. They got everything that was coming to them. Pity we hadn't invented the atom bomb in time for them. And you want to know why?'

Not really. Although most agreed with his statements, the main collective interest was instead the Reeperbahn in St Pauli. Those who knew it were impatient to return to its delectations. Those of us who did not were impatient to sample them.

He told us, nevertheless.

'Me old man told us a bit about a concentration camp he and his mates went into,' he said. 'They were the first ones in. Didn't say a lot to us, of course. But he wouldn't, would he? We was just kids. But we heard him tell our Mum how he and some of his mates did their bollocks and did in some of the guards. Arrogant, well-fed bastards, he said. Our mum says he still has nightmares about it. Not about the guards. Fuck the guards, he said, well, he didn't say that to our Mum, of course, but it's what he meant. No.

167

More the smell, like. Like bad pineapples, he said. Bloody Hun bastards! Nah! Stuffed if I feel sorry for any of them. What else could they expect? They started it. Serve the bastards right. Aye, serve the bastards right, I say!'

After that the solitary line through the non-existent street assumed a sombre singularity each time I saw it or others like it. I also sometimes fancied I could smell bad pineapples.

The Reeperbahn was celebrated by generations of seamen. Even the young man who regretted the lack of the atom bomb luxuriated in its delectations. The events of the rest of our stay — nights of lager, music, song; brassy Brigid, go-getter Irma, et al — are better left in the Café Canadian. But they were notable events. They also afforded endless recollections over the ensuing celibate months.

However, my more enduring ones concerned reserved, blonde Annelies, who I met in a place far removed from the Reeperbahn and with whom I fell in love and remained in that condition for some months.

I recalled her telling me that during the war, she and her friends collected meat bones to be made into ingredients for explosives. When I told her that at the same time my friends and I were collecting ergot which had something to do with treating wounds, I don't think either of us realised the total contrast in our war efforts.

Another night, sitting among the rubble of a bomb site while on the way to her home where she lived with her mother — her father had been lost in a submarine — she told me that during the air raids, a discord of noise, fire and charred brickdust, she had believed each bomb was aimed directly at her.

Funny, that. Joan in Liverpool had once said the same thing. And in New Zealand at around the same age I had sometimes thought that the Japanese would come straight for me when they arrived (despite my only war experience being flour bombs dropped from a Tiger Moth during occasional air-raid practices during which everyone left their trenches to gaze at the roaring aeroplane, which then stopped the raid in case anyone was injured).

Joan and Annelies, however, were imperilled by each other's relatives. I had been in singular jeopardy from total foreigners.

This notion had stemmed from my mother. She had believed her family in England was safer than we were in New Zealand. Japanese were much too foreign for her liking. Germans and their European cohorts, while still foreign, which was bad enough, were more or less of the same race. The Japanese, well, they were more than foreign. They were *alien,* completely beyond the pale. Small men of a completely different race, colour and visage with long rifles and longer bayonets. The image still lives with me to some extent.

(There's a postscript of sorts to all of this: some years later when I read Anne Frank's diary I was struck by several coincidences — Anne's full name was also Annelies, there was a likeness between them and both were born in Frankfurt. And while Anne died in the Belsen concentration camp, Anne, Annelies, Joan and me, although of the same generation, we each belonged to a world none of the others could possibly have imagined.)

⚓

At Freetown in Sierra Leone we embarked our 'Kru boy' cargo-handling gang, short, stocky Kru tribesmen from Liberia, Sierra Leone and the Ivory Coast. Graham Greene described them as 'the great sailors of the Coast, whose boast it is that they have never been slaves, and have never dealt in slaves.'

They would unload our cargo into surf boats — many ports were then ocean beaches — and later load our homeward cargo. They would live in large tents suspended from the derricks above the hatches at night. Meals would be cooked in coal braziers on the steel deck. Toilets would be make-shift wooden and canvas affairs suspended over the stern.

Order would be maintained by headmen with stentorian voices, fists or lumps of wood depending on the level of sanction required. The sternest measures were often needed to settle disagreements fomented by bouts of a brew comprised of ingredients over which some sort of secrecy seemed to be exercised. The bosun, an old

Coast hand, warned all hands to not even sample it. Rots the guts, he said. Putrifies the brain, he said. Turns you into idiots, he said.

At many ports we anchored beyond the surf line, a mile or more from the beach. Fleets of boats arrived early in the mornings. Each was crewed by chanting and sometimes naked oarsmen, their blades flashing in the sunlight, harsh even at that hour, as they raced from the distant shore to be first alongside.

They were experts at laying their heavy craft beneath the derricks from which the winchmen lowered their slings of cargo, usually at the run. All the time ship and boats rolled and pitched unsynchronously in the heavy Atlantic swells. Occasionally the boat crews fought each other with their long wooden oars in fierce dispute of others' claims to the next load. But the winchmen were invulnerable to appeal and dropped the load into whichever boat happened to surge beneath the waiting sling.

For particularly heavy or bulky cargo two boats were lashed together with timber to form a catamaran. Crews then sat astride the gunwales and with rhythmic chants set off for the beach. But occasionally the heavily laden boats disappeared beneath the breakers as they neared the shore. The spluttering men were left floundering until their cargo-less boats popped up beside them like emerging depth charges.

The West African coast was once deadly to European seamen. Malaria, yellow fever, scurvy and dysentery were common. Royal African Company slave ships sometimes lost more crew than cargo. In the eighteenth and nineteenth centuries British seamen were enjoined to:

> Beware and take care
> Of the Bight of Benin;
> For one that comes out,
> There are forty go in.

Which was probably why at Accra, shivering and sweating with malaria despite the quinine tablets issued daily and swallowed by all hands with almost religious fervour, I was lowered by a derrick into a surf boat and ferried through the breakers. Half-carried by two black men I tottered up the beach and went to the hospital on the back of a lorry.

An African nurse held out my hand to take a blood sample. With her other hand she pulled a glass slide from her pocket. She broke it against the bedrail and poked a jagged edge into my thumb. She smeared the blood on a second slide, also from her pocket. What it proved beyond what may have been in her pocket or on the bedrail was not made known to me. But it was enough for me to be immediately put to bed. For several days I didn't care if I never left it.

The hospital matron was the epitome of An Englishwoman of Example. She was the type of Briton who survived all climates and latitudes and was immune from malaria and dysentery. She was a lady who like marriage had to be taken carefully. She ruled her mainly African staff by the firm tramp of her solid legs and the raspy swish of her thickly starched uniform. She displayed an unremitting stare and pursed lips whenever someone or something displeased her, as it did her when I asked what had laid me low. She regarded me as if I had spoken out of turn.

'The usual African stuff, my boy. Malaria and a bit of this and a bit of that. All you need to know is to do as you're told and take your medicine.'

Her manner forbade any further enquiry although she implied God had conscripted my body for a gash bucket.

At night the vaporous darkness outside my window was alive with clicking and grinding African insects, the bright paths of fireflies and the thump of oversized beetles hitting the mosquito meshing.

During the day a small monkey sometimes sat at the bottom of the bed cadging pieces of fruit. When anyone approached he sprang to the windowsill and scratched himself until the nurse left. But he disappeared into a nearby tree when the matron bore down the corridor like a Kru surfboat.

As must be expected of An Englishwoman of Example, the matron was not fooled.

'He's been here, hasn't he?'

'Who's that, matron?'

'Who? That dratted monkey, that's who!'

'Well, yes, he was here. But he left.'

'Obviously.'

'Yes,' I said, 'I suppose it is.'

'Oh, being sarcastic are we? Anyway, he's been around for months, you know. He never stays when I come along. Yet nobody else seems to worry him. But he's a nice wee fellow, I believe. The nurses tell me he's taken a particular shine to you. I'll send some fruit for him if you like.'

Apparently the matron's ferocity was rather less than skin-deep. Towards small monkeys, anyway.

Others suffered Africa's ailments. One man was bitten by a large fly. Its eggs incubating under the skin caused days of intense pain until the suppurating mess was cut away by the chief steward in accordance with the Ship Captain's Medical Guide. It left a deep hole the diameter of a small cup. Others were bitten by different things with painful results. A few had bouts of feverish illnesses which put them in the ship's hospital two or three days at a time before returning to the chief steward's ministrations, including his lime-spiked iced tea cure-all.

Some of the ports were scabrous places far from the sea. Tiko lay beneath the 13,450-foot Mount Cameroun in the British Cameroons (now the Republic of Cameroon). Surrounded by the African hinterland, the heat and humidity were all-enveloping and inescapable. About five o'clock every morning brilliant multi-forked lightning and ear-ringing thunderclaps preceded a solid, vertical downpour which flooded the deck and flowed over the side in torrents. The phenomenon struck again at about 3 p.m. Each brief respite from the heat and humidity quickly dissipated as the storms' cooling residue evaporated in shimmering waves of steamy mist and our bodies again streamed with sweat.

Sapele in Nigeria lay even further inland, at the confluence of the Benin River with the Ethiope and Jamieson Rivers, nearly a hundred miles from the Escravos bar. The air grew even more stifling, liquid almost, as we wound our way slowly up the sluggish chocolate-coloured waterway, its riverbank's thick bush and palms cleared only here and there for small villages. Even the Kru lay around the deck in almost utter dormancy.

To negotiate sharp riverbends the nautically capped, barefooted and bare-backed native pilot, chosen earlier by the captain at the rivermouth from a group clamouring for the job, steered us directly into the bush and matted undergrowth lining the muddy banks. Trees sometimes overhung the ship as far astern as the boatdeck. The engine was then worked alternately astern and ahead with the rudder hard to starboard and then to port. In this way we were swung around the bend.

At night the ship anchored in midstream or lay firmly wedged into the riverbank's malarial mire. Off watch we lay in our bunks sweating and grumbling in fitful sleep with portholes and ventilators closed against all manner of nocturnal African mysteries.

In Sapele we were tied to the nearest and biggest trees in the tropical forest. There we lay in suffocation for a week loading bales of rubber, abura, obeche, sapele and mahogany logs, plywood, veneers and palm oil. Some of the logs weighed more than two tons. They came from the interior lashed together as floating rafts. Their African crews lived on them in palm-leaf huts as they guided them downriver.

After taking his photograph the chief headman invited me into his deck-tent for a smoke and a sip or two of jungle-juice brew. Mr Bagwana — I doubt that was his name but it was what it sounded like — was an elderly man from a village near Freetown. He had a shock of thickly matted white hair. His rumple-textured skin was the colour of coal, his teeth toothpaste-white and the palms of his hands pink as a child's freshly scrubbed face.

He was an interesting man, wise to the ways of his native African and colonial European worlds. Although reluctant to admit the same of the French, Portuguese, Belgians or Germans, he firmly believed British democracy had done much for Africa. But he maintained that democracy could never properly take root in Africa. Ancient and deeply held tribalisms would ultimately defeat such notions. All his experience, including some years as a fire-man on British and French ships, had taught him the truth of it.

Mr Bagwana's relative warmth for the British may have stemmed from Freetown itself having been established in 1792 in expiation for the afflictions of the slave trade. It had the first rail-way and hospital and provided a university education for over a century. It was also the first diocese in British West Africa. All the same, he said, the old African ways remained barely beneath the 'fruitskin' of European influence. One day the fruit would de-compose, leaving only infertile pips.

It struck me, despite my growing befuddlement, that he and the Poplar shipping office man were bedfellows. Each straddled two worlds. The white official in his high chair and scratching his ear with a pen, foresaw a collision between his British world and its imports. The Kru headman squatting on his haunches foresaw the same between his African world and its imports.

Our discourse was interrupted by the shrieks of a quarrel out-side the tent. Swearing a slow and complex African oath, the big man rose to investigate.

Two naked Africans sat face to face on the deck. Their legs were braced against each other's powerful bodies, hands gripping their opponents' genitals and doing their best to wrest them off each other. They twisted and pulled with deep growls and were incited to even greater effort by whooping and stamping onlookers.

Mr Bagwana puffed his pipe and surveyed the scene for a few moments.

Then he whacked the nearest across the back with a heavy piece of wood. The man immediately let go his opponent who seized the opportunity to give a final twist before himself receiv-ing a resounding blow across the chest. They lay on their backs a moment or two before disappearing on almost crossed legs to their respective tents. The onlookers followed them after Mr Bagwana, still puffing his pipe, swung the piece of wood as a warning to anyone who disputed his action.

His potency lay not only in his handiness with a piece of wood. He had the ultimate power of summary dismissal. As far as we knew he never exercised it during the many weeks on the Coast and its various countries. Both parties fully appreciated the economic and physical consequences of being left high and dry so far from home. And so with implicit agreement by all concerned, quarrels were satisfactorily resolved by whatever means deemed appropriate. We returned to his tent and added crime and punishment to our interrupted discussion.

Later that evening I staggered to my bunk, my stomach, bowels, bladder and what was left of my brain vowing to never again touch African jungle juice.

Next morning the bosun was totally unsympathetic as he roused me from my bunk after the rest of the crowd had turned-to.

'Serves you bloody right,' he said, his every word thundering through my skull like a hammer blow. 'Told you not to touch the fuckin' stuff. Now you know what I meant. Stupid young buggers. Think you know everything!'

I was strongly minded to agree. But I hadn't the stomach to do so.

⚓

'All those films you're firing off, Kiwi,' the ship's carpenter (Chippie) said, 'the heat and humidity'll stuff 'em up by the time we pay off. You should ask the chief steward to keep them in the meat cooler.'

'I had thought of getting them developed somewhere,' I said.

'Out here? Christ, man, they'll stuff 'em up even worse. Better to do them yourself.'

I had always believed what happened between clicking a camera shutter and receiving the pictures was a matter best left to others since it involved chemistry, a school subject in which I had been acutely uninterested.

'But surely it's a chemist's job.'

'Chemist be damned,' Chippie said, and detailed the rudimentary materials required. 'Might even find 'em here. Or we might have to wait until Lagos. But we'll find them somewhere. Come ashore after work and see if we can find them around here somewhere.'

We were at Calabar. Fifty-odd miles up the river of the same name, Calabar was once an infamous slave port from which the last illegal cargo left in 1839. It was still a miserable place. We searched the shanty shops around the docks. We eventually found the materials in a large tin hut seemingly otherwise stocked only with old tools and lengths of rope (stolen off ships, you thievin' bastard, Chippie said, although the proprietor spiritedly denied it), a couple of stuffed vultures, bottles of aspirin and packets of cough lozenges.

Chippie was unsurprised at our successful search.

'When you've been coming out here as long as I have you'll know you can find anything anywhere if you look properly,' he said. 'You just have to dig deep enough. A bit like finding water in the desert or understanding a woman,' he said. Not that he was ever likely to do either, he admitted cheerfully.

In his cabin he measured the developer and hypo into two soup plates of water. Then he folded a piece of red paper around the bunk light, pulled the curtains across the porthole and closed the door. In the ensuing suffocation he seesawed a film in the developer until it turned milky. He repeated the process in the hypo until the negative images appeared. After washing it for a few minutes in a bucket of water, he dried the developed film against the fan.

'Now we'll make some prints. Turn on the main light when I tell you. And off again on my count of seven.'

He placed a piece of photographic paper in the printing box, laid a negative over it and closed the glass lid. I turned on the light to expose the negative to the paper. On his count of seven I turned it off again. He then rocked the paper back and forth in the developer. As the picture began to appear I was seized with a passion which remains with me. Even today producing pictures from a film retains a sense of the abstract despite its mystery being stripped in a couple of soup plates in a steamed-up ship's cabin on the West African coast. When the picture was judged suitably developed he swirled it in the hypo for a minute or two. I was too captivated by the business in hand to be bothered by the stinging sweat running into my eyes.

176

'Now turn on the main light.'

He held a dripping picture of the second cook swinging on a tree branch as we had charged into the riverbank on our way to Sapele.

'You do the rest while I have a smoke.'

By the time we paid off in Greenock after seventeen West African ports, malaria, insect bites, miles up sweltering bush-lined muddy rivers, ploughing into their riverbanks and wet forest, villages with vultures picking at dead dogs, quarrelling cargo workers and boatmen, raging sunsets, lashing rain, crashing thunderstorms, streaming sweat and other assorted rigours, I had a pile of Box Brownie negatives and prints.

Like *Gitano*'s Pompeii-expert Scouse fireman, *Lagos Palm*'s carpenter was another I came to hold in high regard. Especially later, when what he had taught me helped me earn a living.

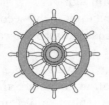

19

I never stuck too long to one ship, said the Sea Rat.
One gets too narrow-minded and prejudiced.
Kenneth Grahame, *The Wind in the Willows*

A ship's captain is her undisputed chief man. Beneath him are lesser chief men: chief officer, chief engineer, chief cook, chief steward and sundry others. Rank is ordained by virtue of the force of law. It needs no assertion, brooks no challenge. Whether some chief men are otherwise idiots is beside the point. They are sublime in their wisdom if for no other reason than they are chief men.

No such formal leadership exists in a ship's messroom. There's still leadership nevertheless. But it's a subtle thing, covert and difficult to define. It doesn't necessarily come to those of superior intelligence. Simply being there usually shows a modicum of their intelligence has been left ashore. And only occasionally does it accord solely to size and strength. And on the rare occasion that it does, generally he is little more than a de facto leader and is instead manipulated by another, the real leader, who leads from behind.

So in general terms, whoever assumes the real leadership, it's because he possesses the inherent character quirk loosely defined as 'leadership quality'.

During later years in the corporate life ashore with its office politics, meetings, committees and general jockeying, bitching and sniping, I was to observe this latter fact was not uncommon in the affairs of leadership. It led me to sometimes ponder the real power ownership of prime ministers and chairmen and chief executives — many may be in office but not necessarily in power.

But so far as we are concerned here, I had not known messroom hierarchy to be also communicated according to the placing of cups and chairs.

Queen Elizabeth's messroom's only other occupant sat hunched over a cup of tea. My g'day mate extracted only a grunted answer. His countenance was that of a man who had never smiled in his life and had no intention of doing so for the rest of it.

I reached for a cup hanging at the head of a long row of cups on hooks.

'That's Taffy's,' the man said. He spoke like a grand piano played by someone who could not play a piano.

I bypassed several and reached for another.

'Not that one.'

The cups bore no definitive marks of ownership. So it must be their placement, and thus the status of their users, rather than the cups themselves, which mattered.

I bypassed several more and reached for another.

'And that's Yorky's.'

An edge in his tone underscored the desirability of not even to begin asking impertinent questions. The monolithic Glaswegian visage, thick simian neck and tremendous arms exuded the charm and grace of a butcher. I moved still further down the row.

Eventually reaching an apparently ownerless cup, I filled the forlorn creature from a large steel urn and moved to a chair.

'That's Jacko's chair.'

'Sorry.'

I didn't mean it. He was the sort of man who stretched credibility too far to believe he could have been the creation of even passionless copulation. An ovum with any *amour-propre* would have aborted the bastard at the first attempt at conception. He must therefore have been composed of the debris of evolutionary accidents some time before Adam and Eve began toying with apples. He was a man without whom the world would have been better.

'And that's Hollywood's.'

'Hollywood?'

'Aye, mon, Hollywood. Johnny Gable . . . Hollywood.'

'Oh.'

By the time I was seated, the cup and chair *führer* was at one end of the long messroom table and I at the other. His thick fingers encircled his cup as if to prevent its escape.

'Where're you from, mon?' he called, without great interest.

'New Zealand.'

'Och aye. Colonial, then.'

The flat statement allowed no debate.

'Yeah . . . suppose so,' I said, a trifle truculently despite my caution.

'Suppose so,' he mimicked. 'Signed on yet?'

'Not yet. I was told to come and get a cup of tea first. How long have you been in her?'

'A long time, mon.'

'What's she like?'

This was a question among seamen designed to ignite a general commentary about their new ship.

'Suits me, mon.'

In the end I decided *Queen Elizabeth* was not my cup of tea. 'Teas,' Shelley said, 'where small talk dies in agonies.' Quite so.

Later I regretted not signing on. However, one of *Gitano*'s sailors had sailed in her and washed windows every day. Some, he said, spent most of the voyage in the baggage rooms and others never reached the deck between Southampton and New York.

But I should have liked the stamp of the world's biggest ship — 84,000 tons; 13 decks; 37 public rooms; four propellers each weighing 32 tons; three whistles weighing a ton each and audible over 10 miles; 1200 crew; twice as many passengers; her hull pierced by 2000 windows and portholes; everything held together by over ten million rivets — in my discharge book.

In a pub waiting for a London train I learned from one of her crew that while seemingly the messroom leader, the cups' guardian was dominated by another, Taffy from Newport, who while much less physically substantial, patently possessed the leadership quality mentioned earlier.

It seemed Jock was little more than a carbon-based life form, one that might have merited a subsidy from some anthropological research fund. His intellect having stalled at the level of most of us at the age of about eleven, he had been given a job as messman. His main task was washing cups and wiping the seats of chairs. Especially those of the messroom's real chief man, Taffy. And the chief man's cronies, in descending order according to the placing of the cups and chairs.

'Aye, Taffy's the real head serang. Peculiar bugger. Never has much to say for himself. Calls himself a Christian. Reads the Bible and believes in God and all that crap,' my informant said irreverently.

I asked why in believing all that crap Taffy should be regarded with any more than reasonably good-natured derision. It would have been the normal reaction to such zeal. My informant regarded me gravely.

'Just as well Jock couldn't hear you say that,' he said. 'It's a funny thing, but for some reason Taffy's the only one who can control that Scottish git.'

I began to ask a question but was interrupted by an upraised hand.

'No, don't even begin to ask. I don't know why. No one does. But there's something. Someone called Taffy a Bible bangin' bastard once. And stuff me if Jock didn't flatten him. Taffy took a dim view of that and read Jock a page from his Bible. Don't know what effect it had on Jock. But no one ever called Taffy a Bible bangin' bastard again.' My informant looked puzzled. 'It's just that, well . . . no, stuffed if I know, really . . . anyway, mate, I'd better get back aboard. It's nearly time to turn-to.'

There still being time until my train I had another beer and forgot all about Jock. Well, I never quite forgot him. Whenever I met a man I disliked, I compared him with Jock and found I disliked my newer acquaintance that much less.

When I returned to London I got measured in an East End Jewish tailor's shop for my first-ever new suit, the last word from Aldgate, a smart affair for three pounds and ten shillings, a fitting tomorrow and ready in three days. I bought a couple of white van Heusen shirts, a Burberry overcoat, a thick woollen scarf, a pair of leather gloves, a pair of black shoes and a suitably matching tie. My ensemble was completed with a small, round, silver Merchant Navy badge from the Poplar shipping office and a small silver fern badge from New Zealand House in the Strand.

Then, while deciding where to go next, I spent evenings in the gods at the Royal Albert and Festival Halls in my new gear reviving a boyhood enthusiasm for the great symphonies and concertos I knew from the radio or gramophone records at home. I had whistled their themes while delivering telegrams in Russell.

After a concert the ghosts of the long-dead composers accompanied me back to Dock Street as I hummed their tunes. The intellectual stimulation also sanctioned acceptance of my Spartan room and few possessions.

In lighter moments I saw Al ('Right Monkey') Read and the Joan Tiller Girls in *You'll Be Lucky* at the Adelphi Theatre in the Strand, Anton Walbrook in *Wedding in Paris* at the London Hippodrome, and Jimmy Edwards, Vera Lynn and Tony Hancock in *London Laughs*, again at the Hippodrome.

All in all, life was pretty damn good.

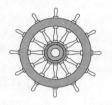

20

The want of a thing is perplexing enough,
but the possession of it is intolerable.
Sir John Vanbrugh

Following several more voyages to here and there I resolved to embark on a longer excursion than anything so far, one that encompassed the world in one voyage. The Poplar shipping office man said that would mean calling on a tramp or tanker company. I said I might try a tanker company.

'Up to you, I suppose, but I can't imagine why you want to be away for so long,' he said. 'Tankers are often away for the whole of their two-year Articles. And I hope you realise tanker men are peculiar. They should never visit a zoo.'

'Why?'

'They'd need two tickets. One to get in and one to be allowed out. Completely round the bend, most of them. They're only in port a day or two. Sometimes only a few hours. So all they do is booze and have a woman or two if they've any money left and are still capable of it. Still, if you want a long voyage I suppose a tanker is the way to do it . . . but don't come back here and moan about it!'

A few days later I journeyed by North Sea ferry from Harwich to the Hook of Holland and by train to a Shell tanker about to complete her survey in drydock in Amsterdam.

Norrisia belonged to the Anglo-Saxon Petroleum Company, which ran the Shell fleet. Shell was founded in 1892 by two brothers named Samuel. Their main business was importing sea shells to adorn trinket boxes. When the trade was overtaken by the oil business, centred on the Dutch East Indies, they became an oil company. To run their ships they formed the Anglo-Saxon Petroleum Company in partnership with Royal Dutch. They retained their company identity by naming the ships after sea shells.

Because of the exigencies of oil supply and demand, tankers were often re-routed during their voyages as companies responded to the market or more likely engineered it to arrive where the cargo was required, presumably at a better price, or to where one was waiting, presumably at a lesser price.

And so no one was surprised when we left Amsterdam in ballast for the Leeward Islands in the West Indies, our nominal destination 'St Kitts For Orders'. Somewhere along the way a radio message would reroute us to a loading port.

In mid-Atlantic we changed course for the Caribbean from whose Willemstad refineries we later sailed deeply laden for 'Panama For Orders'. Everyone said that like 'St Kitts For Orders' it meant very little.

'But since we're going that way it could be Australia or New Zealand. Or maybe Japan or Hong Kong, or Chile or Peru,' the older hands said. 'Who knows? Could be anywhere once we're clear of Panama.'

But within hours we were ordered to Casablanca. Talk immediately turned to recollections and the relative merits of this or that bar or bordello. But hours later the radio operator came to the bridge with orders for Rio de Janeiro instead.

The men who knew Casablanca swore but agreed Rio was a reasonable alternative, although the Brazilian police were always a problem. Drunken or troublesome foreign seamen were routinely jailed for the night. Next morning before returning to their ships they were made to sweep the streets. If they became obstreperous they were fined as well. It was commonly believed the money went into the policemen's pockets. Few could pay on the spot after their heavy spending on the booze, which made them obstreperous in the first place, so the fines were collected from the ships' agents. As well as taking money from their wages to repay the agents, the annoyed captains fined them, too, because their escapades usually meant sailing was delayed.

Despite all that, however, everyone looked forward to Rio de Janeiro. But next day we were turned back to Willemstad to discharge and proceed empty to the Gulf of Venezuela. We were to take on a full cargo from the Punta Cardon refinery, whose oil was likely to be spilled into the sea because of a local revolution, and carry it to Pernis, near Rotterdam. But no one complained or even said very much. By now those familiar with tankers — which was most of them and who so far as I had seen were quite normal — had settled back into the Maybe Here, Maybe There, Who Knows? routine of tanker life. Even those of us new to it had ceased to be surprised.

At Punta Cardon a motley gang of Venezuelan soldiers boarded us even before the last line was ashore. They were diminutive, olive-uniformed, swarthy men hung with rifles, machine guns, bandoliers and swords.

Within moments there was a fearful noise from the soldiers' chief honcho. Besides their own, ships also fly the flag of the country they are visiting. It is a mark of international delicacy. In a martial rhumba and waving his sword around as if seeking someone's neck, the chief honcho indicated the apprentice had hoisted the Colombian instead of the Venezuelan flag. Since the countries hated each other's guts his outstanding passion was understandable.

'Bloody fancy flags,' the bosun grumbled when the captain wearily told him to find and hoist the proper one. 'You never know which is which in these damned places.'

There was an even greater display of Venezuelan foot stamping, shouting and sword waving when the bosun hoisted the new flag upside down.

'And you obviously don't know which way is bloody up. Christ, man, you're as bad as the damned apprentice!'

Once international sensitivities were sorted out the chief honcho bellowed at the soldiers to allow no one ashore, all the while slapping his sword against his long skinny legs. He was a lanky, swaggering, Gilbertian figure. Splendidly encased in knife-creased trousers, brilliant, clanking medals, golden epaulettes, shining leather riding boots and a high-peaked cap with a large badge on the front, he looked really rather comic.

As he left the ship, before which he had flourished his sword to the bosun's muttered hopes that he would 'cut his bollocks off at the same time,' he was accorded a round of sardonic clapping. He seemed puzzled, then bowed slightly. Then he tossed his head effeminately and pranced down the gangway to his beflagged car. He was borne away at high speed in a further show of noisy bombast.

'Fuckin' poofter,' someone said.

'Yeah, probably,' the bosun said. 'Dangerous bastard all the same.'

The soldiers soon left their posts and tramped in groups up and down ladders and companionways exploring the strange new world in which they found themselves. They opened cabin doors and regarded the occupants with interest and an engulfing volubility. We smiled politely and told them to bugger off.

Once they had settled down, mostly dozing, someone said 'I'm going for a walk. Anyone coming?'

'You're mad,' someone else said. 'Boogars'll stick a bullet oop ya' khyber.'

'I'm only going to the gates. No harm in that.'

After some discussion, several, including me, nearly to my everlasting regret, agreed to go with him. We milled around the gangway to be sure none of the ship's officers or a stray guard was around and then followed our ringleader quietly onto the quay. Arriving at the gates without incident, we poked our heads outside and ventured forth.

A few short steps later a shouted '*Amigos!*' was followed by a loud bang. A bullet hit the road in front of us and ricocheted away with a screaming whine. Within moments a second slammed more immediately in front of us. We waited like statues as two soldiers we had not seen sitting on a box outside a distant building trotted up with their rifles stiffly in front of them. Their stained teeth exposed in sneering grins, they took turns poking the nearest in the ribs with their gun barrels.

186

'*Americano?*' one enquired belligerently.

'English.'

'*Si. Inglisi.* From ship?'

'Yes.'

'You have cigarettos?'

'Some.'

'You give me cigarettos.'

'OK,' our ringleader said to the soldier, and then quietly to us, 'We'd better give the bastard every ciggie we've got.'

The man snapped erect and pointed his rifle at the speaker.

'What you say, *señor?* Me? *Bastardo?*'

'Shit, mate! No! Not you, s*eñor, amigo,* sir. No! Us! We all *bastardos,*' the ringleader said with a quick wave around the group. The rest of us nodded. We were absolutely stupid *bastardos.*

'*Si! Gringo bastardos!*'

The soldier raised his rifle.

'Sure, *amigo,* if you say so,' the ringleader quickly agreed. 'We all *gringo bastardos!*'

'*Si!* All *gringo bastardos.* Now, cigarettos! Come! Hurry! All cigarettos,' the soldier barked.

We handed over all we had. Then he gestured towards the gates with his rifle.

'You go back ship. Vamoose!'

As we vamoosed the two soldiers began quarrelling over their spoils.

'Hope the bastards murder each other,' someone said.

'Aye, and some bastard hangs them for it!' someone else said.

'Nah!' said another. 'I hope someone cuts their fuckin' heads off and then buries them . . . where they can't find bloody find them,' he added as an afterthought.

The captain fined us each a day's pay.

'For being completely stupid,' he said. 'Didn't you realise how dangerous it was? And you could've caused the ship, and the company, and me all sorts of trouble!'

'Seems more dangerous to hoist the flag upside down, captain,' one of the braver souls ventured.

'Do you really think so?' he rejoined angrily. 'All the same, you're damned lucky you didn't all get a bullet up your arses.'

For the rest of the time the guards attended the gangway like a vice.

Venezuela, so-named by Amerigo Vespucci because Indian stilt houses on Lake Maracaibo reminded him of Venice and its canals, has had an unhappy time of it over the centuries. The Spaniards wiped out the native Indians by the millions. In the fifteenth century South America as a whole had about 50 million people. About 4 per cent survived the Conquest.

It was not until Simon Bolivar came upon the scene in 1811 that Venezuela was rid of the Spaniards. But as often happens the newly independent country quarrelled among itself over the years and successively spawned its own crop of unsavoury leaders. These included one Marcos Perez Jiminez. It was his South American *bastardos* who shot up the road in front of us and stole all our *cigarettos*.

For the first days of the three weeks' voyage to Holland the weather was fine. In the tropical mornings the four to eight watch scoured the decks for flying fish. Lured by the ship's lights, the brightly coloured fish thumped aboard during the night and expired in the scuppers. We gave them all to the cook who fried them up for our breakfast.

But life became wet and tiresome as we moved into the greyness of the mid-Atlantic. In bad weather the deeply laden tanker was little more than a tidal rock. Seas swept across the decks continually. The flying bridge, too, above the deck from the stern, where we lived, to the bridge 'midships and from there to the fo'c'sle head, was always swept by spray and sometimes immersed beneath incoming seas.

⚓

Pernis was a picturesque town with a canal down the main street. As far as we were concerned, however, the most useful part of Pernis was the nearby Seamen's Store at Nieuwe Maas. It was 'open all day from 8 o'clock with a lot of sailor articles and services. Sunday open from 13 o'clock with a Special Edition of British Sunday Papers. Barber stays open at sailor service, he fixes you after your trip, so you look swell for your good time. Haircut, Shave, Head and Face massage. Different lotions and eau de cologne. Seamen's Store and Barber. Honest Sailor Service.'

After a haircut and looking as swell as we could and having as good a time as was possible in the freezing Dutch winter, we sailed back in ballast to the Caribbean refineries for another cargo of oil. After the usual round of route changes we finally headed for the North Sea and Baltic ports.

We entered the Elbe and passed from Brunsbuttelkoog into the ice-covered 60-mile long Kiel Canal. The canal was built between 1887 and 1895 to save the German Navy the extra 200 miles around Jutland for the passage between the North and Baltic Seas.

Its gaunt, featureless Schleswig-Holstein hinterland was a scene from which nature seemed to have been banished, a place surely the last the sun found and the first it left, a monotony relieved only by skeletal trees and season-beleaguered buildings dimly visible through the heavy sullenness of winter fog. At Holtenau we passed into the Baltic Sea, whose even more frigid air was an elemental chill, beyond any cold I had ever known. It bit deeply into unguarded flesh and seemingly beyond bone level. It overran the body and left it stunned. Ice covered the steel decks in a thin, treacherous layer. The steam whistle froze and icicles hung from everywhere moisture could drip.

In Stockholm we bashed ice off the mooring ropes with heavy hammers before they could be passed on the ends of heaving lines to the dockside mooring party. We bashed them again before they could be wound around the windlass drum after our heavily gloved but still freezing hands had pulled the slack through the fairleads from the all but frozen water.

'Y'wouldn't know what cold was,' said Tom, an older AB, as we hunched together in the engineroom fiddly to revive in the warm air eddying up from below and smelling of hot oil. We complained that nobody could be colder than we were.

'Bollocks,' Tom said through chattering teeth. 'I mean cold with a capital C. Like on an Arctic convoy.'

He told us about uncovered fingers sticking to steel and frostbite sometimes turning gangrenous. He told us of bones snapping after slipping on ice-encrusted decks, breath freezing as it was exhaled. He told us how the wind cut through even the heaviest Arctic survival gear. He told us how hot tea and cocoa froze within moments if brought on deck. And how spray froze on deck beneath your feet.

Even ships sometimes did not survive the cold, he said. Many Liberty ships, because of their welded construction, as *Leicester* had been, had sometimes cracked and fallen apart when the mild steel plates turned brittle like glass at their welded joints.

'Yeah, stuff that for a load of fluffy ducks,' someone agreed. He was struck by a fuller realisation. 'Especially if someone was trying to blow y'bloody bollocks off at the same time!'

'You'd be bloody right, mate,' Tom said. 'And if we'd got done in I wouldn't be here telling you dozy young buggers what forty or fifty below was like. No one stopped to pick you up or they'd've been done in as well. And once you hit the water, a couple of minutes and then . . . dead, mate, frozen bloody dead.' Tom waved his gloved hand in a goodbye gesture.

During a later fractured, beery conversation in a South American bar, he told me he had spent much of the war on tankers.

'And on the Murmansk run when those of us left got there the Russian bastards wouldn't let us ashore,' he said. 'They were supposed to be on our side. Yet they guarded the gangways with bloody bayonets to stop us going ashore. Sometimes they wouldn't even give us our mail. So why did we bother? Stuffed if I know, mate. Fuckin' commos . . . allies be buggered. Worse than bloody Wogs. I'll tell ya'something ya'didn't bloody know! D'ya know that bastard Stalin once lived in Whitechapel? Right near the Whitechapel Bell Foundry. And d'ya know one of the bells they made there? The Yanks' bloody Liberty Bell!'

I began a discussion about the sometimes ironical juxtapositions of history but after asking the meaning of juxtaposition he transferred his interest to a robust black girl sitting alone at a nearby table. Her thin floral cotton dress enhanced the chunky curves and bumps of her expansive body. She toyed suggestively with the rim of a glass of cheap lolly water. Smoke from a cigarette dangling from her thick lips drifted across her ebony face as she sat back indolently and gazed challengingly around the bar signalling her availability to its mostly seamen clientele.

'Jeez, she'll do me, mate,' Tom said. 'The best I've seen this trip. Bet she'll go off like a hot potato.'

As they reached the door he looked back and gave a leery wink before following her waggling gait outside to some backstreet alley, her massive bottom wiggling under her cotton dress like a tethered balloon.

God Almighty, I thought, anyone surviving Arctic convoys could have found a better hot potato than that. Perhaps his eyesight had been impaired by all that Arctic cold. But apart from that, Tom, like most seamen, was hopelessly skewed by a life that taught them to take their pleasures in brief, frenetic interludes.

From Stockholm we crunched our way back to the sea in the wake of a small icebreaker. Rounding Sweden's southern end we reached Malmo in Norway to discharge our remaining cargo. We returned through the Cattegat, around Skagen and down the Skagerrak and North Sea fog to the Pernis refineries to load diesel oil for Bergen and Oslo.

Bergen's cold was even more bitter. Ice closed around the ship even before we finished tying alongside. Back down the coast and through the Skagerrak we steamed up the long fiord to Oslo to complete discharging.

As we pushed back to the North Sea through open pack ice and compacted snow the ship, empty except for water ballast, reverberated like a huge empty drum pounded by a thousand hammers. For several days we pounded and crashed through one of the century's worst northern storms. Much of England's east coast was flooded and many in the Low Countries were drowned. We lay hove-to for several days off the Dutch coast in screaming winds and high seas before we could journey up the Maas to the Pernis refineries. With a full cargo we headed back to sea for another as yet undetermined place. Hopefully on the way we could again have flying fish for breakfast.

⚓

Many tanker men suffered from 'Abadan fever'. The ailment, named after the Abadan refinery in the Persian Gulf, arose from long passages and being unable to go ashore very often — most oil terminals were distant from the cities they served and tankers were alongside sometimes little more than a day. As well, the continual smell of oil, and its fumes inhaled over years of tank-cleaning, did little for their brains. Sometimes it seemed their senses had been tagged 'Not Wanted on Voyage'. Broodiness at sea was matched by aggressiveness ashore where all they needed was some form of ignition to set them alight.

Mick was a man with iron fists, a rock-hard head and a brain to match, an intellectual void filled by a body, the sort of man who had lost his virtues, whatever they had been, and had acquired no others. He sought fights ashore with the passion and patience an astronomer seeks comets. He was undeterred by being regularly bested by his opponents and wore his cuts and bruises with some pride. He was beaten, he said, only because he was too drunk to even the odds to better than about three- or four-to-one. Otherwise he would have done the lot. They were only foreigners, dammit!

I tried to rescue him once from a barroom brawl. It was a futile gesture. Friend or foe was unrecognisable under such conditions. Anyone within reach was automatically unfriendly. Because I was in reach I received a gut-collapsing wallop. He did not thank me the next morning for guiding him back to the ship despite my distinct inclination to leave him in the bar being battered into insensibility. He recalled none of the events. But when my bruises corroborated his blow to me, he apologised for several days.

Bongo was a similar lunatic. He had a cauliflower ear and a thick red beard. Unlike Mick, who needed an hour's drinking and several provocations, imagined if not otherwise forthcoming, to set him off, Bongo needed only a few drinks and a single provocation to become the sort of man who made reality worse than a nightmare.

Bongo invariably went ashore with a dress and a string of cheap artificial pearls stuffed in his dungaree pockets. After finding the roughest bar and after several whiskies, the first gulped, the rest at leisure, that is, two or three gulps, he would don his dress and pearls with elaborate palaver. Inevitable comment from the bar's habitués left most of them in a scattered chaos of distress and injury, following which he left to search out the port's homosexual fraternity.

Unlike Mick, Bongo generally returned with a satisfied and unmarked countenance. He discouraged interrogation beyond a single discrete query. 'Bonged a few,' was all he ever said. Whether he meant a satisfactory fight or satisfactory partner was never clear. He was generally a silent man who carried his silence with him. To that extent Bongo was a gentleman. A very complex gentleman. He had been a commando during the war.

Edwin, a steward, made no bones about his own homosexuality. He was essentially a well-meaning, almost cultured man. All hands regarded his mincing ashore as merely Edwin being Edwina.

Despite their shared sexual proclivities, however, Bongo and Edwin detested each another. Bongo, I think, because Edwin was unashamed of his homosexuality and in Bongo's eyes flaunted it. Edwin, I think, because Bongo in Edwin's view denied his behind over-masculine belligerence.

Edwin also criticised Bongo's dress sense. He declared witheringly, but never in Bongo's hearing, that cheap dresses and even cheaper pearls were sure signs of a 'right blinking poofter, darling.'

'But please don't tell him. He'd kill me. He's a mad man,' Edwin grumbled, slightly emphasising the last word as if secretly wishing Bongo would accord him the same after-drink treatment accorded to unknown foreigners.

It was an interesting state of affairs. And given the circumstances, easy to understand. Except in one detail. What the hell was I doing there?

21

The Sea is Woman, The Sea is Wonder
Her other name is Fate!
Dante Rossetti, *The Sea Limits*

It's a fact. Destiny often turns on an impulse. Elizabeth was a girl who dangled a man on a string until she either cut him loose or hauled him in. Its progressive shortening signified great promise abed. And so as we walked arm-in-arm down a London street the shipping offices were of no interest. Passing the Port Line office, however, I was overcome with a sudden impulse.

And like the impulsive decision to leave Mr Papa-something-or-other's café which led to my chance meeting with *Pamir*'s chief officer who had subsequently provided the way to the sea, I was about to set in train as great a consequence.

The crew superintendent inspected my seaman's papers.

'Yes, I've an AB's job in Canada,' he said, as he handed them back.

He disappeared into his inner office and a few minutes later poked his head around the door, telephone in hand.

'Can you can pick up your gear and leave tonight?'

I hesitated. I had not reckoned on a pierhead jump.

'Well?'

I steeled myself against the promise of Elizabeth. She was an English peach if ever there was one.

'Yes,' I said, at the same berating myself for being mad.

He spoke into the telephone.

'Yes,' he said. 'Tonight.' Then there was along pause, and then he said, 'Really? First? Goodness me! Still, I've got to get the ship away. Yes, he'll have a company order form . . .' followed by various details to which I was deaf — I was too preoccupied with how to explain to Elizabeth outside on the pavement.

When I asked the superintendent what he had meant by First he looked unhappy and said I was about to be treated beyond the imagination of an AB. I told him I had a splendid imagination and that moreover I would be as well dressed as his managing director and act similarly. He seemed to doubt it, despite my van Heusen shirt.

That evening, after an emotional leave-taking at Elizabeth's front door in Canning Town, I boarded the BOAC (now British Airways) flight for Boston. From there I was to travel by train to St John in New Brunswick and replace an injured man who had just been paid off an otherwise ready to depart Australia-bound freighter.

Named after a small southern Australian port, the Port Line's twin screw refrigerated *Port Fairy*, built in 1928, was one of the oldest in the fleet. In 1930 her refrigeration system was changed and she carried the first chilled rather than frozen meat from Australia and New Zealand. Like most older ships belonging to established British lines, she was built of the best steel. It shone with a gun-blue sheen when we chipped paint through to its surface. Her masts and funnel leaned back at the rakish angle of a liner. But despite her cruiser stern her bow was old-fashioned, ramrod-strong and straight — and dangerously so; during a 1940 North Atlantic convoy a Canadian destroyer, HMCS *Margaree*, formerly HMS *Diana*, made a sudden and unexplained turn in front of the ship during squally weather and *Port Fairy*'s sharp steel bow sliced the warship in half.

It had been a tragically ironic accident. *Margaree* had been a replacement for another Canadian warship, *Fraser*, which had been similarly cut in half by HMS *Calcutta* only four months earlier. Forty-seven of *Fraser*'s 187 crew were lost. But nearly all *Margaree*'s crew, many having already survived *Fraser*'s loss, were drowned.

In 1943 west of Gibraltar *Port Fairy* was badly damaged by

German bombers. She was escorted by a Royal Navy warship to Casablanca where she was temporarily repaired.

⚓

Even allowing for the impudence of advertising language, a brochure in my ticket wallet well described the airline's North Atlantic Monarch De Luxe Service as:

> *Travel Royal . . . the very last word in luxury air travel. Everything . . . is superlative — the atmosphere of luxury and elegance, the superb comfort, the excellent food and drink, the impeccable service . . . the gay atmosphere of transatlantic air travel at its best.*
>
> *The interior of this magnificent double-decked airliner, tastefully decorated, with good yet restful lighting, fitted with luxurious dressing rooms, is so spacious it seems like a flying hotel. In the main cabin you relax — really relax — in the perfect comfort of a foam-soft armchair; when you feel like a change of scene, you have but to stroll down the spiral staircase to find yourself in the sociable, club-like surroundings of the large bar–lounge on the lower deck.*
>
> *The cuisine is a speciality — every dish an epicure's delight. The seven-course dinner, prefaced by cocktails, is served with wines, including champagne, and rounded off by a choice of liqueurs — all with the compliments of BOAC.*
>
> *If you wish, for a small extra charge, you may sleep your way across in the wonderful comfort of a full-length private berth, awaking, of course, to the pleasure of breakfast in bed.*
>
> *Menus are as varied as we can make them; breakfast will usually consist of fruit juices, fruit or cereal, a main course, bread, butter, preserves, tea or coffee. For luncheon and dinner, there will be 3 courses followed by cheese, fresh fruit and coffee. Light refreshments consisting of tea, coffee or fruit squashes, biscuits and cake will be served during the morning, afternoon and night, and on request. All comparable to the cuisine of a 1st-class hotel.*

Also supplied on request was a long list of everything from safety or electric razors, newspapers, magazines, 'ship's library', sewing kit, sunglasses, fans, barley sugar. And 'anything on BOAC stationery or postcards, please give them to the Steward who will arrange to post them for you.' Travel Royal indeed!

The phrase explained the almost deferential treatment from the moment I arrived at the Victoria Coach Station to board the airport bus. And the fresh orchids given to the ladies as they stepped elegantly up the aeroplane's gangway. And the Port Line's crew superintendent's manifest unhappiness at having to send me in such company.

On all counts, therefore, the flight was a civilised affair totally unlike today's cramped discomforts. Proper meals were cooked in a proper galley and served on proper plates with proper cutlery and proper napkins. There was ample space between seats to stretch out and sleep. The captain came round at intervals enquiring into his passengers' well-being and inviting anyone interested to visit the flight deck at any time. And the downstairs lounge was a place to socialise, to enjoy a drink, snack, game of cards or a smoke, although while 'cigarette and cigar smoking is permitted on all our aircraft, pipes are not allowed as they create more smoke and some passengers object to this.'

As we droned through the night stretched comfortably in our seats — the superintendent had been irritated enough over providing epicurean delights without the added pain of the 'wonderful comfort of a full-length private berth' — we came upon the Northern Lights off southern Greenland.

They hung from the sky in an inexpressible magnificence. They waxed and waned like waving, folding theatre curtains with trailing ribbonlike streamers, sometimes delicate, sometimes bold, a drapery of gold, magenta and lime green itself; a delicacy of colour beyond the ability of any earthly painter's palette. It was as if it issued from heaven itself.

Science would have explained it as streams of mainly atomic hydrogen solar gas ejected from sun storms and speeding to the earth at over a thousand miles a second. The auroral display was simply the result of the streams' deflection by the magnetic field towards the poles. But such knowledge would have ruined my ignorance as it soared among the spectacle.

Not everyone was impressed.

'Yes, dahling,' a well-modulated voice behind me reproved her excited child, 'I can see it, and yes, it's pretty. But do close your eyes and go to sleep, dahling, there's a good boy, and for heaven's sake let Mummy have some peace.'

Peace? For heaven's sake? In the face of such skyward resplendence? All the same, I was glad when he finally quietened and stopped pulling on my headrest and so bankrupting the 'perfect comfort' of my 'soft-foam armchair'.

Newfoundland's treetops poked through the new morning's snow-blanket below us. We landed amid sheets of flying whiteness at Goose Bay in Labrador to which we had been diverted from Gander in Newfoundland; the pilot made a wry remark about sauce.

Goose Bay airport had been built by the Canadian Government in 1941–42 near a fur-trading settlement at North West River. As we trudged through the snow to the airport waiting room while the aeroplane was refuelled, a husky team and sledge swished past us. The driver cracked his whip and shouted 'moosh!' We really were in the Canadian wilderness.

Aboard a Boston–Maine Railroad train for St John that evening I had a fine dinner then retired to my Pullman sleeping berth. I felt even more like a managing director when a Negro attendant made up my bed, called me sir and shone my shoes sometime during the night while I was dreaming of Elizabeth's legs.

Breakfasting on ham and eggs and freshly brewed coffee, I watched America's sleepy small towns stirring themselves as the engine's hooter blasted through their late-winter frosty somnolence with long, dissonant, mournful cries.

It was snowing in St John and the taxi had some difficulty reaching the docks.

'Where're you off to, mister?' the driver asked.

'Australia.'

'Australia — guess it's summer down that way.'

'Yeah, guess it is.'

'Summer,' the driver said, as if reviving a frozen memory.

⚓

A brown-haired South Australian lawyer's typist sat with a group of girlfriends in a Port Pirie milk bar. Sidelong glances signalled a mutual chemistry. It was confirmed that evening at a local dance. Afterwards I asked to take her home. She said she was going home with the lad she had come with.

'But ring me at work if you like,' she said shyly.

I did. For the rest of the time in Port Pirie when not admiring her litheness playing basketball in a short dress, I took her to dances, and sometimes the pictures because she was in love with Gregory Peck, and kissed her goodnight afterwards. She took care, however, that we were on opposite sides of the front gate. She was either a sensible girl or I was not up to Gregory Peck.

I was intrigued.

⚓

Loaded with Port Pirie lead ingots and other assorted cargo from Adelaide, Fremantle, Geelong, Melbourne, Sydney and Brisbane, *Port Fairy* set off back across the Pacific and through Panama to United States east coast ports.

In Boston I ate baked beans and fed squirrels in a park while parents yelled to children apparently all named Butch or Junior. Passing through the Cape Cod Canal we leaned against the rail with cups of tea and watched highway traffic speeding through a scenery of billboards and small towns. Down the coast Atlantic City was visible only as the tops of skyscrapers upthrusting on the horizon. They seemed to be growing out of the sea like a re-emerging Atlantis. Then around Cape May we went, and up the long Delaware Bay waterway past Salem, Wilmington and Chester to Philadelphia. And then back north to New York.

America is a place you experience rather than visit. Its inhabitants speak the same language but live in a foreign country.

I asked directions from a Philadelphia policeman. He snarled he was 'no gar-damned guide book, mister.' I drank milkshakes nose to nose with a girl I met in a drugstore after asking her the directions the policeman would not give me. While unsure of Australia's location, she thought New Zealand must be near wherever it was. And obviously, as we shared a double straw and blew bubbles in the shared milkshake, New Zealanders had learned to tark English. Ree-al prarper, too.

In New York after my neck ached among the skyscrapers I bought a hamburger in Battery Park and gave half of it to a bum who then protested that I was a bigger bum because I gave him only half; bought thick weekend papers in Times Square; remonstrated with children who said, 'Gimme a Coke, lady,' to an old woman in a small shop near our berth in Brooklyn; asked her why they were belligerent when I suggested they say please and thank you; and was surprised when she shrugged her tired old Greek shoulders and said, 'Thees ees A-mair-ree-ka, my frien'; admired the Manhattan skyline and the New York harbour from an elevated Brooklyn subway station; went to the movies at three o'clock in the morning; walked down Broadway and Fifth Avenue; could not board a bus because I did not have the exact fare — 'Can'ta you reada da bloddy Americano?' the Italian driver demanded, pointing to a notice which said in English 'Exact Fare. No Change.'

As we left New York *Queen Elizabeth* sailed into her berth beneath the Manhattan skyline. I wondered if the cups' and chairs' *führer* was still aboard. It was doubtful he had a heart so it was unlikely the bastard had died of a heart attack.

But I didn't really care as we sailed southeast for Bermuda. There I met a fellow New Zealander in a Hamilton bar. He was an airline steward with a wife and home in Somerset Bay. We spent a pleasant weekend swimming in the bay's warm waters, cycling round the island and drinking beer in local bars or glasses of heady wine in the evening on their wide verandah among the bright, scented flowers whose fragrance smothered the warm Bermuda air with a sweet thickness.

From Bermuda we returned to Canada, journeying 500 miles up the long St Lawrence River past Quebec to Montreal where all hands were paid off and returned to London by a company-chartered airliner. This time the downstairs bar was closed and meals were neither an epicurean delight nor preceded by wine. It had been a pleasant voyage, however. Except for a wild, wet passage across the Great Australian Bight, the weather had been mostly fine and generally warm.

The lissom, peach-tinted Elizabeth greeted my knock on her front door stonily. I should not have been surprised. She had replied only tartly to my letters. I wasted several days trying to retie the string. However, her friend Becky was a friendlier girl for a week or two.

But of greater interest was the handknitted jersey from Port Pirie 'since you always seemed to say how cold it was over there. Affectionately yours, Marita.'

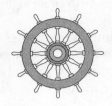

22

Where lies the land to which yon ship must go?
William Wordsworth, *Miscellaneous Sonnets* I.31

The Poplar shipping office man scratched his right ear with his pen while he perused my papers. Since I had known him I had observed that he spoke only after changing to his left ear. Eventually he did so.

'Ah, yes,' he said. 'Didn't think you'd be back here for a year or more.'

'Neither did I,' I said.

I told him about *Norrisia* and how I had paid off at the first opportunity. He said he was not surprised. Nor would he bother saying I Told You So. He said a psychoanalyst could have built a career on tanker crews, but might have shot himself at the end of it.

'Port Line, eh? Australia? New Zealand?'

Australia, I told him.

'Looking for a bit of summer, I suppose?'

'Not really,' I said. 'Anyway, what have you got?'

'Same as usual. Depends on what you want.'

He began his paper-shuffling routine.

'What are you looking for?'

'Don't know, really. A passenger ship, perhaps?'

The man pursed his lips and shook his head.

'Passenger ships are for married men whose wives need to know where they're going and when they'll be home — though not necessarily what they're doing in the meantime,' he said, his mouth crinkling with a smirk as if he wished he could do the same.

I told him about *Queen Elizabeth*. He'd heard it all before. A ferryful of bellboys, poofter stewards and window washers. He kept rifling through his papers. He eventually extracted one.

'But if you really want a passenger ship — by the way, they say the QE's messroom is about as big as the *Mayflower* — makes you think, eh? — well, anyway, here's one that might suit. *Heron*. General Steam Navigation Company. She's in the West India Dock. Sailing in a couple of days. She's a bit of both, cargo and half a dozen passengers. Usually old ducks cruising around the Med on their husbands' insurance money.'

Heron was a small cargo-passenger ship built in Dundee in 1937. We journeyed around the Mediterranean with several blue-haired old ducks. They spent most days in deckchairs drinking gin — their late husbands must have had large insurances — and playing the coquette with passing sailors. Some of the men were old hands at the game and well knew how to avail themselves of some of the aforesaid insurances.

The voyage was a Cook's tour for passengers and crew alike. Often there was only an overnight passage between ports but always with enough time in each to absorb something of their essence. Among them were Gibraltar, Malta, Tripoli, Salonika, Kalamaki, Corinth Canal, Patras, Katakolon, Aiyon and Volos, a very ancient city mentioned by Thucydides and Herodotus in their histories and in which there was the Triumphant Arch built by the Roman emperor Trajan.

In Malta I visited St Johns Church and sat in the Crusaders' Chapel where the Knights of St John were buried. Then I went to St Paul's Bay where St Paul had been shipwrecked. The island itself had at various times been held by Phoenicians, who came in 1000 BC, and later Greeks, Romans, Saracens, French and British with various others in between. Its whole atmosphere was redolent of the fact. It still bore the marks, too, of the incessant air raids by Germans and Italians. Malta's steadfastness in the face of the heavy battering and consequent privations earned the island the George Cross.

In Aiyon, sanctuary of Eileithyia, the Greek goddess of child-birth, and where Agamemnon summoned the leaders of the Achaean League against the Trojans, I spent a whole Sunday with one of my watch-mates, Jack, on a long walk far into the sparse, hilly countryside. Jack was a companionable man. We talked of ships we had sailed in and shipmates we had been with, women we had known, those we wished we had known better, some we regretted having known. We drank wine and ate bread and cheese in small tavernas along the way. We hitched a ride back to Aiyon with a garrulous old peasant and his stout wife and silent daughter on a cart full of firewood. We visited several more tavernas in the village and had to help each other back to the ship.

In Patras I climbed a hundred-odd steps to view the city and the broad sweep of the Gulf of Patras. Then I went to the acropolis where once the ancient festival of Artemis Laphria was held and into whose log fires worshippers cast 'live edible birds and every kind of victim, boars, deer and gazelles . . . wolf cubs . . . full grown beasts . . . together with the choicest fruits . . .'

The twelve to four watch, Jack and myself, both ABs, and Johnny, a 17-year-old junior ordinary seaman, would have been a typical cross-section of *Heron*'s crew.

Newly off-watch and having finished our eggs'n'chips blackpan, we were having a smoke and a hand or two of cribbage before turning in.

'Why did I go to sea?' Johnny said. He was echoing my mildly irritable response to a moan of some sort while he shuffled the cards. Seamen always moaned even if it meant inventing a complaint. For some it was almost an art form. Of course, the complaints could be reflected among any office or factory workers ashore. But they went home at work's end and had weekends off. Aboard a ship there was no such demarcation. Home, job and workers travelled together in intimate company.

Nevertheless, however much sailors complained, few would have opted for any other life, hence my 'Why the hell did you go to sea, then?' irritability.

Johnny was a lanky lad, loose-limbed almost to the point of

dislocation. A mop of unruly brown hair swept across his barely whiskered cherubic face. Not yet having reached the age at which men in defence of their private personas generally shield the motivations of their lives, often as much from themselves as any other, he was also a guileless fellow who approached every issue with an open mouth.

'Because I fuckin' wanted to, Kiwi. Why else?' he said, as he dealt the cards.

'You must've been mad,' Jack said, as he picked up his cards. 'Were you a Vindi boy?'

'Aye, I was that,' Johnny said.

Vindi boys began their careers aboard *Vindicatrix*, a Merchant Navy training ship on the Gloucester–Sharpness Canal. The ship had been built in Glasgow in 1893 and named *Arranmore*. In 1910 she was sold to a German company and renamed *Waltraute*. In 1914 she was used as a training ship for U-boat commanders. In 1919 she was taken back by the British to accommodate German seamen awaiting repatriation. She was renamed *Vindicatrix* in 1922 and lay idle in West India Dock. In 1939 she was towed to Sharpness. The former Cape Horner, as a hulk, replaced the Gravesend Sea School when it was evacuated. She ended her days in 1967, when she was broken up in Newport, South Wales.

With basic accommodation, tough discipline and sometimes hunger, Vindi boys received an uncompromising introduction to the facts of life at sea from their instructors, mostly former Merchant Navy and Royal Navy officers.

'Bit rough at times?' Jack asked.

'Aye, but I stuck it out,' Johnny said quietly, with unusual understatement.

'Yeah, you must have been mad,' Jack said.

'Well, mate,' Johnny said, 'me ol' man said I was. Round the bend, he said. A waste of life, he said. Better to be a bus driver like me brother George, he said. Or a bank clerk like me other brother Harry. A bank clerk? In a bloody office? Cor! What a waste of life!'

Recalling the Russell post office and my resolve never to work in another office no matter what might befall me, I felt a greater understanding of young Johnny, an even greater one of myself.

'Aye!' Johnny said. 'I'm here because I bloody want to be. Simple as that, mate.'

The family lived in Gravesend at the top of a steeply sloping street. For as long as he could remember Johnny had watched the ships as they picked up mud pilots to take them up the Thames or Channel pilots to take them to sea. So it was as natural for Johnny to go to sea as it was for a Rhondda Valley lad to become a miner. The ships had always stirred him with a profound sense of arrival or departure, although he expressed it differently.

'I was always fuckin' wondering, like, where they was fuckin' coming from or was fuckin' going to. Y'know what I mean?' he said.

Johnny's father also used to watch the ships. But *his* father had convinced him the sea held no future, especially if he wanted to get married and have a family.

'S'pose that's why he told me the same thing,' Johnny said as we began our game. 'Me sister Gloria told her boyfriend the same thing when he went to sea. Y'know? The "ships or me" routine, like? Poor old Gloria.'

'Old?' Jack interrupted.

'Twenty-four,' Johnny explained. 'Getting on a bit for a Judy . . .'

'Twenty-four! God strike me! Jeez, wish I was twenty-four again,' he said as he played a card.

Johnny's expression hinted that it must have been a hundred years since Jack was twenty-four.

'Yeah, well,' Johnny went on, 'her boyfriend went to sea anyway. Must have thought, "No bloody Judy's going to tell me what to do." Alan his name is. And every time I see him he asks how Gloria is. When I tell him she's OK he just shrugs. When I tell Gloria I've seen him and he's OK, she shrugs, too. Bollocks! Gloria's never had no other real boyfriend. Alan hasn't had another Judy, either. Not from round our way, anyway. Could have one somewhere else. Who knows? He's a randy sort of bugger. So he must have.'

'What about you? You're a randy bugger yourself. You got a Judy?' asked Jack.

'Well, yeah, sort of. Avril . . . works in a shop up the West End. Nice. But . . .'

'Wha'd'ya mean "nice but"?' Jack interrupted.

'She won't come across . . .'

'Don't blame her,' Jack interrupted again. 'She'd soon be up the duff the way you've been carrying on. And then you'd be right in it, mate! Anyway, no self-respecting Judy'd come across if she saw the ones you've been with this trip. Jeez, Kiwi, you should have seen the one in Malta!'

She had been a thick-thighed, stoutly buttocked girl from the Gut with a face, which, unlike Helen's, would have sunk a thousand ships. Johnny had referred to her as Jalopy.

'I did,' I said. 'A bit big.'

'Big? Nah, Kiwi — comfortable,' Johnny said, as if my comment was not so much untrue as uninteresting. 'Anyway, what about yours in Volos? She was bloody skinny. And so was the one in Salonika. She didn't even have any bloody tits!'

Young Johnny judged girls non-existent unless round, bosomless with less than several handsful.

'Y'prick'll fall off one of these bloody days, me ol' china,' Jack said. 'And y're bloody eyes'll drop out when you bend down to pick it up,' he added as an afterthought.

'At least I'll know what I'm looking for,' Johnny said, implying that anyone of Jack's age must have long since forgotten his own.

Jack smiled an indulgent smile and said, 'Smart bastard.'

'. . . but I've tried hard enough,' Johnny continued. 'But every time I get a hand into her knickers she burbles on about waiting till she's married. Puts a man right off, like.'

He slammed down a winning card.

'Anyway, why did I go to sea, right? Don't really know, except I always wanted to. Like I told you, I used to watch the ships and think about where they'd come from or where they were going . . .'

He paused as Jack looked up after dealing the next round.

'Sounds daft, I suppose,' Johnny ventured uncertainly.

'Like young love's bloody dream,' Jack said. He blew a smoke ring towards the deckhead. A smoke ring following a sarcastic comment, however, usually signified a much less barbarous thought than might have been otherwise insinuated. But Johnny did not understand the significance of Jack's smoke rings.

'Maybe to an old bugger like you,' he said truculently. 'Bloody true all the same. Better than being a bus driver, anyway, or a bank clerk like Harry. Jeez, mate, you should see Harry! Suit and brolly and briefcase. Thinks he looks like a millionaire while he reads the FAY-non-cial-feckin'-TAYmes on the train. And he likes to be called *Harold*!'

'So?' Jack asked in defence of the unknown Harry. 'Sometimes I'd quite fancy a suit and brolly. And being called James for a change.'

Fifty-or-thereabouts and from Whitechapel, Jack was a spare-haired, knotty man with a nicotined, wispy moustache. He viewed the world through uncompromising, sun-squinted eyes. A friendly man, he was at the same time a private man, the sort who unless you came to know him, as I had during our walk from Aiyon, you forgot not afterwards but at the time. The rest of the crew knew little about him except that his wife's name was Mavis, a lady who it seemed had not so much married as assumed command of him.

'I can just imagine you as a bank clerk, Jack,' I said.

My attempted witticism was lost on Johnny.

'God! Stuffed if I can, Kiwi,' he said artlessly. 'But anyway, Harry doesn't *do* nothin'. Most he's ever done was a weekend in Paris once with some of his bank mates. Came home and said all Frogs were pricks and he wouldn't go near the place again. Anyway,' he said reflectively, 'Frogs don't like us English so all Frogs must be pricks. And me brother George, he says he'd never go abroad because all he'd see would be castles and fuckin' foreigners. Says there's enough at home without going anywhere else to see them. A real Londoner, George. Enjoys the buses. But I think he gets a bit pissed off with them at times.'

Johnny examined his cards. He selected one and then supposed everyone got pissed off at times. Even he did sometimes, he complained as he played his card. His sister Gloria did, too. She was pissed off because she wanted to get married and have a family.

'Even me old man gets a bit pissed off, too. Sometimes when I come home and he asks about the trip, I get the idea he's sorry he became a printer instead of going to sea. I think me Mum sometimes wishes he'd gone to sea, too, when she gets pissed off with him.'

'The sea, the sea itself, boyo — do you ever get pissed off with it?' Jack asked mildly, but I knew he was getting pissed off with Johnny's grumbles.

No, mate, he didn't, Johnny said eventually. He didn't think about it much, either.

'Just a fuckin' lot of water as far as I can make out. Fuckin' deep as well. Too deep for my brain to penetrate, anyway.'

'Yeah, probably is,' Jack said dryly. 'It'd probably have trouble getting to the bottom of a bath.'

He gazed at Johnny with a complacent 'explain that if you can' look on his face.

Johnny rose to refill his cup and tried to deflect the course of the conversation.

'Yeah, well, anyway, Jack, what about you?' he called from the tea urn at the other end of the messroom. 'How long have you been at sea?'

'Long before you two buggers were born,' Jack called back. 'Started as deck boy in 1918,' he continued when Johnny returned to his cards. 'Just before the First War ended. Just left school, I had. Fourteen going on fifteen . . . come to think of it, it must have been a thousand bloody years ago. Seems like it, anyway. My old man was at sea, too. So were my brothers. So I suppose it was the natural thing to do.'

His first ship was a collier. He had joined her in Newcastle. *Duchess*. A right bloody old rust bucket. *Duchess*! Blimey! What a name!

'Royalty my arse!' he said. 'Absolute working class, more like. All coal burners. Woodbine funnels. Half a bucket of fresh water a day. For cooking and washing. A tin of condensed milk a week. Burgoo, oxtail, bangers and plum duff. And fo'c'sle accommodation. Us one side, firemen and trimmers the other. Messroom in the middle. We also had to bring our own donkey's breakfast and blankets.'

The Old Man was a Welshman, the chief officer a Geordie, the second and third mates Scousers, the engineers Scotsmen, the sailors mostly Londoners and Geordies.

'And the firemen were mainly Liverpool Irishmen. Real hard

sods, too. Began life as bastards and worked their way down. The only time they were sober was when we'd been at sea long enough for them to dry out. Then they were miserable sods until they could go on the booze again . . .'

Jack carried on in similar vein until Johnny asked what about the war? It was a part of his seagoing life Jack had not mentioned.

'The usual, mate,' Jack said. 'Atlantic convoys, mostly. Usually Liverpool to Halifax or sometimes New York, and back. A couple of trips to Malta. And a couple to New Zealand and Australia with Shaw Savill. But mostly to the States and Canada.'

'Anything ever happen?' I asked, anticipating Johnny's obvious next question but without expecting much of an answer. No one I had yet met had ever talked much about his wartime voyages.

'Not much,' he said.

But Johnny was anxious for some tales of derring-do.

'Bollocks! Something must have happened.'

'Nah! I tell you, mate. Reckon I was just plain bloody lucky. Wherever I was the buggers seemed to miss. They had a go several times, of course. But the bastards kept missing!'

'Were you ever excited?' Johnny enquired.

'God Almighty, Johnny lad, grow up! Scared, more like . . . yeah, in fact nearly all the bloody time, mate. Anyone who says they weren't is a liar or as as thick as two bloody planks. You'd have been, too, knowing there was probably some Nazi bastard out there with y'balls in his periscope. I remember once . . .'

His voice tailed off as he lit another cigarette. He coughed and continued, 'Bloody coffin nails, they'll kill me before I'm through. What was I saying? Yeah, once in the Western Approaches — but never mind, the bastards missed . . .' Jack's contemplation of his cards suggested it had been by a hair's-breadth.

Despite Johnny's urging, however, he had said all he was going to say. Others like him had also said little about such events. *Gitano*'s Scouse, for instance, the Pompeii-expert, who never would tell me about his torpedo, let alone how it earned him a medal. Or *Algonquin Park*'s men, who preferred to talk about women rather than torpedoes, although there were those who had regarded them as one and the same.

To break his silence Johnny asked Jack if things had changed much since he first went to sea.

'Yeah, mate, s'pose they have,' he said.

He played a card and then became almost philosophical.

'Suppose the only thing that hasn't is the sea itself. Y'know what I mean? A pain in the arse at times. You'd think after thirty-five-odd years you'd get to know something about it.'

He blew a smoke ring.

'Nah, mate, bollocks! I tell ya' — y'get to know ships. And shipmates . . . well, maybe not all of them. I've known a few queer bastards in my time, I can tell ya. Some had nothing but a mouth to eat with and an arse to sit on. But as for the sea — nah, mate, I like going to sea. But I don't like *it*. You're only ever likely to drown in the bitch!'

He produced his largest smoke ring so far. Its great, silently spinning circle seemed to last longer than most until it dissipated in wraithlike tendrils against the far bulkhead, like the tired pessimism of a philosopher who had found ultimate causes and purposes to be insoluble mysteries.

Johnny turned to me. I told of working in an office and leaving home on a bicycle because of it and about *Pamir*'s chief officer. But I left out the more intimate childhood motivations. They might have enticed Jack's sarcastic comment, with or without a smoke ring.

My watch-mates nodded and said it was time to turn in. It was already 4.30 a.m. We had to turn-to at eight o'clock and stand by on the fo'c'sle head while we passed between the almost vertical 200-feet high soft limestone walls of the four-mile-long Corinth canal on the way from the Ionian Sea to Corinth for currants and on to Patras for more currants.

'Christ,' Jack said to Johnny as we left the messroom, '*ran* away to sea? On a bloody *bicycle*? Must've read too many fuckin' books, the silly prick!'

⚓

In a Liverpool pub after we paid off in the Huskisson Dock, Johnny sought our best advice on divesting Avril of her knickers back in

211

Gravesend. Dammit, he had bought enough presents. This from here, that from there, the other from somewhere else. And this, this had cost him — he almost spluttered into his beer — two fuckin' quid! What else could a man do? What else could a Judy want?

We both expressed the hope that Avril, since she seemed a nice and apparently intelligent girl, would remain unimpressed by a few trinkets and keep her knickers waist high and their elastic legs tight for some time yet. By the time we left the pub, Johnny was planning to distribute most of his gifts to more likely prospects. Jack and I were relieved on Avril's behalf. I said goodbye to my shipmates as they left for Lime Street Station and I set out through the drizzle up Canning Street for the seaman's hostel in Paradise Street.

Paradise Street was once as unsavoury a place as London's Limehouse and Ratcliff Highway. Some of its more unscrupulous boarding-house keepers had drawn a line across the floor and placed a cow's horn in the middle of the room. Sailors were plied with drink and guided across the line and around the horn a number of times. The befuddled men were then delivered to ships' captains as excellent able seamen who had 'crossed the Line' a dozen times and 'rounded the Horn' at least half a dozen.

Paradise Street was also celebrated in old sea shanties — *As I was a-walking down Paradise Street / Aye-aye — blow the man down! / A pretty young gal there I chanced for to meet / Give me some time to blow the man down . . .*

And it was because of the pretty young gal, blonde, passionate Joan from Aigburth, whom I had met while aboard *Durham* and visited most times I paid off a ship, that I stayed for some time in Liverpool.

But unlike Johnny I did not need trinkets. Joan was unimpressed by trinkets. They were always gladly received but were unnecessary prerequisites for entry to her bed. Despite well-indulged passions, however, I was preoccupied with other thoughts.

Still signed only 'affectionately yours', Marita's letters from South Australia were intriguing me more and more. And a man intrigued by a woman is in greater excitement than if he is merely in love with her.

And so I set off for Australia by car.

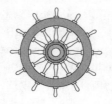

23

Tripping hither, tripping thither
Nobody knows why or whither.

W S Gilbert

It was Aussie's idea. Aussie was a tall, slightly stooped but otherwise angular mid-twentyish Sydneysider whose thick glasses seemed always about to upend over his hooked nose. A stokehold accident had ended his days as a ship's fireman. His compensation money had bought a four-wheel-drive Humber ex-army staff car to return home in what he called 'style, mate, bloody style!'

In seamen's missions and pubs around Aldgate and Whitechapel we pored and argued over maps devising the best routes to Singapore. Post-Singapore plans would be hatched when — Aussie would not countenance my more cautious *if* — we reached there.

A friendly Middle Eastern embassy official also suggested some means of self-protection.

We met shifty characters of every colour and a dozen nationalities in dark, dingy rear rooms of little shops along Commercial Road, in dockland pubs and dosshouses around Limehouse and nameless places along the Mile End Road, in Cable Street and other East End dives and backstreets and alleys. But we had money for a gun and no bullets, or bullets and no gun.

After hearing of our fruitless efforts the embassy official was nervous. He gripped the bars of the grill with one hand and ran the other through his hair.

'Sirs, I thought you understood! Legally! Oh, dear me! You must do it legally! Sirs, you must get a police permit!'

After Scotland Yard's close scrutiny of our visas, lengthy inter-view and considerable interrogation as to our efforts so far, we were each given permits to buy 'one only pistol with 400 rounds of ammunition, for the purpose of export from the United King-dom only.' We were then directed to an address off Leicester Square.

Down an alley and up a long musty staircase to the second floor of a shabby building, we entered a large room. A man with a tweed jacket and goatee beard sat behind a dog-eared old desk.

'A very good orf-ternoon, gentlemen,' he said graciously, like they did in Harrods. 'May one be of assistance?'

'Jeez, mate,' Aussie said, looking around him, 'there's enough here to start a bloody war.'

'There's enough here, sir, because there *was* a war,' the man said with a slight tartness which belied his polite smile.

'Yeah, mate,' Aussie said, 'maybe you're right.'

Amid the odour of gun oil and gunpowder we explained our-selves. The tweedy man stroked his beard while he examined our permits.

'Well, gentlemen,' he said, having finally smoothed his beard almost to a point, 'my main business is hiring to film studios and theatrical persons. But yes, I am licensed to sell to persons with police permits. Personal protection . . . well, yes, revolvers there, and automatics there.'

Aussie picked a 9 mm Luger pistol, I chose a .38 Smith and Wesson revolver. The proprietor oiled them after which he wrote their particulars into our permits, added his name and address and charged us six pounds apiece, including 400 bullets each.

'Good orf-ternoon, gentlemen,' he said as he ushered us to the door. 'Have a safe trip.'

'Too bloody right, mate,' Aussie said.

'Yes. Quite so, I suppose,' the man said.

We left him at the top of the stairs looking down on us and again stroking his goatee beard.

Sliding through West End streets with guns in paper bags had become tiresome by the time we reached Piccadilly. The little pack-ets of bullets in our pockets had also begun to weigh heavily. And so we bought a cheap attaché case. The lone shop assistant seemed on the point of foundering as we emptied everything into it.

'Goodness me! Are they real?' he stuttered.

Aussie poked his glasses back up his nose in a 'you silly bastard' gesture. He waved his Luger under the assistant's nose.

'Too bloody right, mate! Allah be fuckin' praised!'

'Goodness me — but you needn't swear like that!' the assistant said with returning spirit.

In case he became hysterical after we left we showed him our Scotland Yard permits.

We pinned up a notice in the Down Under Club in Earls Court and selected the only three with sufficient money — Vernon and Harry, both Australians, and Ethna, a New Zealand girl. We nicknamed her Joe to make things easier all round.

Almost immediately upon leaving the ferry at Boulogne we were lost. Everyone we asked, even the *gendarmerie*, was unhelpful. It might have been our bad French. More likely, recalling *Heron* and young Johnny's bank clerk brother Harold, it was because they were French.

That evening we pulled into a side road beside a small stream outside Amiens. We washed in the icy water and prepared our first meal — meat, onions and potatoes rendered to a gruelly soup in a bucket over a Primus. We then burrowed into our ex-US Army sleeping bags in the shelter of the car.

The pistols caused some discussion at the Yugoslav border. It was the first time anyone had done other than satisfy themselves our Scotland Yard permits were in order. But this time the guns were sealed in a cardboard box with orders to present them in the same condition at our exit.

Warned to stick to our authorised route and leave by the stated time, we assured the guards we intended passing through as directly and as quickly as possible.

A day later, somewhere after Zagreb as the grey day turned to black night, the vehicle slid off the road. Its four wheels spun uselessly and dug still deeper in the snow. We pushed to no avail and after brewing a cup of tea set off with a torch towards a distant light. It and our torch were the only suggestions of a world otherwise devoid of all but snow, darkness and disagreement.

A horsedrawn sled swished towards us as we struggled through yet another snowstorm. Once the driver understood our car was stuck somewhere behind us and that we were freezing, fed up and far from home, he turned round and carried us back to his village of Sasence Srem.

Selacki Nikola's house was home to a family of six, including four daughters. It had a large kitchen/general living room with an electric light, a combined bedroom/sitting room with an oil lamp and a separate bedroom with another oil lamp. All were sparsely furnished.

The girls talked and laughed and cast us shy glances as their mother directed them at the wood stove. Soon we were presented with bacon fritters, pickled cabbage and dumpling soup.

'Is not bloddy goot,' Selacki said mournfully the next morning after taking us by horse and sled through the still falling snow to the car. It was hopelessly stuck and the battery and radiator were frozen.

For the next several days we became part of the local life. We visited other families for meals and *sljivovica*, a sharp clear plum brandy. After a certain amount of drinking, hosts and guests alike were sometimes driven to hurling their glasses into the open fire where the residue ignited with exuberant, belchy explosions.

Vernon became enamoured with a village girl. We named her Cutie since no one could pronounce her name without causing her relatives great mirth. A neighbouring Lothario took a fancy to Joe who reciprocated with some reluctance. Nada, eldest daughter of the household, mended my socks and we flirted shyly when we went out in the snow to fetch more firewood.

Time passed in such convivial fashion until a party official arrived early one morning. He ordered us to move to a Mitrovica hotel. After he left our hosts more or less said 'Commissar, bah!' A few hours later another official, after studying our passports, spoke briefly to the family and left.

'Commissar OK,' they said, explaining that Harry's and

Vernon's documents were not in order. They had no idea what the error was. But the official had implied the less it was known elsewhere the better, or there would be 'difficulties'.

Our complacency was short-lived. A jack-booted lady commissar ploughed in on a horse. She had a pistol strapped around her bulbous belly. Her arms were like those of *Queen Elizabeth*'s *führer* of the cups. Sitting imperiously in front of our this time silent hosts, she demanded we go to Mitrovica and be interviewed locally. Or if we persisted in arguing about it, we would be 'taken' to a higher authority in Belgrade.

An air of trouble wafted about the square-faced lady. After she left horses were hitched to the car and it was dragged to the village. The battery was given a massive charge and hot water was thrown over the radiator and engine. Still no bloddy goot.

Next morning an increasingly fractious Aussie struggled to Belgrade by train to see if visas could be extended. He returned with the news that they would not be extended on any account. Furthermore, road conditions to the Greek border were difficult and travel through Bulgaria or Albania was refused out of hand.

With time at a premium we managed to coax the car back to life. Early next morning we underwent a round of *zdravo*'s, or goodbyes, and some embracing. I gave Selacki a thick fur cap bought in Canada when I had joined *Port Fairy*. He had indicated modestly that it would be sufficient payment for our stay with his family.

As Yugoslavia disintegrated in the 1990s I sometimes wondered what became of the village and Selacki and his wife and family and the rest of the villagers. I had no idea then, nor do I today, whether they were Serbs, Croats, Christians or Muslims or a mixture of all four. Then, winter appeared to be their only enemy. Not even the arrogant, gravel-voiced, jackbooted, pistol-packin', bull-bitch of a lady commissar could have competed for its bitterness. Why must women who wish to behave like men behave like bastards?

The following weeks were an encyclopedic variety of mishaps in more Yugoslavian snow and then Grecian and Turkish mud, rain and floods. We paid exorbitant prices for dirty petrol in mountain villages. We crossed inadvertently into Bulgaria and beat a hasty retreat. Aussie grew increasingly irritable over everything, including a broken starter motor.

Eventually we arrived in Istanbul. We booked into the YMCA, in the old part of the city. Aussie's complaints increased after an unsuccessful search for another starter motor. They worsened when we said it didn't affect him. Because of his injured arm it was us who swung the crank handle. Anyway, while he had tinkered with the car in London had he looked at the starter? If not, why not? The drama became theatrical. He'd had enough! The car! The stinking weather! Us! Never mind bloody foreigners, rotten roads, terrible food, and hopeless languages. We could take the car and do what we bloody well liked!

The trouble with turning disagreement into drama is that someone else generally writes the Last Act.

'OK! Please yourself! We'll have the car and call it quits. You go your way. We'll go ours,' we said.

He threw us the car's papers and travel carnet, gathered his belongings, including his Luger and packets of bullets, and left with a great deal of noise. We later agreed things should not have turned out that way. We searched briefly for him. He was not to be found. Whatever happened to him I have not the faintest idea.

Joe preferred a quieter life and left by the Taurus Express for Baghdad and a job looking after an English resident's children.

Harry, Vernon and I poked around Istanbul. The YMCA was near the 1400-year-old Sancta Sophia and within walking distance of the 1000-year-old Blue Mosque and the 400-year-old Topkapi Palace, the setting for Mozart's opera *Il Seraglio*. The Grand Bazaar and its 4000 shops lay only a little further afield.

Sometimes in the early evenings we idled on the Galata Bridge. As the sun set across the Golden Horn its orange orb bathed the tips of the minarets with shimmering light. Perhaps their builders had reckoned on such a phenomenon to enhance their creations. All the while the smells, sounds and sights flooding the bridge and the water passing beneath it pulsed with the heartbeat of the rich variety of life bestriding the crossways between the two parts of the sprawling, boisterous city.

Leaning against the bridge rail, we were an integral part of the human mash around us; people, people, people, all lurching without pattern or priority between history and destiny. I indulged my senses in the palatable reality of being far from my own country and still without an assured destination.

My ruminations ranged the world — leaving Russell, *Pamir*'s chief officer, signing aboard *Algonquin Park*, wondering where Ginger was, whether young Johnny had finally divested Avril of her knickers, whether Lillian was already married, what Marita was doing . . .

In more indolent moments we sat with pipe-smoking old men in baggy pants. A popular Turkish pastime, sitting. Sultans, when not lying with their harems, spent much of their time sitting stylishly in pavilions with their ample bottoms and crossed legs spread over brocaded divans measured by the square yard. But the old fellows sitting on the pavements or small stools were unlikely to be descended from sultans. Their ancestors were more likely goatsmen or herders who, when not following their animals, also, like sultans, undoubtedly sat.

Brian, a globe-trotting Canadian YMCA resident, was a master of foreign finance with no intentions of leaving Istanbul for some time. He conducted complicated manoeuvres with a shadowy character he called Madam Fifi. Whether it was her real name was beside the point. Under the circumstances it probably was not.

Brian introduced us to black-haired Madam Fifi. She lived in a Galata tenement room hung with tapestries and lit by two brass oil lamps. Rouged, ringed, long fingernailed, sallow complexioned, high cheekboned and of grand stature, Fifi also had a lust for the virile Brian. In the interests of continued nurture at the fiscal breast he submitted as required.

Madam Fifi hinted strongly that she would also welcome our services. But we conducted ourselves in professed ignorance of her amorous contemplations.

After lengthy coffee-fed conversation laced with oval Turkish cigarettes and carnal innuendo, our transactions roughly involved changing sterling travellers' cheques into Turkish lira and then American dollars, followed by something else, Greek drachmas, I think, or perhaps Italian lira — counted in the thousands whatever it was — and so on until, even with Fifi's commissions, we had more sterling than we started with. The cycle was repeated on further visits.

As profits increased, Madam Fifi, at around forty being of a dangerous age for ships and women, became more resolute in pursuit of our favours and sometimes went so far as to assume the position of a *grande horizontale*. The increasing likelihood of having to explore Fifi's impassioned hills and valleys while she lay on her vast bed palpitating like an animated acre of fertile ground meant it was time to leave Istanbul.

Over the heights of Turkey we went, and then down through the Cicilian Gates Pass, near which was the Triumphal Arch built by Emperor Justinian and through which Alexander the Great marched in 333 BC. Beyond lay the Taurus Range which we later crossed on the way to Tarsus. After crossing the River Cydnus and passing through Adana we arrived in Iskenderun. In Hama we visited the *norias* or water wheels. The wheels are relics of ancient irrigation systems which sent water along aqueducts far inland to dry areas. The largest wheel is of the fourteenth century. It once supplied the town's Grand Mosque. Later we crossed the Orontes. The river flows into the Ghab depression where Pharoah Thutmose III hunted elephants, which 1000 years later Hannibal taught the Syrians to use in war. Then came Homs, dating back to Roman days, before passing into Lebanon and down to Tripoli and Beirut, then a busy commercial and financial jewel of the Middle East, with no hint of the ruin to come in later years.

From Beirut we turned east over the snowy 5000-foot Jabal el Barouk and Jabal el Knisse and on down to Damascus. We had scant opportunity to wonder overlong if this was part of the *The Road to Damascus*. White-robed long-distance truck drivers treated the road as solely their prerogative. We had little time, space or safety in which to conjure up poets' visions.

From the Syrian border at Deraa we passed through an eight-mile no-man's-land to Ramthe. We were stamped for entry into Jordan, into which we dipped only briefly on our way to the Jordan–Iraq frontier. From the Arab Legion fort at Mafraq two armed soldiers were detailed to accompany us to the border.

The soldiers, taciturn and politely refusing our cigarettes, were the stuff of real Arabia. Seaport Arabs never seemed to be sons of the desert. They were much more urban in their inclinations and could have thought of nothing worse than living even anywhere near a desert, any more than most Australians would live anywhere near the outback, or New Zealanders in the backcountry, or the English on the moors.

It is fitting that poets find silence a fertile field for their lines. From my sleeping bag the desert's silence, like Hardy's, was wonderful to listen to and, like Rosetti's, more musical than any song. And where better to behold Byron's *Ye stars . . . the poetry of heaven*! They shone down as clearly as when the wise men saw their star. During such private times I sank into introspection as I had sometimes done during the night at sea. There was a difference, though. An enormous one.

At sea you are surrounded by existence. It is everywhere. The ship's motion, the wind's push, the ocean's immensity, they all signify existence — and one's part in it.

But the desert was a place of nothing. There was no sound or movement to signify anything. The desert is therefore also a place without expectation.

The map to Baghdad showed a rocky lunar plain empty except for an oil pipeline running from Kirkuk in northern Iraq to Sidon on the Mediterranean coast. We followed the line to the H3 pumping station and on to Rutbah. Then we struck out across the desert for Baghdad.

Approaching the city we were enveloped in a forty-day, forty-night deluge. The Tigris River dividing the city was a tawny, swift-flowing flood, its surface stained by the same earth of which the houses and minarets on its banks were built.

At the British Embassy in Karkh, on the riverside behind high walls, we asked for suggestions of where to stay. Officials were so airbsolootly-epper-clawss they could scarcely bear to advise us other than, in descending order, the Regent Palace, the Sindbad Hotel, the Tigris Palace Hotel, or the Semiramis Hotel, whose card proclaimed it as the 'Randazvous of the Gormet with a Specious Lawn Overlocking the Tigris.' Others' cards intimated similar happinesses. But it went without saying that all were quaite airbsolootly beyond our means.

A lower-clawss Briton from the carpool office, however, suggested a Rashid Street establishment near Faisal II Square in the heart of the city close to the Tigris riverbank and the covered bazaar.

'Cheap and reasonably clean,' he said, 'though perhaps a bit bare and probably noisy.'

It was all those things. Well within our limited means. Reasonably clean, although the toilet was a hole in the bathroom floor with a tap next to it. Bare — the room itself held little more than beds. But comfort was a matter of relativity after so many cold desert nights in sleeping bags. The noise levels, however, had been badly summarised. Traffic horns, talking, arguing, shouting and general hubbub raged day and night. At five o'clock each morning and several times during the day the amplified wail of the muezzin in the tall tower of an adjacent mosque called everyone to prayers. Everyone except, apparently, car, lorry, bus and taxi drivers.

During the heat of the day we sometimes sat on the hotel balcony overlooking Rashid Street. We sipped tea and munched dates and watched policemen blowing whistles and shouting at drivers and pedestrians. When no one took any notice the policemen subsided into apathy until they regained their lung power.

In the cooler hours we wandered the streets and byways of a city then happily lacking the architectural proportions that profess to decorate high-rise monotony. In some alleys old Turkish houses overhung the pavement so that they seemed to be almost touching each other. Men in white shirts and ties mingled with craftsmen and small merchants, whose ways had barely changed in twenty centuries, although cruise missiles may have since caused some modifications.

Sometimes beneath the date palms along the riverbank and admiring the setting sun's flaming sky colouring the brown water as if it was on fire, we ate *masquf* as an antidote to bread, goat cheese, dates, oranges, tomatoes and cups of tea. *Masquf* is a centuries' old Baghdad dish. A fish, a Tigris salmon if you are lucky, is cooked over a fire of sticks. Onions, tomatoes, salt, curry powder and oil are then spread around the inside of the hot fish and the juices allowed to penetrate before serving.

In between times we drove out along the dusty Kut Road to Ctesiphon, capital of the old Persian kings, and the Hillah Road to Babylon.

Somewhere in Baghdad's covered bazaar we were appropriated by a hawk-nosed Arab. Barcham visited us in our room and we spent time partying and dining with his family and relatives, friendly, pleasant people, near Baghdad West, where the city was first built in 762 by the Second Abbasid Caliph, Abu Jaafar al Mansur.

But Barcham himself proved to be merely another in a long line of Thieving Bastards of Baghdad. And a brazen one, even for an Arab. He arrived one morning in what Vernon had always reckoned was his best shirt. Following a wild denial that he had stolen it, but still wearing it, Barcham flounced off screaming the assurance that we would die, separately or collectively, he didn't care which, in what we understood to be a pile of camel shit.

The Tigris and Euphrates Rivers are lowest in September and October but flood massively between March and May. This was unknown to us in London although even elementary bookshop browsing would have found it out. The floods, at whose peak we had arrived, meant it would be some weeks before we could resume our journey. And in the meantime our onward visas would begin expiring. After an obstacle course of police, customs, taxation and other opprobrious bureaucracies who all adhered to the old bureaucratic rule — if something is unusual, it is impossible — we sold the car and flew to Basra.

In that ancient town, founded by Caliph Omar in 637 AD and during the sixteenth century an important port for Arab dhows trading to India and the Far East, the Euphrates and Tigris meet to form the wide Shatt al Arab waterway, which then flows some 100 miles south to the Persian Gulf. We spent several days searching for a dhow to India. But like being in Iraq in the first place, it was also the wrong season in Basra for dhows. Nor, even for me as a bona fide seaman, was there a working passage by ship, British or foreign, in any direction. There was only one way to go. North to Baghdad and west to London.

In the rear of a silversmith's shop I sold my revolver in as clandestine a fashion as when I first tried to buy one. But my negotiating proficiency had since been considerably honed. The weapon — its bullets long gone in desert target practice — fetched more than enough for hard-class railway fares and sustenance from railway station hawkers' trays from Baghdad to Istanbul on the Taurus Express, from Istanbul to Paris on the Simplon-Orient Express, the boat train to Calais and the Channel ferry to Dover.

Each moment of the train journeys across Asia Minor and Europe contained its share of commotions and Dover was reached with relief. Except that Harry and Vernon became lost in Trieste and I never saw them again, everything was familiar and back in its familiar place. Even the English rain had a friendly familiarity about it. Had I been a Pope I would have kissed its muddy puddles.

As William Hazlitt, in *Notes of a Journey through France and Italy*, 1827, said:

> *Nor do the names of Liverpool, Manchester, Birmingham, Leeds or Coventry, sound like a trumpet in the ears, or invite our pilgrim steps like those of Siena, of Cortona, Perugia, Arezzo, Pisa and Ferarra. I am not sorry, however, that I have got back.*

Nor was I. It was spring going on early summer. England's green and pleasant land is a tonic at that time of the year.

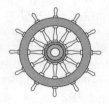

24

To roam
Giddily, and be everywhere but home,
Such freedom doth a banishment become.
La Rouchefoucauld

A sea voyage peters out in time and geography as it drifts home-wards after months of comparative loitering. It ends with the anchor dropping or mooring ropes hauled to the dockside. Each is a leisurely process and either is a very proper emblem of an ending.

A land journey doesn't end. It climaxes. Sometimes almost orgasmically, with a sudden and total cessation of urgent movement and stimulation followed by a collapse born of exhaustion. Or it leaves the traveller akin to lying almost comatose after having wandered through a wine rack. Either way, to regain stability one must slough one mentality for another. London was an ideal place for doing so.

Among the quietness of Hyde Park, the saltiness of the Red Ensign Club, the raucous rowdiness and intermittent fracas of East End and dockland pubs or equally uplifting museums, galleries and West End theatres and concert halls, I ruminated over the sometimes trying but always interesting months of snow, mud, rain, cold, heat, mountains, deserts, strange people, incomprehensible languages and unfamiliar proprieties.

Generally the event-filled months were contemplated with indulgence — the outward-bound crazy paving of countries in some of which we got lost in a sort of medieval soup; encounters with all manner of people, many of whom had not much gone beyond their chimneys' smoke; individual kindnesses in every country, official bastardry in some; ancient cities in combinations of splendour and squalor, like dirty queens clothed in filthy rags.

And the homeward-bound hard-class train journeys. The compound of anticipation and *déjà vu* on boarding the overcrowded Taurus Express in Baghdad. Travelling through Iraq, Syria and Turkey with goats, chickens and Arabs who, when not attending their devotions, chattered and squabbled among themselves and sometimes shared their food with us. Long-winded Middle Eastern railway travel bureaucratic lunacies. People of many nations and as many tongues shoving their way aboard the mid-evening Simplon–Orient Express at Istanbul for the journey through seven countries to Paris.

Coloured boiled eggs, dates, oranges and sweet tea from Baghdad to Istanbul. Crusty bread, sugary cakes and cheap wine from Istanbul to Paris via Venice where there was time enough at the Santa Lucia rail station to see the Grand Canal. Toad-in-the-hole and mushy peas from Calais to Dover.

Harry and Vernon missing the train in Trieste and my never seeing them again. The policeman and his handcuffed prisoner sharing my compartment from Domodossola on the fertile plains of northern Italy and through the Simplon railway tunnel, longest in the world, to Brig on the other side and their mutual gloomy contemplations of the Matterhorn and Swiss Alps' moonlit mountain tops as we travelled on to Lusanne. Paris' Gare de Lyon station and becoming lost on the underground while changing stations to catch the boat train to Calais.

The journey across the choppy English Channel to Dover and another train through the rain and Kentish fields and towns and villages inhabited by familiar people and Morris Minors and back to the musty smell of wet clothes on London's buses and tube trains.

And after so much concentrated travel the realisation that while I may have returned to my journey's starting point, I was nevertheless of another place, another hemisphere.

Marita's continuing letters were not yet love letters. They were still signed 'affectionately yours'. But as John Donne said, 'more than kisses, letters mingle souls.' I was becoming even more intrigued by her.

I was also beginning to realise that going to sea was like flirting with life — you enjoyed a passionate tryst with it in port and then sailed on.

⚓

The man in the Poplar shipping office was still in his tall chair but the sailing ship painting at the back of him had dipped a little more askew.

'Not seen you for some time,' he said. 'Where have you been?' I told him.

'Good God, man! By car? Australia? You must have been mad!' he said — I hoped it was an expression of perplexity rather than a psychological assessment — 'and you got only as far as Baghdad? Lucky to get that far, I'd say. Was it worth it?'

It seemed a genuine question and so I told him, Yes, once the exasperations were passed and the difficulties forgotten, there were things to be learned from such travelling.

The first was that seamen's views of other lands and their inhabitants tended to be elemental. It was a matter of our innate pragmatism. The fact that people were different was part of our daily lives. And so we acknowledged the differences and lived with them as best we could, provided they did not threaten our own mores — like anyone else we erected intellectual bulwarks against others' idiosyncrasies. In this way early romantic illusions were soon dispelled. Experience eventually teaches that places and people are much the same everywhere. But if this is a measure of the sailor's cynicism, the old stimulation of new horizons is not abandoned completely. There is a deep inner excitement, like a lover awaiting his mistress; though he knows some miserable East African port will turn out to be the usual melange of flies, heat and stinks, he still watches it grow out of the Indian Ocean with interest.

But that's about as far as it went. Facing the continuous differences was part of the job and so we became fatigued with distinctions and reduced the unknown to common denominators. Thus all Arabs were Wogs, all French were Frogs, to New Zealanders all English were Poms, and New Zealanders were unknown to almost everyone.

Because seaports were the same the world over we felt at ease within their confines and so seldom ventured into their hinterlands. We therefore rarely met truer representatives of the countries' peoples. The stout German woman, for instance, who insisted we warm ourselves over a free meal in her small village café was a far cry from the Reeperbahn's *frauleins*. The peasant with the horse and cart in the misty Grecian mountains who helped repair our engine and the villagers who later dragged us from a swollen stream were a far cry from the thieves and vagabonds of Piraeus. The shop traders of Baghdad were a far cry from the bumboat traders of Port Said or Aden. And so it went on.

The second thing I had learned was that with so many nationalities, ethnic minorities and majorities, languages, religions and cultures jammed in so small and complex a space as Europe, it was not surprising such an explosive mix caused periodic insurrections, rebellions, genocide, wars, two of which had entangled the whole world, and the bloody rise and cataclysmic fall of states and empires. I told him about the West African Kru headman who had said Europe could afford democracy because unlike Africa, Europe did not have tribes. But I had come to realise that Europe did. White Tribes. Affiliations between them could hang by as thin a thread as between any African tribes. Democracy could itself therefore also hang by threads as equally thin.

So that all in all, I told him, while the rest of the world was an interesting place and I enjoyed it, I was still damned glad our respective countries were islands and the sea our only borders.

The man's reply was almost introspective, like a prophet who would not be particularly pleased to see a prophecy come to pass.

'You and me both, Kiwi,' he brooded. 'You and me both. They're all the same, bloody foreigners — and in this country we live too close to the buggers!'

It was an interesting statement. The man's comment reflected the fact that the British, especially the English, did not see foreigners as different. They saw them as separate.

Once we finished philosophising the man nodded and told his assistant to get us both a cup of tea. As we drank it he asked where I wanted to go next.

'I'm beginning to think it's about time I went home,' I said.

'Why?'

I told him about Marita in South Australia.

'Aha!' he exclaimed as if making a discovery of benefit to all mankind. 'So *that's* why you tried to get there by car! Good God, man, what are you going to do? Marry the girl?'

'Don't really know. Might do.'

'How old is she?'

'Nineteen. Sixteen when I met her. It was during the trip to Australia. She was a lawyer's typist then. Now she's a hospital nurse.'

'And what did her parents think about their daughter going out with a seaman?'

'Not very much from what I could gather. Her mother, anyway. You'd have thought she was guarding the crown jewels. But her father winked and said he didn't mind provided I behaved myself. And that if I didn't he'd cut my balls off. He didn't actually *say* that, of course, but I sure knew what he meant. Anyway, I was on my best behaviour the whole time. I helped do the dishes, too. And she always made sure we said goodnight with the garden gate between us!'

'Jeez, you must have been keen.'

'Well, yes, s'pose I was.'

'Oh well, it happens to us all in the end. It's not so bad if you pick the right one. Picked the right one myself thirty years ago. Probably good luck more than good management. Mind you, it's the only bit of luck I've ever had. Bloody football pools've never been any good!'

He suggested a one-way delivery voyage as a way of returning to my own hemisphere.

'Try Pedder and Milchreest in Fenchurch Street,' he said. 'A ship-delivery firm. Everything from millionaires' yachts to dredges.

All over the world. Occasionally they go your way and you can pay off instead of having to be repatriated.'

'Thanks. I'll see you later.'

But it was the last time I saw him. And I never did know his name. Or whether the sailing ship picture finally fell off the wall. But I would like to think that one day he may have won something on the football pools. He would have deserved it.

⚓

'Yes, we've got one to Australia soon,' the Pedder and Milchreest marine superintendent said. 'A new pilot tender for the Queensland Government. All hands pay off in Brisbane, except the captain and chief engineer. But it's not for a couple of months yet. If you want something in the meantime, I've a new harbour and deepsea salvage tug from Greenock to Aden. *Champion*, for the Port of Aden Trust. You'd be away about a month but back in plenty of time for the Australian trip.'

He gave me a train ticket to Glasgow from where I was to find my own way to Greenock.

Did it ever stop raining in Scotland? Did the sun ever shine? Was it ever warm? Even this time, in summer, the answers were still a sepulchral no. It was always as if Scotland was halfway to entering or just leaving an ice age. Small wonder the Scots invented whisky, played the bagpipes, tossed cabers, danced the Highland fling and spoke as if through a mouthful of hot porridge. It might also have been why they invented the steam engine, as a means of leaving the place, and the bicycle pedal in case the steam ran out, and, in case both were inoperable, television, as a means of pretending they were elsewhere.

From Glasgow's Central Station I took another train through the drenched Clyde Valley to Port Glasgow. I made my way through the evening muck and grimy, deserted, gloomily lit streets to the Star Hotel.

The landlord was as unrelenting as his native weather. And from the same pre-Darwinian stock, apparently, as *Queen Elizabeth*'s Glaswegian cups' and chairs' *führer*.

'Nae, mon, nae rooms. Nae rooms herre, nae rooms therre, nae bluidy rooms airny-wherre. Y'best gae on tae Gre'nock. Och aye, mon, y'best dae tha'.'

'Och aye in-bloody-deed,' I muttered crossly.

'Och aye, mon. Och aye, in-bluidy-deed. But y'best go on tae bluidy Gre'nock all the same . . .' he completed the sentence in what I assumed was Gaelic and which by its tone seemed likely to be highly disparaging.

I waited in the rain beneath the feeble light of a street lamp for a bus tae bluidy Gre'nock. There I found a room in the Inverclyde Sailors' Home. In its canteen a mournful, half-drunk Welshman played a piano. He licked his lips under the strain of his efforts. But his pianoforte skills were not great. The canteen's coffee was even worse. It was too late for a meal, too. I bought the pianist another beer hoping it would shut him up. It didn't. So I bought him several more. He finally fell to the floor and remained there for the night. And bluidy Greenock looked even more gloomy by daylight.

Champion's crew — captain, chief officer and second mate, three engineers, three firemen, a cook-steward, three able seamen and a bosun — met up in the still-falling rain at the builder's fitting-out wharf. After making ourselves known to each other the captain took us to the shipping office to sign on. Then we went to the nearest pub until it was time to start loading stores, including the ubiquitous 'Merchant Navy, suitable for the use of' Battle Axe jam.

We set off next afternoon past the Tail o' the Bank and into the Irish Sea. We were bound for Oran in Algeria and then Port Said, the Suez Canal, the Red Sea and finally Aden.

As night gathered over the grey, wind-whipped water I stood in the messroom doorway with a cup of hot cocoa warming my hands and shielded from the tearing wet west wind by oilskin, seaboots and thick woollen cap.

I was again part of a community I knew well and in which I was at ease as in no other. I felt the deck pulsing beneath me, smelled the salt air, tasted the occasional flick of spray and looked at the passing ships and flashing coastal lights.

I was at sea again.

And counted it life indeed.

We passed the great rocks of Ushant and crossed a foul-tempered Bay of Biscay, rounded Cape Finisterre, threaded our way through tunny fishermen off the Portuguese coast and battled around Cape St Vincent.

The cape and its vicinity are places of maritime history. As they retreated from Seville in the face of the Moors, monks took bits and pieces of St Vincent with them. When they reached the cape they built a small chapel to hold the relics. A convent was later built and the lighthouse atop the 220-foot cliff is part of it.

At nearby Sagres Point, Prince Henry the Navigator built a school of navigation. Among its later pupils were Lourenço Marques and Vasco de Gama. Down the coast, from Palos, Christopher Columbus sailed for America in 1492. Further down, from San Lucar de Barrameda, Magellan set out on his circumnavigation in 1519.

As we passed close to Cape Trafalgar I stood on deck out of the wind and recalled all I had learned of Lord Nelson.

We crossed the Gulf of Cadiz to the Straits of Gibraltar and into the Mediterranean. On the way we passed Tarif Point. It is named after El Tarif, commander of the Saracens who landed and built a fort there in 710 when they were invading Spain. For hundreds of years ships had to stop and 'Pay Tarif' on their way into the Mediterranean. Hence tariff.

Most of the crew worked solely for the company. They called it Pedder's Circus. In between worldwide ship-delivery jobs they engaged in other occupations ashore.

The captain was unmarried but had two dependents, one his mother, the other a matter of some mystery. Between voyages he was president of the local model aeroplane club, having been a Bomber Command navigator during the war. Among his delivery voyages had been a Fairmile harbour defence launch to Singapore, a 36-ton trawler to Chile, a millionaire's yacht to Brazil, and he had had to pick a crew from a Hong Kong jail to bring a small tug back to Swansea.

The chief officer had proposed to his wife five times but was repulsed until the fifth because her girlfriend also had designs on him. Between voyages he worked in his father's North Country hardware store. His family also owned a hotel in Nyasaland and he sometimes thought of taking a job on a Lake Nyasa ferry steamer but his wife was fearful of being eaten by crocodiles.

The second mate was married to a Portuguese and lived in a caravan. 'Like Gypsies,' he said. 'Very interesting. We don't like houses much. Mortgages even less.'

Jock, a fireman, bred greyhounds and canaries. During the season and spare time from his kennels and aviaries he poached salmon. 'Och, mon, guid money, you un'erstan' — ten bob a poon' for two hundred poon' o'salmon a time.'

Harry, an AB, was concerned a British-based American airman was courting his daughter. Harry had been sunk twice during the war and lost two sons in a London air raid. He was in Sydney at the time. When he returned he searched for what remained of his family. He eventually found his wife and young daughter in a Coventry boarding house.

During one of his early voyages as a boy, a sailor fell ill in Venezuela and a local doctor prescribed Epsom salts. The man died and the doctor turned out to be a ship chandler. The man was buried and the skipper sacked. The ship chandler continued chandling.

'I'd like to give that bloody Yank a bottle of Epsom salts,' Harry said several times. 'I'd chandle the Yankee bastard real good. Aye, I would that. Real good!'

Leaving the Suez Canal's yellow sands, we were engulfed in the Red Sea's usual ferocity. Built for local Aden crews, *Champion's* defences against the sun were few. Below-deck blowers only blew hot air around. And so at night we slept on deck, our mattresses trembling with the vibrancy of the great triple expansion steam engine and the thudding twin propellers. Discomfort increased when the ship had to slow down. Sea water was too warm to properly maintain the engine's cooling system at full speed.

The captain said the sea's ochre colouring was plankton. The chief officer said it was oil sludge from tankers. The chief engineer said it was from submarine upheavals when a bubble of oil sometimes burst to the surface. Eric, an AB and so presumably without the benefits of certified education, said it was desert dust. When it began coating the ship the captain shrugged his shoulders. The stuff on the ship was certainly desert dust. Of course it was. Goddammit, even Eric would know that. But the stuff on the sea was plankton. That was why it was called the Red Sea, dammit.

The chief officer declined to comment. The chief engineer reluctantly agreed both the captain and Eric could be right.

No one else cared one way or the other. It was too hot to argue. A heavy heat haze, almost a fog, reduced visibility to sometimes only a mile or two. Occasionally a slight breeze sprang from nowhere and ruffled the sea but died away as quickly as it came, leaving the sea once more a flat, oil-like surface unmarked except for porpoises or manta rays or a shark's fin.

As we steamed through the increasing oppression, Eddie, a fireman, began babbling to himself and refused to work in the engineroom. He climbed the mast instead. For no reason anyone could ascertain, Jock lay in a grunting, groaning, naked stupor on the deck of his hot-house cabin. Paddy the cook took to the bottle. His Irish brogue became less intelligible and he began producing curious dishes of remarkable appearance equalled only by their startling flavour and eaten only under the provocation of hunger. All the while Harry's threat of Epsom salts for his daughter's American boyfriend rose by the crate.

The captain, in underpants to keep cool and gold-braided cap to keep off the sun, said most of the crew were clowns. That was why the company was called Pedder's Circus.

After the ship's formal handing over to the Aden Port Trust, all hands stayed in a hotel in the Crater. This is Aden's old commercial quarter. It lies inside the sunburnt walls of an extinct volcano, its narrow streets crowded and noisy and smelling of spices, curry and wood smoke.

Aden has been a trade centre since antiquity. It is mentioned in the Bible and was a Roman colony in 24 BC. The Turks took control of it in the sixteenth century. Two centuries later the British got hold of it. Later they turned it into a Crown Colony and a coaling centre on the sea route through Suez to India.

When not haggling with or repulsing the omnipresent Arab and Levantine traders, we sat out on the wide upstairs balcony drinking long glasses of ice-cold beer in robust British imperiality and decrying the noisy, white-robed Arab throng. It was different during the steaming nights. While every Arab in Aden was doubtless resting peacefully, we sweated and grumbled in restless doziness.

Several days later we escaped aboard an Arab-crammed Dakota 'airliner' for Asmarra in Ethiopa, Port Sudan and Jeddah. There we boarded another Arab-crammed DC3 rattletrap for Cairo where, thankfully, we boarded a BOAC Argonaut, a real airliner, stewardesses and all, for Rome and London. Thank God we've got proper people up the front now, the captain said.

Eddie and Paddy displayed an almost old-world courtliness towards the stewardesses. The rest of us were surprised. Not only at their comportment, but also at their newly-donned pinstripe suits, sober ties, Persil-white shirts, gold cufflinks, and shiny black shoes — all of which they had carried from Aden in brown paper bags — and faces shaved almost to the point of being polished.

'Jeez, mate, y'gotta have principles y'know! It's not like on them bloody Wog aeroplanes. Y'gotta be polite and dress proper on *British* aeroplanes. Everyone fuckin' knows that,' they explained as they nibbled their smoked salmon and sipped their aperitifs and wiped their mouths with linen napkins.

⚓

Matthew Flinders' crew assembled on Waterloo Station and entrained for Southampton and thence by ferry to Cowes on the Isle of Wight. The thirteen-strong group comprised seamen seeking their fortunes in Australia.

The brand new ship's two hundred feet of flowing lines were a statement of all that embodied a fine vessel. Her 800-ton blue-black hull and white superstructure shone with her shipyard maiden-hood. Her teak decks and mahogany rails glowed with her Samuel Wright & Co shipwrights' craftsmanship. Her job would be to lie out in Moreton Bay as a base for the pilots who brought the ships in and out of Brisbane.

The captain was the same who had taken *Champion* to Aden. He and I were the only members of Pedder's Circus. Everyone else was new.

'Thank God you're the only one of that last lot,' he said in a Cowes pub the night before we sailed.

'Surely they weren't all that bad,' I said. 'I've been with worse!'

The captain agreed that at heart *Champion*'s crowd had been a reasonable bunch, considering.

'Take Eddie and Paddy, for instance,' he said. 'They're old hands with the company. They've been with me on several trips. Hang-men at times but good blokes, really. Even gentlemen sometimes, especially when they're flying home at the end of a trip. It's just that the heat gets to them. I've sailed with worse, I suppose.

'A few trips ago, to Antofagasta, I had to lock a couple of firemen in separate spare cabins after we left Panama. Boozed to the gunwales and the chief engineer said they were mad and bloody dangerous. Chileans they were, being deported after they jumped ship in Hull. I let them out when they sobered up but the silly buggers stuck knives into each other. Couldn't stop them and couldn't do anything for them once they'd finished.

'Completely bloody dead. The pair of them. Cut up like steak. Horrible sight. Even after we washed down the deck there were stains on it for days. The company wouldn't let me bury them at sea. Had to wrap them in sacks and keep them in the chief steward's freezer until we arrived. But the Chilean police weren't all that fussed. After I made a statement they just carted them away and I heard nothing more about it. But it took a bit of explaining to the company, I can tell you. Wasn't too stuck on steak, either, for a while.'

On a late summer afternoon we passed down the Solent and into the English Channel. Men off-watch leaned against the stern rail.

Most were silent, contemplating the last views of the homeland they were abandoning for the promise of a new life at the opposite end of the world. I joined them in their silence . . . after what seemed a lifetime ago, *Algonquin Park* had passed this way in the opposite direction at the end of my first voyage . . .

A feeling of echo reached out and left an intangible essence hanging in the dusky Channel air.

Six weeks later we sailed up the Brisbane river dressed by flags from stem to stern and accompanied by other ships' whistled greetings and pictures in the newspapers (some years later, when her time was up on Moreton Bay, *Matthew Flinders* became a luxury cruiser around the Great Barrier Reef and the Fijian Islands).

I travelled to Adelaide where I got a job delivering furniture on a truck and Marita and I renewed an acquaintance nurtured over several years with long letters spanning great distances.

At night when she was not on duty at the hospital we went to the movies — she was still in love with Gregory Peck — and afterwards held hands on the banks of the Torrens. But apparently I was no Gregory Peck, and despite my high expectations things eventually turned out rather differently, as things generally do.

And so I went home to New Zealand.

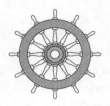

25

When that which drew from out the deep
Turns again home.
Alfred, Lord Tennyson, *Crossing the Bar*

My British seaman's papers ensured automatic entry to the New Zealand Seaman's Union. But the man in London's Poplar shipping office had no counterpart here. Unemployed seamen stood 'on the corner' outside Government shipping offices. As its name was called, those fancying a particular ship detached from the crowd and stood in line. Chief officers nodded or pointed to those they wished or in some cases because of union stratagems had no choice but to engage.

The New Zealand Seaman's Union was ruled as an almost personal fiefdom by its president, Fintan Patrick Walsh. He had taken it over in 1927 after physically ejecting the incumbent from his office. In later years he also became president of the Federation of Labour and a close associate of the country's political leadership almost until the day he was safely in his grave. One newspaper (*Evening Post*, Wellington 7 July 1994) described Walsh as 'a power behind the throne during the Fraser, Holland and Nash governments.' A union member told the same newspaper in 1988 that 'he used all kinds of personal abuse and intimidation. Men were afraid to go against him. They could lose their jobs and also get beaten up.'

An unsettling feature of New Zealand seafaring was the compulsory monthly stopwork union meetings. They were often little more than vehicles for officials' and shipboard wannabe officials' own agendas. Their unabashed militant politicking induced continual minor uproars (stick-ups) for very occasionally genuine but usually fatuous claims of injustice. Shipowners always surrendered. Tied-up ships were wasting assets. They needed to be at sea to earn their keep.

Complaints and demands came mostly from expatriate British rather than local seamen — New Zealanders were often in the minority anyway. The Britishers were still plagued with the 'them-or-us' history of their former social and industrial lives, which they claimed to have come to New Zealand to escape. But persuaded of their rights, they were obsessed by the belief that even antipodean authority was continually cheating them out of them.

It was a deep-seated obsession. Despite the perils of 1940 four million working days were lost because of strikes. Scottish miners struck because of 'inaccuracies of a weighing machine.' During the Dunkirk evacuation aircraft workers in Manchester struck over an employee dismissed 'because of falsification of the recording of his time of arrival at work.' At the peak of the Battle of Britain over four thousand working days were lost at a De Havilland aircraft factory because of 'the transfer of four capstan fitters from the firm to other work of national importance.' In that same fortnight the RAF claimed 180 German planes on one day alone. At least some men were working.

It was a pernicious state of affairs and life at sea lost its sense of vocation. It had become a mere job. In port crews spent their time in waterfront bars such as Gleesons, Ann Powells, the Ambassadors, Chicks. There they argued and sometimes fought with each other, or caroused with females of various ages, reputes and health hazards against which even Ginger at his most libidinous would have adopted a defensive celibacy. Sam would not have bothered even asking.

As its shipwreck record shows, New Zealand ships sail in waters as dangerous as any in the world. And so, as there must always be at sea, there were spurs of excitement and moments of potential disaster. But they were generally so much part of seafaring as to be scarcely remembered. Life at sea is only a small percentage of crises. There is an impression ashore that the job is somehow synonymous with a life of action. Not so. Although remarkably reliable, most of them anyway, seamen are not heroic figures. Every part of their job is a matter of avoiding the need for heroism.

Marita and I later renewed our courtship. The circumstances do not concern this story. But they would have made a good romantic novel. We were married in Port Pirie with little money and high hopes.

My new wife, regretfully, was a complete invalid during the sea crossing to New Zealand. Her debilitating seasickness afforded no scope for shipboard romance, despite the reality of my having at last surpassed the promise of Gregory Peck. The seas of matrimony, however, provided opportunities even Mr Peck might have envied.

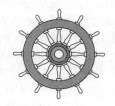

Epilogue

Man's yesterday may ne'er be like his morrow . . .
Percy Bysshe Shelley, *Mutability*

My fortune had multiplied. I had joined *Algonquin Park* with ten pounds. Now I had a hundred. My possessions had tripled, from one to two suitcases and a kitbag. I had also acquired a wife. And a change in tax bracket.

Neither of us not really knowing what else to do — both of us fearing offices and Marita not wanting to continue her nursing career — we became lighthouse keepers. The job had its moments of drama and was not always comfortable. But we enjoyed each other and remote islands afforded a mutual fulfillment unavailable elsewhere. We saw the sunrise and sunset together and knew the difference between day and night. We may not have been in heaven but we could see it from our lighthouses.[9]

An accident ended it all. I was carried by stretcher across the island, down a cliff and across the beach to a small seaplane and flown to Auckland and several months in a hospital bed with a badly broken knee. Unfortunately, the injury, including several months' dependence on a crutch, meant we had to leave the lighthouse. And that was how, despite every effort to avoid it, I became a government department office worker in Wellington.

We stayed in a Wellington hotel for several days until we could find a house. It was an ironical circumstance. It was the same hotel I had stayed at on my way to the sea. And as if to completely weld the circle, the three children were in the same room I had been in a lifetime ago. That evening, standing at their door propped up by my crutch, I contemplated my sleeping family and wondered what would befall *them* from this room onwards.

Marita, however, viewed our changed circumstances with the same composure with which she had met the idea of lighthouses in the first place. As for the children, well, childhood is a happy time for being young, ignorant, thoughtless and so much less apprehensive than their parents. I reflected that I had been of much the same disposition the first time I had been in this room.

In somewhat of a mixed humour I went out and got slightly drunk.

For a time our suburban house, the bus to work and back again and Wednesday's rubbish collection, was as bread and water after the banqueting years of sea life, and office life a matter of intellectual self-defence rather than a firm conviction in the value of much I was required to do. I felt like an actor in a play without a plot.

The chief administration officer suggested that since I apparently needed to reinvent life I could start by taking it easy and observing what went on around me. His words had a strange echo . . . 'Well, you're here now,' the sailor in *Algonquin Park*'s messroom had said on my first day at sea. 'Just do as you're told, learn, and you'll be OK. Otherwise you'll soon fuck it up.' Good advice then, doubtless good advice now. And so I took it.

Time had its way as it usually does and we settled into the new life. After a couple more stays in hospital I was able to discard my crutch. My job began expanding, too, and I travelled widely throughout the country. I also became involved with politicians and cabinet ministers, although having had politicians in my own family did not make them any more comprehensible. Their black-is-white arguments were convincing enough to believe, but when I later found that black was neither white nor even a shade of grey, they explained patiently that the problem was my eyesight. Between us we would have caused chaos in a paint shop.

'Yes, probably,' the chief administration officer said. 'But you'll learn to live with it. It's only politics — and they are only politicians.' I was unsure if his comments were to explain or excuse them. But he once said, in a moment of complete exasperation, that anyone actually wanting a job as a politician should be automatically disqualified.

As I became more accomplished in the intricate choreography of office life I began to enjoy it. But my sea-nurtured let's-cut-the-crap-and-get-on-with-it approach, regarded by some as pushiness, others as rudeness, a few (fortunately those who promoted people) as initiative, sometimes got me into trouble. Then, buried in bureaucratic sediment, my efforts degenerated into the gloomy sadness of Noble Attempts whose results were more easily conceived than described, as someone once said of the visitor's baby.

At such times I gazed out the window if there was one or at my pen if there wasn't, and lost myself in a vicarious return to the sea as if seeking assurance that those around me, or myself for that matter, had not always been marooned in a mass of silliness.

But I got the hang of it in the end. While it was hard to imagine a problem to which a committee could be a solution — the ability of a committee to make sows' ears out of silk purses was at times breathtaking — as a member and sometimes chairman of various committees I played the game with some skill, even when engaged in things everyone knew were futile but in which, because everyone else was doing them, everyone fought to take the lead.

Eventually I arrived at an office of my own. On the top floor, just down the corridor from the chief administration officer. With a high-backed chair of my own. And my name and designation on the gold-lettered personnel directory in the mezzanine foyer.

I had finally been allowed to dine with the grown-ups. Even more, I was able occasionally to alter the place settings.

My scepticism remained, however. Inevitably, probably, since it was spawned in conditions unrelenting in their demand for things to be seen as they are, not as they ought to be. The sea's absolutes allowed no room for bullshit. It was an early truth imposed upon me aboard *Algonquin Park,* reinforced during the monumental ocean storm aboard *Leicester*, and validated during all the following journeys between offices. In short, the seafaring life imposes in every way what become lifetime values, especially during a man's formative years. They become intrinsic and make it bothersome later conforming to a diametrically opposite way of life, however critical it may be to do so to earn a living in what is sometimes a common-sense-free zone.

It was something the chief administration officer sometimes found a little difficult to understand. Or occasionally at first to even tolerate. He once announced, after tapping his blotter with his upturned pen for several moments longer than normal, that while 'swallowing the anchor' may no doubt be difficult at times, I could perhaps try doing so with rather less indigestion than I sometimes exhibited.

All the same, while the seafaring life had ill-prepared me for later years it had, paradoxically, enabled me to cope with them. Everything learned at sea had stood me in good stead in my grapple with the office, which I had found to be as much a container of human comedy and tragedy as a ship.

And so I had good reason to thank the seafaring men in whose often boisterous and occasionally unsympathetic fellowship I had grown up — libidinous Ginger, phlegmatic Old Scouse, quarrelsome Ted, companionable Jack, even artless young Johnny, and even, although it must be said only occasionally, that prick Southern.

It was a symposium from which I had profited, not that I always understood the lectures and sometimes incurred high bills as a result. But its most enduring lesson had been to remain unsurprised by human conduct — which still constantly turns out to be not what I had expected.

And where are they now, those sailors?

Retired, probably, most of them. Drowned, perhaps, a few of them.

Our ships?

All gone. Most to the breakers' yards. Some wrecked.

The sea?

Unchanged.

Its tides still ebb and flow and its currents still run. As if none of us, men or ships, had ever been upon it.

THE END

Well, not quite. My share of the National Debt is now around $13,000. *Thirteen-Bloody-Thousand!*

Endnotes

1   *Decoy*, Dudley Pope, Secker & Warburg, London, 1983
2   *Supership*, Noel Mostert, Alfred A Knopf Inc, New York, 1974
3   *Instructions for Forraine Travell*, James Howell, 1642
4   *The Liberty Ships*, L A Sawyer & W A Mitchell, Cornell Maritime
    Press Inc, Cambridge, Maryland, 1970
5   *Leicester*'s epic battle with the hurricane is told in Farley Mowat's
    book, *The Serpent's Coil*, Michael Joseph Ltd, London, 1962
6   *Notes of a Journey through France and Italy*, William Hazlitt, 1862
7   *Sailor Town Days*, C. Fox Smith, Methuen & Co., London, 1923. There
    was also a well-known Tiger Bay in Cardiff, Wales.
8   *The Atlantic Campaign*, Dan van der Vat, Hodder & Stoughton, 1988.
9   *As Darker Grows The Night*, Peter Taylor, Hodder & Stoughton, 1975